PORTS

OF CALL

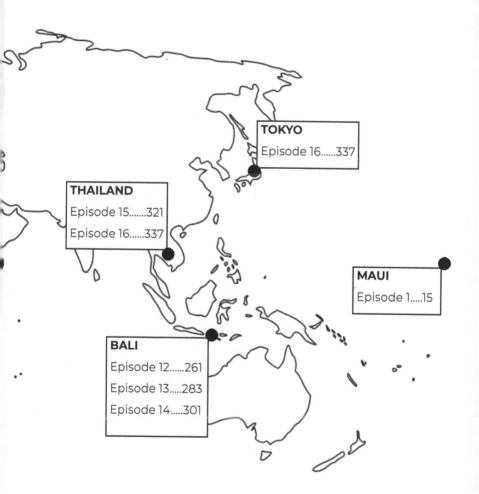

HOW I MET MYSELF

AN ODYSSEY IN MODERN ADULTING

By Jonathan Restivo

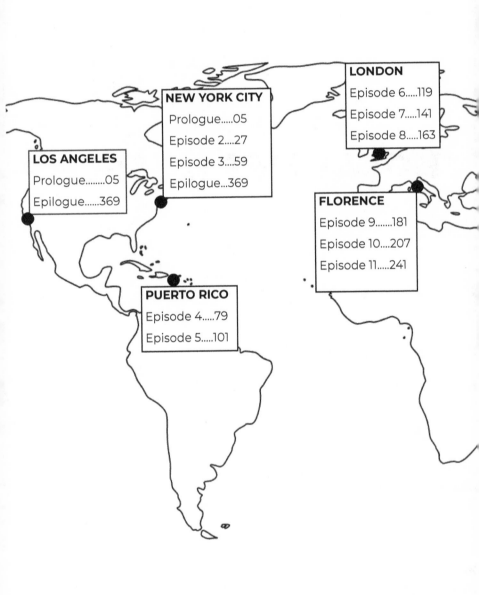

STAGE SETTING

prologue

Pop.

Pop.

Pop... the last bubble to burst snaps my consciousness back into the present moment, a modest reminder of the task and scene before me, sprawled in bustling congregation across the streets of Central Park West on this unseasonably warm late-March morning in New York.

I toss out the gum I've been chewing and popping, and trade it for a cup of coffee in the tent behind the main stage, a necessary shot of caffeine to the system after a mostly sleepless night. The soothing playback of meditation music eventually knocked me out around 3 A.M., just one of the many changes to the old lifestyle I've recently implemented. I've found that the soft sounds help me sleep easier than calling it a night to the sweet melody of episodes of *The Office* on Netflix. Although, I did enjoy starting every morning by confirming with a symbolic click of the remote that yes, I am still here, thanks for asking.

Yet despite running around the world the past year, learning new ways of approaching and handling this crazy, beautiful, fucked up blessing called life, a faint, all-too-familiar anxiousness lingers inside this morning.

How much have I really changed in my time traveling? Am I back to being the same stressed, scattered, insecure person I was before I left? As a new friend from abroad, Bali Rob, asked me the other day: can we really change that much out on the romanticized road, or do we fall back into who we truly are upon our return to reality?

They're fair questions, but the fact that I'm even here right now is self-assurance that I'm stronger today than I was a year ago. That even if I don't have all the answers now after my soul-searching sojourn, I can take on anything life throws my way. At least I hope so. I believe so.

I mean, wouldn't anyone be feeling a little nervous in my position? Looking out over the parallel cross streets terminating abruptly in the famous park's green reprieve, filled with people stretching from Columbus Circle for so many blocks that I lose count?

With tense but determined energy, I check my pocket for the 387th time this morning, just to ensure that my paper speech has not fallen out in the thirty seconds since I last confirmed its presence. From my other pocket I grab another stick of gum, just to keep things fresh and my mouth feeling light and loose for when I get on stage. I blow another bubble.

Pop.

The story I'm about to share is one of actual, legitimate struggle. It's a far cry from my junior year of high school in the sleepy, sheltered suburbs of southeastern Connecticut when I wrote my college application essay detailing my struggle in overcoming the seemingly simple but somehow insurmountable task of being able to blow a bubble.

Open FruitStripe, remove wrapper, chew, purse lips, spit out directly onto an unsuspecting passerby or my friend Jeff.

Eventually, though, I figured out the trick, as most people over the age of seven usually do. For some reason at the time, I thought using this mini-tale of toil and triumph over the challenge would demonstrate to the Admissions offices at Notre Dame and North Carolina that if I could best that beast of bubble-blowing, surely I could accomplish anything in this world. I saw it as a fun and illustrative parable that appropriately conveyed my personality and life experience.

Ironically, it did, but not in the way or to the effect I thought it was.

That essay (or lack thereof) landed me a fallback gig at my home state university, a disappointment to this wide-eyed and wanderlusting first-time adult, not for the school itself but for its 45-minutes-away proximity to the place I grew up. Though to be fair, everything in Connecticut is 45 minutes from anywhere else in Connecticut.

When it came time to look at next steps after college, my vaunted and impugnable Political Science degree provided me with two potential career paths: law school, or turning tricks on the street for cash. And while the latter seemed like the more respectable of the two, I had packed on a few extra pounds my senior year and was not sure I'd have the commercial appeal necessary for a successful career as a gigolo. So, law school it was for me then, and I was for damn sure finding a place far from the cozy corner confines of New England. I went clear across the country to Pepperdine, finally setting out on my own as only an overly-driven person with independent first-child mentalities can.

I was never really sold on Los Angeles, though, or Los Angeles on me. I knew from the beginning that it wasn't a place where I would ultimately settle, always aware that we had an expiration date. Sure, there were the occasional highlight-reel, "only in Hollywood" stories that keep you coming back, like the time we made it onto the *Price is Right*, or the time a friend and I were invited to a Halloween block party in Malibu Colony and somehow ended up hanging out with Cheech and handing out candy to Denise Richards and the Brangelina kids, while Brad caught up with Courtney Cox and David Arquette next to us. But I just never felt like the city and I were a good match.

Where L.A. was sprawling and unorganized, I was one-track and linear. Where L.A. was eclectic and complicated, I was straight forward and whatever the exact opposite of trendy is. Where L.A. was cutting edge and pushing boundaries, I was conservative and reserved. Where L.A. was laissez faire and laidback, I was reactive and emotional. Plus, fuck that traffic. Seriously, fuck the 405.

The thing that kept me there for the better part of nine years was the people, a large and close friend group that consisted of guys and gals all in similar situations: newly out of college, not entirely out of the college mindset, from places far less exotic than the beaches of Malibu, ready to work hard and play hard as basic bros and bitches know best. Our crew went together as well as a Prius and a Coexist bumper sticker, the combination of which we saw with seemingly every other car that passed on Pacific Coast Highway.

One of those Pepperdine friends texts now, having recently made the permanent exodus from L.A. to New York as well, and wishes me luck from her position in the crowd near 77th Street. My dad also texts, in his typical old-person-style, complete with humorously fractured sentences and unnecessary abbreves, as if each line of text is subject to the pricing structure of the telegraph. "Just got 2 Grand Cent. Ur mother getting coffee and will walk over. Good luck, c u after!" Thanks Dad, I forgot my decoder glasses back in California, but I think I follow you. A third text from a friend who knows what I'm up to today alerts me to the fact that Paul McCartney is apparently out amongst the masses in front of me.

The moment hits me again. Given my age, obviously, I never got to see The Beatles, but Paul McCartney is now about to watch me on stage.

A slight smirk of implausibility quickly turns to appreciation, purpose, and resolve. A reality gut check of why I am here. And how.

Not that long ago, like many of my peers, I was facing down the barrel of life's typical maladies, and not handling it all that well.

As a red-blooded millennial, I committed a large chunk of my day to putting dog ears on pictures of things, sipping on overpriced coffee at brunch while waiting for my avocado toast to arrive. I spent far too little time concerned about The Sword of Damocles' Student Loans dangling perilously over my financial future, and too much time indulging an aversion to retail space by buying needless items with my Amazon Prime account. Most of my money was dedicated to trips for bachelor parties, showers, weddings, and the gifts that go with it, though I love jumping up and down to "Shout" on a dance floor, so I don't mind that part. I developed an affinity for adding "bro" before regular words to make funnier combinations like "bromance" and "brosè all day", overused the term Basic, and tried weird new workout classes, as I moseyed through my everyday life on the west side of L.A. during my transition year from the fresh, still-got-it age of twenty-nine to the abject staleness of the dirty thirty.

Then one morning, it was like I woke up to a Facebook news feed that showed me the world had passed me by. All of a sudden, everyone around me was doing their part, moving around the *Life* gameboard, fulfilling the roles of proper adults and productive members of society: stocking up their 401K, moving to the suburbs, running in an endless stream of 5K races, reproducing appropriately as if straight out of central casting for a town called Pleasantville.

And social media was there to broadcast it all. Staged engagement photos on a beach at sunset in outfits strategically designed not to be too matchy-matchy. Baby announcements using baked goods. Pictures of pregnant friends together at weddings with their hands all on their stomachs in odd uniformity, just making sure everyone out there knows they're developing a child and not a beer gut. More half marathon finish line posts than my double tapping finger could keep up with.

Even if it was a façade put on as easily as an Instagram filter to a selfie, everyone around me seemed to project a story of having this adulting thing figured out. Yet, there I was spiraling down, unfulfilled in work and in love, spending too many nights out at the bars, too many drug-influenced ones toward the end, hampered by a general lack of focus and confidence of purpose in everything I was doing. And it really pissed me off, not knowing how to deal, and where or how I fit into the modern adult life.

"Was there a boat to Grown Up Island I missed somehow?" I wondered, looking around in hungover confusion on my private island for misfit boys.

Okay, so I may have upgraded the posters on my bedroom walls from unframed pictures of movies, sports heroes, and women in bikinis to framed black and white shots of Italy and New York City, but where was the rest of the adulting progression?

I needed someone or something to blame for my general malaise and waywardness, because God forbid I point that finger at the aging man standing across from me in the mirror, reciting rehearsed fabrications to make the reflection feel better. Defensive lies I tell when I'm feeling vulnerable and exposed, like how I always assure my dentist that I floss every day. Or that I've ever actually read a single Terms of

Service. Or how I say, "guys, I don't really like Justin Bieber." Instead, I turned the finger, probably the middle one, on my surroundings and contrived a plan to break up with L.A. in dramatic, one-way fashion.

I've typically viewed friends who get into relationships when, from the start, there's a clear lack of a future and wonder why they do so. What's the point? I suppose my relationship with L.A. embodied that scenario, though, and I kind of get the compulsion. Despite our differences, the many years we spent together helped me grow as a person and have some fun along the way, even if I knew it was not "the one". L.A. taught me to be more mellow and outgoing, and have a better appreciation for the role of the avocado in my life. And we did share some qualities that helped us get by together. We're both entrepreneurial and creative. We both love great weather and the presence of beautiful women all around. I also think we both know we can do better.

At one point, we even took some time apart to work on ourselves, and I flirted and got serious with Newport Beach, Chicago, and Dallas, before returning to L.A. for one last go-around. I had seen what else was out there and knew more about what I was looking for. Still, I thought we could recapture the magic of the old days, in that played out way that every broken relationship thinks that this time around, things would be different. It should come as no surprise that I was wrong, and it was time to break up for good.

When I first developed the idea to drop everything and hit the road in the few months prior to leaving, my objective was almost entirely surface level. Working and moving around to multiple countries for a while appealed strongly to my adventure-seeking and unsettled mind, and I liked the thought of getting away from it all. I did not set out with the goal of finding the meaning of life, or my place and purpose on earth, or to play centerstage in some grand voyage of self-discovery and self-realization in that cliché way that would cause people to sneer and make *Eat, Pray, Love* jokes.

Honestly, I was just ready to move on. I wanted to live in London and maybe become friends with the Queen; to take a selfie in front of those cool-looking offshore islands in Thailand; to go clear across the world to Bali and be as far away from my normal as I could. I wanted to let destiny guide my way, into a coffeeshop where I'd meet the woman of my dreams, or to a cozy little neighborhood in New York, and get that deep down feeling that this was finally where I was supposed to be or the one I was supposed to be with. And I really wanted to get back to Florence, ten years removed from a study abroad experience that changed my world.

I had a "work from home" job that never defined what "home" actually meant, so in Kerouac fashion, I stuck that home into a suitcase and that suitcase onto a TSA conveyor belt.

In an act of stubborn defiance to all the pre-ordained social constructs that swirled around me mockingly, I said "fuck it, why not?" as has always been my style, setting out on the road with the branding of a lone outcast, putting very little thought toward the consequences of the future or the real motivations from my past.

It was like I had gone to the bar and ordered another round, but when I turned around with Titos-and-sodas in hand, everyone had gone home, so instead I chugged all the drinks on my own.

Now that world tour, through an entirely unpredictable course of events, brought me to this improbable moment. And now I have to tell a bit of my story. But really, it's our story. And to me, that's what makes it all the more worthy of telling.

I check the security of my speech for the 388th time this morning, with the crowd before me growing to an extent beyond my comprehension. Still, the 200,000 people out there are less scary to me than if I had to speak in front of 200, the sheer size acting as a buffer to the intimacy of public speaking that typically terrified me. I'm ready now, and it's my turn on stage.

One more deep breath in, one out, and away we go.

PART ONE

"Our battered suitcases were piled on the sidewalk again; we had longer ways to go. But no matter, the road is life." – JACK KEROUAC, ON THE ROAD

"I have wandered all my life, and I have also traveled; the difference between the two being this, that we wander for distraction, but we travel for fulfillment." – HILAIRE BELLOC

"Not all those who wander are lost" – EVERYONE ON INSTAGRAM WHO HAS EVER POSTED A TRAVEL PHOTO. ALSO, TOLKIEN.

THE CHAPTER WITH ALL THE BAGGAGE

chapter one

This is the life.

I kick my feet up on the condo balcony, still dressed in the casual floral décor of my Hawaiian luau outfit. I look like Jimmy Buffet's biggest fan. Across the channel, across the same Pacific water that looks so much better from this angle than from California a week ago, in that exact shade of blue that an ocean should be colored, the sun falls gracefully over the Molokai island. It's been another day worthy of the scrapbook, if anyone still used scrapbooks anymore, in a setting so perfect it would probably be on a postcard, if anyone still used postcards anymore. I can't stop smiling. I can't stop smirking. Since this is my last night in Maui, I make a valiant, some might say heroic, effort to put a dent in the seven-gallon barrel of Kirkland vodka that I hauled out of Costco a week ago. I spend the next few minutes getting the framing just right on my vodka-and-something. I set it against the fading sunlight to generate the maximum jealousy effect when I upload the picture to my Instagram Story. Satisfied with my efforts in self-promotion, I lean back in the balcony lounger to fully absorb the storybook scene laid out before me. To spend a minute in calm pleasure and peace of mind. To leave the world behind... My eyes wander to the resort's very frameable setup. The U-shape forms the border of this early evening vista to Maui's neighbor perched elusively just off-shore. I take a few more photos. Some portrait, some landscape, I need the options. I'll play with the filters on those later and turn one into a new post tomorrow. I've got to be strategic. There's no recovery from the shame of violating society's one-post-per-day rule. My temporary home here at the Honua Kai condo complex has me pin-dropped in the northwest corner of the island, a soul-satisfying ride up the port-side coast along the Hono... Honap... I grab my phone and pull up Google Maps... Honoapiilani Highway. I love to study maps. It's a cheap way for me to feel like I know where I am. And where I'm going. I trace my steps from this past week along the impossible-to-spell highway down to Lahaina. It's a small village that delivers a shot of reality to the wishful fantasy of a simpler island life, free from the trappings of modern America. An untouched and abundantly green nature preserve sits to the east, drifting me into a daydream of a *Jurassic Park* or *Lost* scenario where I can play the hero for a group of struggling survivors. Its mountains crest at the sky and provide at least a little protection from plunder by the rest of the world. I continue to scroll around my handheld landscape as I sip my drink and the sun dips a little lower. I close the Maps app and take a few swipes on Hinge. My target location is still set to L.A. for dating purposes, despite my recent jailbreak from the city. I won't be back there to date for a few months, or hopefully ever, but the muscle memory is still built into my fingers. Ew, she likes pineapple on her pizza? Pass. I set the phone down and peep Molokai again. Incredible... Islands have always been a fascination of mine, either from a prior life as a pirate roaming free on the high seas, or a childhood imagining a Peter Pan role in a magical place where I'd never have to grow up. My phone buzzes and my heart adds a beat to its regular pace. It's from my friend Penelope, who I'm kind of into, responding to my Story with a heart eye emoji. I bask in my triumph in social relevancy with another smirk. The sky sways a harsher orange in front of me. Almost reddish, like the blaring light of Sirens. Back and forth, the waves crash the shore. Never stopping, always moving. Since I've got Instagram open, I check my post from this morning for the latest "Like" tally. I just passed triple digits, so I'm content now. It's a sunrise picture of my laptop from the beach, as I embrace and advertise my new remote work lifestyle. One month at a time, around the world, wherever my (broken) heart desires. No holding me back. No one to tell me where to go or care what I do. No one to care... I leave this balcony view to get a refill on my drink and to grab my laptop. While it's on my mind, I might as well keep plotting my course. All the locations I will conquer in my undefined journey. Setting out on my path to prove that this is what I want. That I'm happy being the wild-card. The maverick. The one who doesn't play by the rules to the point where I can offer that trademark smirk whenever people ask with genuine curiosity or passive-aggressive concern "what is your life, exactly?" It makes me feel for a minute that I'm doing something right after all. Let everyone in my social circle allocate their resources toward other question-able priorities like paying rent and saving for the future. I'm taking my checkbook out on the road. My figurative check-book. The real one is stowed away in the back of my Venice Beach storage unit somewhere, having not been put into use since around the time MySpace was still relevant. This is a really nice sunset. I never got these in L.A. I mean obviously they were there, I just never paid attention... The sun has done good work on my tan this week, my Italian skin getting a solid base for the beaches I will surely soon visit. Down be-low, the families are emptying out of the pool for the day, carefree and sunkissed. I check my phone to see who else has viewed my Story. I don't know if I want kids of my own anymore. Come to think of it, it was exactly this time, one year ago, when I first developed that skepticism. It was on Thanksgiving in The Bahamas, at Señor Frogs, the bastion of tourist debauchery and cheesiness. The type of place that makes you question all of your life decisions. I shoo away a mosquito or fly that's distracting me. The anxiety had been growing all night as I sat at the bar, chugging strawberry margaritas like Pepto-Bismol, trying to tame the pit in my stomach as my phone sat in silence after my girlfriend Calyp-so had gone dark on me. Then the text came. After months together, I got a breakup text, then one more to twist the knife, and that was the end of that. The sip from my vodka drink now is a little heavier this time. I distinctly remember my overwhelming emotion not being sadness, but disappointment. In having to go back out into the dreaded dating arena again. That moment was the first time I can say I actually paused to question whether I wanted all of that in my life. Having to start that relationship process all over again when I had convinced myself she was supposed to be the one. I rarely date, and I certainly don't fall in love. But Calypso was different. She'd appreciate this view, by the way. Maui was her favorite place to visit. I knew I would love it here too. We always had that level of connection. Like the first time we hung out at Disneyland, bonded over our lists of the best Disney movies, and I found myself increasingly gravitating to her throughout the day. So much so that when in line, I made sure I was standing near her when the time came to board so that we sat next to each other on the ride. Yeah, I know, adorable. It sucks being single... I pull up Instagram on my phone and check who has viewed my Story. No Calypso. It's been a few months since I've seen her name pop up there. I think she has a new guy. But I can't bring myself to look. She's probably doing better than I am. In the last year, I wrote a dark sitcom pilot, went overboard on a strict workout regimen, unfollowed her on my social media feeds, and found a few rebound women that I left behind in L.A. without much change to my feelings meter at all. She's that one that I just can't quit. Like Jen with Brad. Or me with mozzarella sticks. I return inside, grab another drink, and plop back on the lounger. We had talked of taking a trip to Disney World this year. World is definitely better than Land. You've got all the unique parks, and that mini golf course I love, and the easy transportation all around the complex, and the feeling of being young again everywhere you go, and Epcot with all the different countries you can visit. Mexico, France, Germany, Italy. Ah, I can't wait to get back to Italy soon. It's been ten years since I was in Florence. I'm really looking forward to that. That sunset view from Piazzale Michelangelo, looking down over the city... where else can you get a view that good? I stare out for a moment. I wonder when I'll actually get to Italy on this trip, maybe Florence in the spring for like a month? My phone buzzes again and it's a friend from home in Connecticut. He asks when I'm going to be back in Cali. East coast people always use the word "Cali". I want to respond with: don't call it Cali. We hate that. It's NorCal, SoCal, CA, or spell the whole thing out. Insider tip. But I just say, "Tomorrow." It's the return of Friendsgiving with my L.A. family, an idea I captained with my law school mates who were also marooned on the west coast. There's always a ton of food, football, Fireball, and friends drinking too much Fireball. I missed it last year having a shitty time in The Bahamas, but our ten-year tradition is fading anyways. Our hosts are leaving L.A. Others are getting engaged, married, scattering. This may be our last one ever. I scope the sun sailing a little lower in the sky, and take a stiff drink. You might even say this little Turkey Day ritual we've carved out for ourselves is cooked. I smirk at my ability to at least make myself laugh. I can't wait for that, though, to get everyone together again, even for just a day. I pop on my phone for a minute and take a few swipes on Bumble of the Maui crowd one more time. It's peak sunset now, this is the final moment to take it all in. I really do feel #blessed. All the incredible sunsets that lie ahead for me in the places I'll go over the next however long I'll be traveling... Actually, I'll be going to a lot of international spots, and I think they prefer Tinder to Bumble, so I start to download that app and head back inside for another drink. Back on the balcony, dusk is setting in and I can hear the tide on the beach below. It's struggling. Fighting its natural direction... I like lakes better than oceans. My motto for the ocean is similar to that of any decent strip club: stay away, but if you must be there, look but don't touch. Although, I roved from that stance this week when I finally tried surfing in Lahaina. Spoiler alert- surfing is overrated. At least I got a good picture to post, though. I'll probably put that up on Friday. My phone buzzes with a check-in reminder for my flight. I browse through my emails, eliminating notification bubbles with determined precision. There are two types of people in this world: the people who somehow have 4,668 email notifications in alarming fashion, or people that have no notifications anywhere. Those red dots are as annoying to me as people who incorrectly place the toilet paper on the roller so it pulls from the bottom and not over the top. The wind is picking up on the balcony, and my cool Tommy Bahama look has quickly aged beyond its purpose. One thing about Hawaii I don't really like is the con- stant wind, tossing my rapidly thinning hair out of its very specific placement. I shake my head at the douchiness of that thought. I set a reminder on my phone to do some volunteer work while I travel, as penance. The November breeze is chilly and salty, but my vodka cardigan is keeping me warm for now. All in all, it's been a great trip to Maui. Lots of stops constructed on Memory Lane... Yesterday's drive on the Road to Hana was certainly one. The switchbacks and banana bread and waterfalls along that black rock coastline. The massive unfettered waves of the Pacific crashing onto the stage at... I need my phone again... Wai'anapanapa Park. The relentless ocean violently meeting that jagged and unfazed terrain. The refreshing mist floating over the blackness of the rock and sand contrasted against the toupees of bright green vegetation perched calmly and steadfastly on the domes of the natural lava forms. The trees hanging over the beach, what are they called again? I grab my phone and poke around. They're either algarroba or banyan, apparently. Either way, they're iconic and beautiful. What an experience... I put my phone down. The encroaching darkness of night sets the charming scene before me now. I pick my phone back up and play with different lighting settings before I frame a few more pictures. And I take another drink, down to the bottom. I send a Snapchat to a few friends who will appreciate the artistry and poignant message of the emptying of my drink set against the backdrop of the end of my last night here. I open my newly installed Tinder app and start setting up my account pictures. The most recent shot of me is golfing at the stunning Plantation Course at Kapalua a few days ago. That smiling picture of course came before I started playing. On one hole, after depositing what must have been my thir- tieth golf ball out of bounds into the thick, welcoming forests, I promptly launched my seven-iron down the fairway further than my previous shot traveled. There are things I've learned to be more mellow about from my years in California, and competition is absolutely not one of them. The sky has turned darker, deeper, bluer. Periwinkle permeates the air. I can still see Molokai looming and hear the waves crashing and receding below... It's too chilly now for this outfit, despite the vodka surplus that sustains me. Inside, I rummage through my luggage for a hoodie to throw on before settling back on the deck. The scene tonight needs a background soundtrack, so I open Spotify. Springsteen, "Glory Days", nah. Miley Cyrus, "Party in the USA"? I love you girl, but not the right mood. Under the stars tonight, it feels like I need some Eric Church or Jason Aldean. I hit shuffle and let my Country playlist wander. A particularly bright light pierces the new-ness of the night like a beacon. It's too bright to be a star, it must be a planet. I download a sky mapper on my phone and check to confirm it's Mars out there. I near the end of my drink. The rest of the stars start clocking in for the night shift. They pepper the sky, but there's a little too much light pollu-tion to make out too many. Nothing will beat that time I went to my ex Stella's family cabin outside Eureka. I've never seen so many stars in my life. That was a great trip... My phone buzzes with a message from a buddy, responding to my Sto-ry and asking what's next after my twenty-four hour expedi-tion to L.A. tomorrow. I rattle off a handful of places that fill mine and many bucket lists. If I put my full bucket list on paper it would be longer than a CVS receipt. All in the realm of my seemingly open-ended possibility now. "What's next" is one of my favorite phrases, borrowed from one of my favorite shows, *The West Wing*. What I love about it is the attitude of both past and future accomplishment, recognizing that what was done is done, and what lies ahead is a moment left to be seized. To my compulsively planning, ambitiously progressing personality, it's note-perfect. I'm ready to call it a night now. What an incredible sunset and starry sky for me to remember Maui by. What an opportunity to have that moment, to take it all in... Inside, I prep for my next ports of call. I rotate the tropical gear into the back of my suitcase, front-loading the winter cargo I'll require next month in New York. With so much uncertainty around where this trip is headed, I'm heavy on the baggage... But that's okay for now.

This is my life.

THE CHAPTER WITH ALL THE AVOIDANCE

chapter two

I drop the lime into the vodka and soda, use my mini-straw to push it underneath the floating ice cubes, toss the straw in the trash behind the bar, and take a sip. I prefer not to squeeze the lime into the drink because then the lime taste becomes the overwhelming flavor, and I'm drinking Tito's and soda for a reason: I want to get drunk, and quickly, and don't really care what it tastes like. Also, carbs.

I pass my buddy Agamemnon a matching vodka soda, this round is on me. He takes a sip of his drink and we stand side by side, scanning the crowd at this secret bar above a Five Guys in the West Village of Manhattan. I catch eyes with a super cute brunette on the other side of the bar. Italian heritage is oozing out of her, exploding my attraction meter. After almost a decade of chasing blondes up and down the beachfront bars of southern California, I'm returning to my roots. Or at least the color roots that first perked my pubescent parts into man-mode, back in my early days growing up in the land of Volvos and weekends at the Cape.

We play eye tennis across the room.

Look, look away, look back, she's looking, hold it there for a second, too long, she looked away, she looks back, I look down, look back, look away, look back, she's gone, oh well.

That confident, natural instinct to strike up a conversation out of nowhere with a complete stranger of the female persuasion has always been lacking from my genetic repertoire, save for the few nights a year when the right amount of alcohol causes me to trip over myself into some hidden swagger or coolness I keep repressed deep within my personality.

Back in college, things were easier for me. These were the pre-Netflix days, but it took very little effort to hop on Instant Messenger and hit up a girl from class or the floor above to come over and How-to-Lose-A-Guy-in-10-Days-and-chill.

But I've always abhorred the cliché of being "that guy" at the bar. I can't stand "that guy". I'm not sure if it's more that I don't want to be that guy, or, if I'm not that guy, I know I'm not, and wish that I could be. Chads hitting on a girl at a bar are a dime a dozen, though, and I never like to feel that way, in anything I do. And I won't go the negging route, it's very off-brand for me.

If I approach someone, I can't help but think the first thought going through her head is, "Great, here we go again." I imagine most women have their guard up at all times, and it takes quite the confident, or cocky, guy to break through that shield. Or Channing Tatum. Seeing as how I'm none of those options, I generally avoid the situation entirely, waiting to see if she initiates or if some lucky force intervenes like she asks me to take a photo on her phone of her friends and I have my opening, or if a polar bear comes into the bar and I knock it out with one punch and she comes up to me to thank me for saving her life.

I'm usually waiting around a lot.

Tonight is another one of those nights, but my wingman for the evening is up to the task. Agamemnon has no shame bone and makes the obvious move on the pack of three next to us. Being outnumbered three to two, though, is never a great proposition, as whoever's left out of the equation will feel slighted and ready to leave, dragging the rest of the squad with them. That's how the night plays out, of course, in a scene I could have scripted before we walked up the hidden stairs past the burger registers.

I wouldn't have even bothered. If there's a sixth sense looming in my subconscious, it's the acute ability to judge a night's "Hookup Expectancy Rating", and if I'm not feeling it, well you can forget about getting an awkward and stammering inquiry about how your night's going from me. I probably would have just maintained my wallflower status and popped on a swipe app to feel like I was accomplishing something. And to save me from the rejection. The in-your-face-ness of the bar pickup denial.

Sure, dating apps may be the worst thing millennials have forced on the world, aside from Facebook and an inexplicable affinity for the Kardashian family, but an active profile is as necessary to modern dating as going to the gym and maintaining gainful employment. And in the same way that a friends-with-benefits or relationship backslide keeps me hanging on, escaping to the known and mediocre, and hating myself for all of it, I continue swiping, fighting the futile fight in ashamed resignation. As just another nameless face in the crowd, a forgotten fish in a polluted pond. But that's the tradeoff I make in being able to grasp that modicum of female companionship in my everyday without any serious emotional risk or ever having to leave the couch. I'm just not thrilled about it.

Nobody wants their love story to start with, "Well son, you see, one night some Navy pals and I had just returned from the dance hall. I was taking a crap and doing some swiping and I locked eyes with your mother across the room. Well, across the bathroom, down to my phone. And I guess your mother's eyes were digitally locked, but still. And right then and there I knew it was real, so I yelled through the door to my buddies who were munching on Dominos in the other room, 'Guys, I'm gonna marry this girl.' Although I suppose I didn't say 'marry' either."

That's why Tinder is the worst of the bunch. And of society. Both the original trendsetter and with the sleaziest reputation, despite this profile I'm reading from a woman named Ligeia right now that pleads, "NO HOOKUPS. I'm looking for something real and meaningful". On Tinder? Oh, honey.

That seems to be one of the biggest issues with this whole miserable dating existence. A clusterfuck of mixed expectations, objectives, and seriousness across the platforms that results in a self-fulfilling prophecy of exhausted lonely hearts shorting the whole experience, committing to the prospect of love with the same level of game-playing optimism as the daily and impossible-to-win *Hamilton* lottery. But at least when you get a buzz on Tinder you know what you're doing that night. Or whom.

I've never been much for the one-night-stand, though. My "number" consists of only two, maybe three, of that description, but that's not what I want now. The inappropriate and random bar makeout at a younger age, that's a classic. But I'm too much of a hopeless romantic at heart, sucked in by many a rom-com storyline, to settle for the uninspired and meaningless hookup. Most of the time. Now, I'm searching for my person, my one, my soulmate, all that gooey shit.

As my profile reads, I'm looking for my partner in crime... because I plan to rob some banks in the near-future and could use a good getaway driver.

But this is the state of the dating landscape now. An online world where apps are a surface level escape, commitment is non-existent, and intentions are blurred beyond recognition worse than this girl's duck face selfie from inside her car where her head takes up the entire screen. I swipe left, close the app, then delete the app. I deserve better. So does she.

In this city with so many eligible women, successful with East-coast personalities that match my own and great educations and senses of humor, I should be able to meet someone here that meets my difficult and probably over-inflated standards. Right?

One of the ways I try to feel comfortable in a new area is by finding and frequenting its best coffee shops, laptop in hand, productivity in mind. There is something about venturing out into the people, sitting down amongst the locals, getting shit done while those around me are none the wiser to my newcomer status and infiltration of their scene, and walking out a conquering hero of the moment. One area I want to try is in the heart of West Village, a few blocks to my west, and the theoretical setting of the show *Friends*. There is not a coffee shop, but a restaurant on the ground level of the famous apartment building at the corner of Grove and Bedford, and I overpay handsomely for a delicious meatball appetizer that is the real-life restaurant's signature dish. Still, I want to continue to indulge this New York-life fantasy for a day, and I find a coffee shop in the Village a few blocks away from "Central Perk" for an afternoon of work in my new 'hood.

As I maintain my "work from anywhere" status, I pause to look up from my laptop and latte and study the scene. An eclectic blend of the city's prototypical characters surrounds me. The two middle-aged businessmen in power suits, breaking out of the office for a late lunch. The hipster who apparently was lost on his way back to Brooklyn and found relief in green tea. A mid-twenties brunette dressed entirely in Lululemon, splitting focus between the phone in her left hand and the over-sized mug of some steaming beverage in her right, having just taken a photo of the heart-shaped foam the barista artistically created on top of her drink and sending it to some invisible person(s) on the other end to admire. Come to think of it, just about everyone in this place appears committed to the digital world they hold eighteen inches from their face. Some are clearly wasting time fruitlessly swiping through their dating app of choice, others knocking out a quick email or scrolling through their Snapchat feeds. A few people have their laptops out like me, typing away and mooching the free WiFi. After about five minutes of pausing to take in the environment, I catch eyes with an older woman, probably sixty, sitting alone with only her cup of tea in front of her and who appears to have been watching my amusement with her own amusement. We smile at each other in an unspoken acknowledgment of shared sentiment. I wonder if she's single...

It's funny to think about the contrast in this type of scene from that of a 1990's sitcom episode. How would the conversation of the characters have changed if people were only halfway present in the coffee shop, and halfway distracted by a Buzzfeed list of the top 26 ways to create a topic for a new Buzzfeed list? What kind of hijinks could be had when you can no longer blame an answering machine mishap or forgotten note in the pocket for some important missed appointment? How long would arguments last over the origin of some phrase or who really was the MVP of the 1989 NBA Finals if Google already had the answer and was only a click away?

Ding ding ding! We have a winner, the Bumble app yells at me, interrupting my wandering musings. And now, we pause in our regularly scheduled odyssey for an episode of "My Modern Love Story", guest starring my newest match, Leucosia.

My Modern Love Story with Leucosia:

"Hey, how are you?" she asks.

I hope she didn't strain too many muscles to come up with that opening zinger. My interest level immediately shoots from midnight to six on the clock.

Bumble was intended to shift the gender balance of power, letting the women go first in the conversation and potentially shielding off dudes whose opener is a variation of a "Wanna bone?" line and/or a dick pic. But after years of guys getting a bad rap for nasty or lame opening lines on dating apps, this type of message is all too common of a potential relationship starter. And in four words from her, I'm already bored.

Over the years of dating and socializing in Southern California, I developed a bit of a... I really don't want to say test, but more of a standard, for evaluating my interest level in potential mates. Admittedly, it's douchey on its face, but demonstrates my attraction to wit. It's called the Clueless-to-Crazy, Stupid, Love Scale, and it's based on a real-life example from law school.

Here's the scenario: Say a girl from class tells me, "I have a ton of reading to do, guess I have a hot date with my Contracts book tonight," and I clap back, "Yeah it looks like you guys have been getting pretty serious. Will you be updating your Facebook relationship status soon?" in my mind there are four ways of responding after that.

The first type is what I would call the Valley Girl or Clueless response: the "Wait, what, I don't get it?" The joke going completely over someone's head is the type I could barely be friends with, certainly not date, and is unfortunately all too common in the City of so many Angels. The second response would be something like a basic, "LOL" or "haha yeah". Okay she gets it, she laughed, but doesn't really add to the banter. Or just straight up is not interested in playing, which is also a bad sign for my prospects. I might be able to date this person, but not for very long. The third type is very dateable and probably the most common. It would be on the level of "Haha, that would sure make my ex jealous". Gets the joke, can play along and have some fun repartee. I probably operate on this level most of the time. Overall, really solid, but that kind of ends the exchange. The fourth response, though, oh the fourth type is marriage material to me. It goes like: "I'm not sure we're there yet but we did have a convo yesterday about sending Christmas cards together". I love the clear-as-day chemistry of that natural back and forth. No need to tell me you're laughing, the response says it all, and keeps me on my toes with a good return volley.

That's the Gosling-Stone level. Or in the Aughts, the McConaughey-Hudson standard, or in the Eighties and Nineties, the Meg Ryan-Hanks, or Meg Ryan-Crystal, or Meg Ryan-with-everyone status. That last response was actually from my law school girlfriend Stella, and we dated for two years after that and might have gotten married if we met in an alternate timeline. Calypso fell into box number four too, and thus, a further explanation for my smitten feelings and inability to let that level of connection go.

"Hey, how are you?" registers a One or Two on the scale.

Long story short, I don't respond, and that's the end of Leucosia and this episode titled "The Yawn".

The rapidly intruding darkness of the early December

evening triggers a restlessness in me, and it's time to move on to another spot to keep the work productivity flowing. That perk of inspiration and ambition that's been lying dormant for years is bursting through in my new life on the road, even if misplaced or without a certain objective yet. I actually prefer to work at night like this anyway, and the late-night coffeehouse session is my ideal office of choice. I try a new venue tonight in Greenwich Village, and this one has a better balance of WiFi warriors and casual chatters. I enjoy the people-watching aspect, developing a game of trying to determine from body language and the conversation topics I overhear, what date number the couple at the next table is on. Part of me gets a little lonely watching all the connections unfold in real time. I have no core group of friends here, no go-to wingman or steady date to take out. I left that all behind in L.A. to pursue whatever this is I'm doing now.

Ding ding ding! My phone buzzes with delight. And now it's time for another episode of "My Modern Love Story", this time with Thelxiope, a new match on The League.

My Modern Love Story with Thelxiope:

I like The League as an app because it limits the number of potential matches I see in a day. So, I can't just sit there mindlessly swiping through faces and passing easy judgments in the thirty seconds of downtime I need to fill while waiting for the train or in line at Whole Foods. When I first joined The League, I had to go through an approval process, including revising my pictures to make sure my face was showing clearly, i.e. no sunglasses or hats, Mr. California bro. It includes a prominent "About Me" section that allows for a non-looks-based expression of personality. It also allows me the chance to issue immediate Swipe Left verdicts any time I see someone that says, "I love to laugh". Oh really, you enjoy laughing, do you? That's your defining quality? Do you also love your family, puppies, the beach, pizza, your friends, sunny days, breathing air, and being happy?

Thelxiope has a funny profile that catches my attention, something truly important, something that confirms our shared interest in nachos and other cheesy treats. It takes multiple attempts to find an open date on her calendar, though, since there always seems to be a late work meeting, a much-needed night out for drinks with the girls, or other "appointments", before we finally meet at a Korean BBQ restaurant for dinner.

I suppose there was a time, maybe five-ish years ago, when I really enjoyed the thrill of dating. Sitting across the table from someone I don't really know, getting to hear her story and share things about myself with a sort-of stranger. The excitement of where should we go, would she like dinner or just a drink, could we try something different like a hockey game or a hike, what should I wear, where could we go for a drink or a stroll after, the will they or won't they, this is good conversation but do I see a future here, is she feeling it, let's do this credit card dance when the check comes and I can slyly set her card aside and play the hero, do I go for the kiss, okay that went well, now do I text her, do I wait for her to text, ah crap, I texted and she didn't respond for a day, she's busy this weekend, is she blowing me off, okay she's free on Monday, now what do we do?

But I can't even remotely recall the last time I've been excited about a first date. My meeting with Thelxiope is no exception, and unfortunately, she only reaffirms my pessimism. Sitting across from me is someone clearly going through the motions, reciting a personal history spiel she has rehearsed at a crisp two minutes and forty one seconds, hitting on all the important topics including where she grew up, where she went to college, what she does for work, how she came to New York, and how frustrated she is with the New York dating scene, almost as if she had given this speech before and as if it was her third date of the week, which it is, even though it's only Wednesday. The vibe in the room has a distinct air of distance and apathy. No inquisitiveness, no back and forth, no trying to be relatable and make a connection. Just a talking past each other on the way to the next date tomorrow night attitude that really makes a guy feel special. When we hug goodbye at the end of dinner, I put it at 50-50 odds whether she's meeting someone for drinks later.

And thus ends the tale of Thelxiope, The Speed Dater.

Using these apps, my overall ratio of number of first dates to the number of fifth or sixth dates with the same person is roughly equivalent to the number of times Lucy pulls the football away from Charlie Brown to the amount of times he actually kicks it. Basically, the limit does not exist.

But I soldier on. Into the bitterly cold weather bound for home now. My first winter back on the east coast is really chilling my bones after years of Californication. Normally, I don't like talking about the weather since it's pretty much the lowest form of communication. It's something that I generally reserve for conversations with Tom at the office, since I really fucking hate Tom but it's much easier to just wax poetic about the sunshine last weekend than to tell him how unbelievably annoying he is when he chews or talks about his gym routine. Or, for long elevator rides when the boxed in, forced awkward silence between me and this stranger becomes too deafening to avoid.

If I had a stand-up act, I would do a bit about elevator rides that goes something like this:

"How awful are elevator rides, am I right? I mean, that's the Super Bowl of Awkwardness right there. Or at least it is for me. Like I'll be waiting for the doors to open and they do and I'm stepping on confidently like, 'Hell yeah. I am getting to where I'm supposed to be.' And then the doors open enough to see another person there and I'm like 'son of a bitch!' Seriously, my body language goes from 'Da da da da da, I am killing it right now' to 'Ah Shit! Why are you here? 15th floor, press number 15, asshole.' And then every elevator ride from there is the same, like it takes 20 seconds to get to the 15th floor and those are the longest 20 seconds of my life. Standing there next to this stranger two feet away with nothing to say to each other but you're both trapped. You know how some of the elevators have the numbers you can watch as you go up, as if that's something interesting to see, so you just stare at the screen? Like 'oh 2... nice 3, wouldn't have expected that one... ah 4 wow, we are really making progress'. But if that's not there and there's no postings or anything to read, I play a game of 'how many times can I look at my watch in 20 seconds?' (Acts out looking multiple times at watch) HOW IS THIS STILL GOING UP?? God bless phones though, it makes killing the time so much easier. Now I just pull that out and pretend like I'm Instagramming really hard the whole time. Like, awesome baby photo Kim, your kid looks exactly the same as yesterday, double tap. Cool, you don't look like a douchebag in this mirror selfie at all Derek, double tap. Whatever I can do to pretend to be occupied and avoid talking to this fellow hostage. Sometimes I'll get really bold though and actually try to talk to the person, beyond my standard head nod half-hearted smile. You know, where you're both acknowledging 'this sucks for both of us, let's just get through this and get out of this hell hole.' But I even suck at that conversation. It's always like the most mundane bullshit. I'm like 'nice day today, huh?' And I couldn't get away with that in L.A., talking about the weather, because what the hell can you say? 'So, the weather's exactly the same as it's been the last 300 days. Crazy right?' And he'd just be like, 'we're at the 15th floor, asshole.'"

Out of the frozen tundra now, I ride up to my apartment solo, and I may or may not have, but definitely did, hit the closed door button as quickly as possible so the slow folks entering the building would have to take the next awkward death box on their own. Back in the comfort of my month-long digs, it's time for another round of my favorite game.

Ding ding ding! Molpe, come on down, you're the next contestant on "My Modern Love Story".

My Modern Love Story with Molpe:

I open the Hinge app on my phone to check my latest love connection. Hinge is my preferred dating app of choice, sort of in the same way that I'd rather go to the dentist than the proctologist. Hinge was originally started with the premise of matching you up with friends of friends, which is legitimately a decent idea. "Well hey, this guy Mark is friends with that other guy Bill I know, so there's only a slight to moderate chance he's a Fuckboy and/or an axe murderer. Yes please (swipes right)".

Molpe and I start off with some fun conversation. She acknowledges my profile detail on the languages I speak, which I list as: "English. I'm really good at English". I heatedly engage her Most Controversial Opinion topic that "they were not on a break". As the week marches on, hours of gaps in between messages leads to half-hearted attempts to meet, followed by the inconvenient reschedule and the unfortunate cancellation. We pen pal for two weeks before she fades into the obscurity of the rest of the names in my list of matches, a digital monument to the voluminous, uncommitted, and what could have been.

Molpe, for her efforts here on this episode, goes home with a new title: The Fizzle Out.

This entire dating scene has me thinking about reinstituting my membership in the He Man Womun Haters Club, a lost but not forgotten sentiment from when I was a little rascal who still believed in the power of cootie shots.

But it's a new city and a new day, and I hoof it over to Little Italy to meet my parents for lunch. My family is located right on the dividing line between Boston and New York, but at no point in time has my allegiance to one city over the other ever been in question. When my great-grandfather came over on the boat from The Boot as a teenager in 1921, he came through Ellis Island and didn't stray very far, like most Italian immigrants. As we dine at one of the delicious but overpriced establishments on Mulberry Street, I like to imagine my family in this scene, shifted north a few miles to Arthur Avenue in the Bronx and a few decades back, walking through the outdoor fruit stands underneath clothes drying on lines overhead, the smell of tomato sauce and pastries and city in the air.

There's nothing better than Christmas in New York, and an annual family trip on the Metro North for a day of window-peeping and Central Park-strolling is a holiday tradition for us on par with wearing new pajamas while eating too much French Onion dip on Christmas Eve. After battling the tourist throngs and admiring the festive Midtown decorations, I bid ciao to my parents at Grand Central and hop on the 6-Train downtown.

I'm a subway stander, partly because I self-identify as a polite gentleman, but mostly because I like to train surf. Riding without holding on serves the dual purpose of blending in like a subway-experienced local while also avoiding all of its nasty hand germs. As the cross streets fly by with practiced precision, I dabble in my favorite pastime of people-watching. The commuter-heavy crowd may skew the anecdote, but as I survey my fellow riders, no one is interested in interacting. Everyone is closed off to the world, headphones in and head in phone. Could you imagine if I approached the gorgeous woman across the train rocking the tight-fitting peacoat and cute-as-hell beanie, and interrupted her Pandora session to introduce myself and ask if she wanted to grab coffee some time? I might as well be asking her if she's listening to Nickleback and if she's as big a fan as I am. You just can't do that today. Meet strangers like that, or listen to Nickleback, though the latter I agree with.

Ding ding ding! My Bumble is blowing up. Who is the lucky lady this time?

My Modern Love Story with Aglaope:

Aglaope never sends me a message. The End.

That is what we call The Looky-Loo. But that's okay because...

Ding ding ding! A recurring character makes a new appearance in the latest episode.

My Modern Love Story with Parthenope:

I am a great texter. I've always found it easier to write my thoughts and feelings (and witty or sarcastic comments) than to verbalize them. Parthenope and I get the banter going early and ramp up the interest at the right pace to result in an actual live date, believe it or not. I like the way she laughs at my attempts at humor, and it makes me feel reassured. The in-person conversation flows well also, spilling out onto the street after a solid two-hour dinner session.

New York has a tricky goodbye scene to deal with, though, more so than goodbyes in L.A., for instance. After a first date in L.A., I'm most likely walking her to her car or apartment, or ordering an Uber that's on call and whose arrival we can track. In New York, we're out on a busy street, maybe a big intersection, hundreds of people around, hailing a taxi or searching for the correct corner where the Uber is arriving, and then oh shit, the ride is here and the light in front is green, and okay, uh, quick kiss I guess, do I go for the lips or the cheek, let's go lips, okay good quick kiss, and I had a great time too and yes let's do this again and she hops in the car and see you later, end scene. This is going to take some practice.

We meet up later in the week for post-work drinks, and as much as I like her, I just don't like her. Not in that way, anyway. Not in that way that when we pull back from a kiss, I see that look in her eyes and get that indescribable feeling that I haven't even tried to explain yet, but you already know exactly what I'm talking about. The penetration deep within the eyes. A softness and welcoming and longing and conviction that something legit just happened. That spark.

A few days go by and I think we both know it's not quite there. With my leaving the city soon as well, it just makes sense to go our separate ways. That lightning bolt of fate that would cause me to drop everything and stay in New York because "I gotta see about a girl" never strikes. We agree to become Instagram friends as social consolation.

Unfortunately, Parthenope is The Just Not That Into You. My southern friends might know this person better as The Bless Your Heart, though I'm not sure I'm using that term correctly.

My buddies Helios and Poseidon come to visit, and we join the thousands of twenty-something revelers who love Christmas and love alcohol even more that gather together to don Santa costumes and get white girl wasted, wreaking havoc on the bars of East Village in the age-inappropriate tradition of SantaCon. With a margarita in my hand at the sweaty and impossibly crowded Blockheads bar, I stand by the wall observing the festivities with one pervasive thought on my mind: I don't belong here.

All around me, in annoyingly intrusive fashion, are kids with the world at their fingertips, unlimited potential in the pockets of their skinny jeans, stars in their eyes, other people's tongues in their mouths. Young, loud, drunk, tiresome, reminiscent.

Then there's me, off to the side. Sulking, probably.

Another thought materializes through the alcohol vapor haze. I don't belong on the couch staying in for the night either. It's Saturday in the City. I'm unattached and not adulting very hard or very well, why shouldn't I keep enjoying myself with these types of adventures? That's why I'm out here, that's why I left L.A., another place where I didn't belong. To see the world and create some memories, and maybe let fate serve as the cruel but decisive mistress to my unfulfilled heart and head.

But is this really enjoyable? Is this really what I left everything behind to do? I've staked a decent amount of personal and social credibility on this entire experience. I may not have had much in mind as far as goals or larger objectives when I started, but it had to be more substantial than this.

A man without a home, in every sense of the word. A man with no direction, no matter what the itinerary says.

I've had a few memorable moments in my life that came out of nowhere. Moments that would be otherwise unremarkable if not for that ineffable emotion that clicks from an unknown place within the soul, and the monumental but unpredictable impact that eventually affirms the value of that inkling. There's that moment pause after pulling back from a first kiss that tells me everything I could possibly want to know about a future relationship. There was the time in college when I snuck away from a party in my friend's basement to check my LSAT scores on his computer and announced with my first words of reaction that I'd be going to Pepperdine Law. There was the time at my girlfriend Stella's house outside Eureka where the emotion bubbling up within me, metaphorically while we were in the hot tub, was more than I could handle, and I told someone for the first time that I loved her. There was the time I sat at Señor Frogs in embarrassed defeat and first questioned my ultimate goals in life.

And much like that obnoxiously incongruous setting in The Bahamas, there was the time, now, waiting for thirty minutes on the cramped steps leading to the underground bathrooms of Blockheads on Third Avenue, where the moment strikes me from somewhere inside and I ask a loaded question that has long deserved consideration: what exactly is my end game here?

After I avoid peeing my pants in this line, of course.

By thirty, I was due to be happily married, have made my first million, be gearing up for a run for Congress, have a second child on the way, be operating my own business, have visited fifty countries, be unreasonably fit for my age, have golfed at Augusta National, be spending summers at my lakefront second home in New Hampshire, and have control over every aspect of my life. That was the plan. There's always a plan. Having accomplished approximately 4% of that ambition, I may have missed the mark just a bit.

At least this travel adventure is doing... something. It's not sitting still and just taking my beating. That's my motivation. I'm fighting... something. Complacency? The Man? Maybe my own expectations? An uncertain but determined something. An exciting but anxious something.

My origin story is replete with plot points that nurtured my type-A personality into not accepting the minimum and always seeking out the best. To achieve. My mother, the early childhood educator, encouraged me to engage in playful imagination and develop a sense of independence from the start. Combined with my cautiously practical father, they fostered a ceaseless drive in me to succeed. "A's" on the report card get taken out to dinner. "B's" get "what the heck happened?" "C's" and below don't exist. Ever. Mixed into and in between semesters, our family was always on the move, learning about the world by being active in it. From multiple trips to Orlando, Myrtle Beach, and Cape Cod, to exploring all over New England, or San Diego, Arizona, and Virginia.

Go to Disney World as a family, create a lifelong traveler with a sense of wonder. Sit on the couch with your kids all summer, create a future of heart disease.

I was born to run, trained to go after it. It's an instinct I am stuck with now, like how I became an "exclamation point guy" because I used one in an email to a colleague one time and am now forced to use one every time, so he doesn't think something's wrong.

In my hometown area of Norwich, Connecticut, I'd come across folks in their twenties and thirties, still hanging around the local food and beverage establishments and refer to these "Townies" in a derisive manner. There were even some who were legends on the basketball court or in the party scene, only a few years older in school and whom I previously looked up to, but now had a few less hairs up top and a few more inches around the waist. I never understood the mindset of a Townie, and what would drive someone to settle unquestionably in the same location where it just happened that their parents decided to settle. The key in all of that, to me, being "settle".

For someone who always has at least one eye firmly fixated on the next destination to conquer, the mentality of settling is almost offensive to me.

I've been told, by those around me, by my generational stereotype, and by my dwindling bank account, that I have a clear case of wanderlust. Engrained within me is a desire for exploration, going back over thousands of evolutionary years, when the first Neanderthal emerged from his cave and said, "I keep getting the same girls popping up on Tinder, I need to branch out and see what the ladies in the village down the Tigres have going on." The original Manifest Destiny. It's the same exploratory mindset that drove so many of my expeditions on the Oregon Trail game in Fourth Grade until I inevitably died of dysentery.

But despite my recent flirtation with the maverick character that has arisen for my storyline in the last month, I don't fit the free-wheeling, exotic-minded, off-the-beaten-path archetype.

I order my pizza with cheese or pepperoni and put ketchup on my cheeseburger, and that's enough. I went from college straight to law school. All of my cars have had a navy exterior and a tan leather interior. My parents are happily married at the head of a pretty nuclear family. I consistently "lose" at the game Never Have I Ever. I embrace a bougieness level just below that of the ruling class. Sure, I like my fancy water, and go wine tasting at vineyards. But I'm drinking Smartwater, not Pellegrino, and choosing my winery attire from a wardrobe of monochromatic T-shirts and jeans from the Banana Republic collection of two years ago, not the Connecticut casual with pastels and slacks that would seem to be my natural uniform.

As much as my dating profile shows a man of the world and my tagline reads about a partner in crime on the run, I'm a boring homebody at heart, looking for a place or way to be grounded, something that's my own, even if everything feels foreign and out of place right now.

To me, the thrill of travel is to venture out in exploration, and return in achievement. But always to return home.

And maybe that's what I can get out of this in the end. Some prize to return with, earned in the zones outside of what has been comfortable in the past, in situations and locations I would have never chosen otherwise.

But there is no prize to bring home tonight from these drunken shenanigans, just the slices of cheese and pepperoni I scarf down at Joe's on my way back across the city. And speaking of prizes...

Ding ding ding! My time is running short in New York, but I've got one more shot at finding love in this hopeless place, perhaps with my latest Hinge match Peisinoe in the latest episode of...

My Modern Love Story with Peisinoe:

I want to get cute with this last first date, so I take Peisinoe to the quaint Restivo Restaurant in Chelsea. I think she might get a kick out of the name like I do, but she's too busy talking to realize the family connection. From the start of the date, where she's late because she went to happy hour with a friend and had a few glasses of wine first, through the entirety of the meal and the street corner goodbye challenge, I'm not sure she ever stops talking. At least there are no awkward pauses to worry about. Yet, at no point do we discuss anything real that I would feel weird talking to the barista at Starbucks about.

The physical attraction is there, though, and before she hops in her taxi, she makes the driver wait as we get a solid makeout going in plain view of our Manhattan audience. She has a few more things to say on her way into the cab, but I've long since tuned out.

That doesn't scare or shame me from sending the day-after template message on Hinge: great time last night, yada yada, hope to see you again soon, yada yada, (insert inside joke from the night before), yada yada, what are your plans this weekend?

Ironic silence.

To be continued...

I hop on the train to the airport for my long-awaited Global Entry appointment, then hit a serious snag when the issue of "Permanent Address" comes up in the processing.

I've ditched the home address for a life of travel, and explo-ration, and boundless possibility and adventure on the open road and skies, but the agent interviewing me doesn't give a shit about that, and I struggle to find evidence of a living sta-tus that will satisfy him to stamp my application. Eventually I'm able to show proof of my parents' address in Connecticut as my own, and though it may be the first, it will certainly not be the last time that this nomadic life becomes a hindrance to operating within the norms of the system. Health care, taxes, insurance are sure to become more complicated by this rather innocent diversion from the standard that seems to obfuscate the paper-pushers in front of me.

I don't know why what I'm doing needs to be considered so revolutionary. With the emergence of a more digitally con-nected people, third world advancements in infrastructure and safety, and an expanding, easily-utilized travel culture and industry catering toward Europeans with too much holi-day time and Americans with too much income and parental resentment, the world has never been more accessible. Re-mote working is trending as well. WFH is now an acronym in our daily vocabulary, as people look for opportunities to ditch the commute, the stuffy office space, Fred stealing your lunch from the fridge, and too many awful jokes about "Hump Day, am I right?" in favor of a home workspace. Combining those two concepts, working from abroad while traveling, as my laptop can testify, is now dubbed being a "digital nomad" or "location independent". Cowork, coliving, and remote work programs like WeWork, WeLive, and Remote Year offer a bit of structure to the digital nomad population, making it much easier to live and travel the world while maintaining a sense of community and work productivity.

It was these types of programs and opportunities and social media accounts showing a remote life of wonder and wander that inspired my recent foray into the non-tradition-al. The people I see on Instagram alternating from computer on the beach to glorious waterfall hike to coffeeshop session to island sunset make it look so easy. Everyone looks so joy-ful. Certainly, I can be too if I follow this path, through the jungle and along the beach as well. With my consulting job being entirely remote, the opportunity is there for me, and with each post that hits my feed, I feel guilty about my life for missing the moment that's out there for the taking. Without really doing anything, all these people are doing something.

I want in. I want that life. And I don't want to waste my chance with this.

Call it Catholic guilt. Blame it on a birth order over-achiever mentality. But while I'm living this remote life, I want to accomplish something too. I need that prize at the end. It could be financially meaningful, or my own *Eat, Pray, Love* story, but I can't allow this journey to just be a passive one.

And while I'm off experiencing this #wanderlust life, maybe I can show everyone that I'm doing things better this way, by not settling. To prove... something. To someone. That's my motivation, I think.

Ding ding ding?

Now for the series finale of My Modern Love Story, Part II:

It's been a few days and I have yet to hear back from Peis-inoe. Maybe she's been busy. Maybe she typed out a response and forgot to hit send. Maybe she's hiking Machu Picchu. All valid excuses. I send a second message, asking about drinks and hitting some golf balls at Chelsea Piers, Thursday night?

No response.

I can't send a third message here. That's social suicide. It's like when you get introduced to someone at a party with a name that's difficult to pronounce.

"Hi, I'm Jon."

"Hi, I'm Falghefn."

"I'm sorry?"

"Farlgshem."

(Long pause of confusion, eyes racking the brain)

"Okay."

You get two shots at it, then it's time to give it up.

Verdict: Ghosted.

Peisinoe, like so many others and certainly a role I've played before, is The Casper.

And who can blame her? When the basis for a relationship today is generated in an environment where seconds-long decisions are made on a person's worth, the mindset is established that potential mates have earned only a cursory amount of my time, attention, and energy. What we owe to each other is very, very little. And in the face of conflict, it's so much easier to hit ignore than to deal with a possible confrontation. Even from my first time with the sex, following my sixty second performance in the freshman dorms at the University of Connecticut, my natural instinct was an abrupt phase out. It wasn't until after an ominous AIM away message that I took for a pregnancy scare when I felt compelled to the noble act of saying, "hey".

Ghosting may not be page one, but it's probably the theme of the first chapter in the Millennial Handbook.

Discouraged, by Peisinoe, by dating as a whole, by myself, I delete the rest of my swipe apps and announce to myself in indifferent fashion that my love life and I are on a break. I have a new focus now.

For the last few weeks, a thread has been running through the background of my mind as this ill-defined voyage sets sail, about my motivations and a self-doubt generated from a fear of the easy escape. Without a determined objective, with a background that is conditioned for flight, am I not just running away?

That begs the next question: is having an overly strong desire to travel like this, to do what I'm doing now, a good thing, as the common perception might imply, or a bad thing, as some bitter Baby Boomers might overtly rant?

So again, what exactly is my end game here?

Wanderlust sounds like such a wonderfully pleasant word, perfectly created for a hashtag or travel documentary. But couldn't it also be a crutch, a defense mechanism employed under the pretext of exploration when confronted by a challenge? Whether the modus operandi is a trip around the world, quitting a job, or flaking out on a relationship, the end game seems to be the same: avoidance, and non-committal behavior.

I wonder if I should write about all of these questions. To tap that curious ambition, festering guilt, and innate desire to accomplish something of value with my time on the road, and observe life outside of the world I've always known but never truly, honestly explored.

As I walk back from the gym one frigid winter evening, I give my mom a call to discuss the latest action.

My mom tells me to go for it, embrace the challenge. To just write, see what happens, see what I learn and who I meet along the way.

This feels like a scene in a show where a friend gives another friend absurdly simplistic advice to solve a problem.

"I don't know, I think I really messed up. He's going to be so mad at me."

"Just talk to him, I'm sure he'll understand."

"You know what? You're right. I'll do that."

And that is how I met myself.

PART TWO

"*I saw my life branching out before me like the green fig tree in the story. From the tip of every branch, like a fat purple fig, a wonderful future beckoned and winked. One fig was a husband and a happy home and children, and another fig was a famous poet and another fig was a brilliant professor, and another fig was Ee Gee, the amazing editor, and another fig was Europe and Africa and South America, and another fig was Constantin and Socrates and Attila and a pack of other lovers with queer names and offbeat professions, and another fig was an Olympic lady crew champion, and beyond and above these figs were many more figs I couldn't quite make out. I saw myself sitting in the crotch of this fig tree, starving to death, just because*

I couldn't make up my mind which of the figs I would choose. I wanted each and every one of them, but choosing one meant losing all the rest, and, as I sat there, unable to decide, the figs began to wrinkle and go black, and, one by one, they plopped to the ground at my feet." – SYLVIA PLATH, *THE BELL JAR*

THE CHAPTER WHERE FOMO IS REAL, AND NOT SPECTACULAR

chapter three

Left or right?

For the first time in a while, this isn't related to a swipe decision.

Layered in winter wear to shield the cold from creeping in and the gym sweat from emanating out, I survey the options laid before me. I have the chance to choose my own adventure back to my apartment, as the night rudely wraps Manhattan's early evening skyline on one of the darkest days of the year.

To the left, my favorite route home. I could take a short walk down Bowery on the edge of East Village, then hang a right on Bond Street for a quick taste of cobblestone streets where the light reflects off the wet old stones, twinkling with imagined nostalgia in a way that makes me fall in love with the city all over again, before cutting down to Bleecker and my apartment.

To the right, another can't-lose option. Straight along 4th Street through NYU country, along the southern border of Washington Square Park and the *Friends*-famous Arch until I turn down Sullivan.

There are more choices for food on the latter route and I need to do something about dinner, so I opt for the bustle and take a right, a crisp but manageable bite imbuing the December air. Alongside me, newly-freed workers make their way to their respective happy hour establishments, the city being a particularly safe haven for the single and aged.

Everything about the street experience here is enveloped in a tangible quality of frantic energy and some kind of important business. New Yorkers walk with a pace of purpose, taking any opportunity to find an efficient time-saving maneuver in their pursuit of the next block, whether it's crossing on a red light and narrowly avoiding a hard-charging taxi, or aggressively pushing through a family of slow-walkers from Nebraska (probably) who don't understand proper sidewalk protocol. This is my natural pace, and my time in L.A. has never slowed that street aggression and quest for ultimate walk-time efficiency, although I'm still spelled by an irrational fear of the large and ominous steam grates that I find on my route. It is thoroughly enjoyable to be able to blow through "Do Not Walk" signals again without hesitation, after almost a decade in California of impatiently waiting on street corners for permission to move.

People in New York, visitors and residents alike, most often use the comically cliché word "energy" to describe the vibe of Manhattan, as I have already. But like most stereotypes and conventional wisdom, the meme comes from somewhere and carries on for a reason. There really is something about the rush of being in the City that is unlike anywhere else in the world, and is likely why it's also the place where people never sleep. It's either that, or the constantly needless horn-honking from taxi drivers at all hours of the night, anxious to get to their destination and another fare, hustling for their next dollar just like the Wall Street trader or Murray Hill pizza shop proprietor they carry impatiently in their back seat.

Should I pick up food now? And if so, from where?

Pizza, Thai, Argentinian, ramen, Greek, pizza again, Mexican, kebabs, and oh yeah, American, aka fast food. It's all here, in this epicenter of variety. It all sounds good, but nothing sounds good.

I'll just get something at home. But I do want to pick up a Christmas tree first, to give my apartment more of the holiday vibe. I stop at one of the frequent pop-up stands along the way.

Which tree?

I like my Douglas Firs, and I like 'em full-bodied, with a little cushion for the ornament pushing. I've only got time, space, and arm strength for a mini two-footer, though, so I select my Charlie Brown tree and finish my route, ready to hibernate for the night, fire up the Yule Log on Netflix, and get into the holiday spirit.

People that start the Christmas season immediately after Halloween, disrespecting and cutting short the end of Fall (which is, in fact, the best season) and diminishing Thanksgiving (which is an underrated and fantastic holiday) are, quite frankly, monsters. You want to listen to the occasional Christmas song in November? I'll allow it. Maybe break out the Red Apple Wreath and Frosty Gingerbread flavors of Yankee Candles? Fine with me. But come on people, have some respect for the falling of the last autumn leaves and a day centered entirely around turkey and mashed potatoes please.

My stomach is grumbling now. I thought I had more in the kitchen to cook. I'll need to order delivery.

What am I vibing for dinner?

Since I am ceaselessly weight watching, food is constantly on the brain.

Malcolm Gladwell theorizes that with 10,000 hours of practice at a particular objective, anyone can become an expert at anything.

I'd like to challenge that assertion, because I've easily spent 10,000 hours, roughly in the last week alone, at trying to have a healthy relationship with food. Yet, I'm still just as unfailingly a failure at that endeavor as the Trump family is at everything.

My mind approaches food with the same inattentive fervor of a kid in a Candy Crush store, and with the same amount of ineptitude. It's just one of the constant struggles between my better angels and the self-sacrifice of the short-term selection. A succumbing to the inherent inability of the mind to operate in rationality.

One of the three sections of the law school-required LSAT test is called Logic Games, and the questions typically involve a scenario where rules are provided in a hypothetical world with the charge of figuring out how people will act within the confines of that world. A "for instance" would be: Aaron can't sit next to Blake on a plane, but must sit behind Chris and to the left of Danielle. A bunch of additional rules are given... where will Aaron sit? To solve the questions, you have to map out the constraints and possible choices, using logic to deduce the final outcomes. A difficult Sudoku puzzle requires a similar diagramming strategy, and is probably more relevant to a broader audience, but I get to humble brag for a minute this way.

I aced this part of the LSAT. All 24 questions. The rest of the test is where I bombed. Within this isolated world of rules and rationality, things make perfect sense to me. In the real world, with all of its imperfect chaos, the choices people make and the way people act, particularly this guy here who can quickly knock out the Sudoku in the back of the airline magazine but takes an hour debating menu options for dinner, elude my full understanding and thought processing.

In my everyday, there is a constant confrontation with impediments to the benevolent choice, my mind naturally being skewed toward the irrational. It's subject to temptation (if you put bowls of chips and salsa out at a party, I'm probably going to keep eating until they're gone, even if I'm not even hungry, just because they're there: the "take these away from me" mentality). Or misplaced overconfidence (I always think some new relationship or business idea is going to succeed, even when faced with steep odds against: the "yeah but this time it will be different" mentality). Or susceptible to framing (a doctor saying I have a 95% chance of living versus saying I have a 5% chance of dying, with the latter being disproportionately affective to me: the "your bedside manner could really be improved" mentality).

My mind is consistently failing in its search to find meaning and adapt to the real-life, non-Sudoku complexities of the world.

If I encounter turbulence on an airplane, my first inclination is to tense up into a firm grip on the armrests thinking of the recent plane crash that's easily available in my short-term memory bank.

If I was told not to think about a penguin wearing a funny hat, you better believe I'm conjuring that image in my head and working on a name for him. For the record, it's Harold.

If a group of women are grabbing dinner at the next table, my friends and I might guess jokingly about the trivial things they might be discussing, like their outfits or the loser boyfriend one is dating, while they laugh to themselves about how we tough guy, big brain manly men debate football and the proper role of the Fed. The cheap stereotype is the easier narrative because it "makes sense".

All of it is, in some manner, making judgments. Being presented with a million things at once and trying to process the next move. The right choices. Making sense of the world and how to operate in it from a place fraught with these natural mind fails in abandonment of the rational.

At any given moment on any given day, I am faced with some decision, whether largely immaterial like what toothpaste to purchase at Rite Aid, to slightly more important considerations like whether I should move to San Francisco for a significant other.

And sometimes, the easiest choice, the option that's going save me from all of that unwanted heartache and uncertainty, is to just make no decision at all.

In high school, I always sat in the same seat (and played Tetris on my TI83 calculator) even if there was no seating chart. I'll get subscribed to an email list one time and then keep receiving messages for years after because, well, it's too much effort to cancel so why not? Then there's the iPhone. Firstly, everyone has the same phone, so there's a lack of choice in and of itself. But when I'm walking out of Verizon with my new phone, how many default settings do I actually change, or does the ring tone and message alert that I use now match that of everyone else? I'll pause here while I go change my ring tone settings.

It may not be what I really want or what's best for me personally, but the "Default" option becomes the standard because I have no real impetus to change, or to make a choice that cuts against the grain. The status quo earned its place for a reason.

Tonight, I should probably choose something healthier, but why rock that ancient jukebox? This feels like a pasta night and my usual order of spaghetti carbonara.

Which delivery service do I use?

I spend the next twenty minutes bouncing through my phone from GrubHub to Caviar to UberEats to Seamless to Postmates, hunting for the best deal and delivery rate on this meal. While I wait for my Caviar order, I open my computer.

Which Christmas movie should I watch?

Elf, Love Actually, Home Alone 1 and 2, *Jingle All the Way, The Santa Clause, Christmas Vacation, The Grinch Who*

Stole Christmas, A Charlie Brown Christmas, A Christmas Story, It's a Wonderful Life. All on the seasonal bucket watch list. But in order to see anything, because I haven't bought a DVD since MTV was still playing music videos, I need to find a streaming source.

Which streaming service should I use?

I spend another twenty minutes flipping through Netflix, Hulu, Amazon Prime, and HBOGo to see what's available, and where I might be able to create a new Yahoo or Gmail address in order to snake my way into a "free trial".

Unable to pick one that feels right tonight, I give up on the idea and lay back with my new book by Michael Lewis. This most recent release is a story about the relationship and ground-breaking research findings of two Israeli psychologists, Daniel Kahneman and Amos Tversky. Kahneman and Tversky are essentially the Godfathers of modern psychology in the field of choice and decision-making. And let's face it, I need help with navigation, so here's how they map it out.

On the surface, it would make sense to a layman like myself that having more choices and the authority to make them is a good thing. According to economists and pure conservative thinkers, having more options to choose from generates a more optimal decision, as the hypothetical rational person would have more of an opportunity to make the logical choice that maximizes her benefit. However, these theories and the idea of a completely logical decision-maker fail to recognize that we're all idiots. Or put more nicely, irrational. Having too many choices, too many opportunities, too many possible outcomes to weigh can be a stressful and paralyzing experience instead.

Being the one in control is a role I am very familiar with in all of my personal, professional, and social circles. But despite my acceptance of, or in reality my type-A desire for, that call to action, it often comes with a debilitating dichotomy of dithering indecision on one hand or abdication of a decision on the other.

The latter, these "mindless defaults", bother me, but are mostly harmless and often caused simply by my own inertia. Oh, is the next episode of *The Sopranos* starting automatically on this stream? Well I guess I'll watch one more. Or if I'm out at the movie theatre and order a popcorn, the large order being roughly the size of a toddler, chances are I'll default into finding the bottom of that bucket eventually, even if unintentionally. Portion sizing, and the inability to appropriately manage intake accordingly, is one of the main reasons the entirety of America is testing the sturdiness of any chair we sit in, while the French are rail thin while maintaining a diet consisting entirely of carbs and cheese.

Far more haunting to me, though, is the former, the pain of indecision. The anxiety of affirmatively making a decision and being wrong, with the possibility of letting people down, letting myself down.

If you gave me the choice between two options...

Item A: a sure thing gift of $500.

Item B: a ticket with a 50/50 chance of winning nothing at all or $1000.

... in that scenario, I'm choosing Item A, the guaranteed cash. But when the values are flipped, and the scenario is changed to the setup below, I'm choosing Item B.

Item A: a sure thing <u>loss</u> of $500.

Item B: a 50/50 chance of losing nothing at all or $1000.

This is because the pain of a loss hurts so much more than the pleasure of a gain, by quite a large margin in fact. If someone were to just hand me $1000, it would have the same emotional and physiological impact of losing $500 from my wallet, so the ratio is about two to one in terms of the overvaluation of loss to gain. Because of this, I'm naturally wired to be loss and risk averse, since the effect is so disproportionate when all other factors are accounted for. I know that feeling of loss, and have attached strong negative emotion toward it.

I choose Item A in the situation where a gain is involved because I don't want to take the chance of feeling the pain of losing a guaranteed $500. Basically, I pay a "pain premium" in the odds department in order to avoid the mental anguish that comes when a fat zero shows up in the lottery, thinking about what I could have had and essentially turning a gain into a loss. So, I'll take the cash in the first scenario, and head out for a mimosa and avocado toast brunch, and call it a day. No need to play with gambling when guacamole is on the line.

In the second scenario in which loss is now fully in the picture, I have the opportunity to avoid that loss entirely, and a decent 50-50 shot of it, so I take the gamble and become risk seeking. When the situation is framed in this way, as a losing proposition, I will do what I can to dodge that negative feeling if possible. In short, I am already in the loss column with my circumstances, but there is an option (and only one) for avoiding it completely, and that is the gamble, so I choose

B and take my chances to avoid loss entirely. My actions would be described in the second scene as loss-adverse, or as loss avoidance, while ignoring the loss <u>minimization</u> strategy of Item A that would seem to be more logical and rational.

And in that choice, and this is incredibly important so make sure you're paying attention, I'm not maximizing my optimal outcomes or my happiness level. I'm simply following the path that might allow me to miss the worst feeling: namely and overwhelmingly, regret. Regret...

I fade to sleep as the taxi horns honk their accompaniment to the urban milieu fifteen floors below, while visions of plum decisions dance in my head. Financial questions, romantic, geographical, professional. All the best possibilities I need to figure out tomorrow, or soon, or now.

Where should I work this morning?

Which neighborhood should I visit?

Which coffeeshop should I try?

I love my West Village regulars, but after my default dinner last night, I'm feeling frisky and in need of a shake-up to the standard. But first, I need to tap one of the many resources available to organize, rank, and visualize my options, assuring me of the best coffee and workspace combination. I pull up Yelp and Maps, checking reviews, ratings, and pictures for outside validation. I want backup sources, so I google articles on the best coffee shops in Chelsea, the best places to work from in Gramercy, the most Instagrammable locales on the Lower East Side. I download an app that caters to writers and remote workers in specifically evaluating coffeeshop work spaces, taking the guesswork and uncertainty out of the process. I settle on a quaint spot with large tables and fast WiFi in Tribeca, which I think will satisfy me.

I pack my reading material on decision-making into my laptop bag, a feeling of curious security coming from keeping this newfound guidance close by and ready for more exploration.

It seems that it's that possible regret, the overarching emotional aspect of choice, that exists in the real world but is what's absent from the hypothetical plane ride scenarios being offered in LSAT logic games. And yet, the human element drives so much action. In that world, maybe I don't know that the reason Aaron can't sit next to Blake is because Blake slept with his sister and Aaron is still upset about it, or that Aaron wants to sit next to Danielle because he wants to ask her out to mini-golf when they land. To say that we act without some emotional influence is nonsensical. It would be like saying I like the movie *Rudy* for the fall scenery of South Bend, Indiana, and not the fantastic way the plotline tugs at my heart strings and causes me to cry every time Rudy runs onto the field at the end.

The pressure that I feel in making a choice for myself is almost entirely created by that decision-making bias centered on avoiding regret. Piggybacking on that emotion is the related feeling of responsibility, particularly when I'm upsetting the status quo. The pain of getting it wrong in this scenario is so much more impactful than a loss within the existing status quo where no change was made, because the loss is seen as a direct result of a choice I made when I could have potentially been happy doing nothing. Because of this, when facing a choice between the sure thing ($500 cash, the status quo, etc.) and the unsure gamble, it's natural to be skewed toward the former because of that asymmetrical valuation of winning and losing. It's hard to regret the steady status quo. The usual, normal choice.

How do I get to Tribeca?

There's no larger, existential threat to my psyche in this choice. I just need to decide if I want to walk, or Uber, or taxi, or Subway. Usually, I enjoy the stroll through the city, a brisk pace of aimless admiration guiding my step. But I'm feeling particularly impatient to get there to check out this coffeeshop this morning.

Being restive is in my nature, and in my last name. I'm the one who would rather read the spoilers for The Bachelor than sit through the nonsense every week, while also annoying my friends with the tease of an unwanted reveal of the "winner". I'm always rewatching the same shows and movies, even though and because I know the ending. I want to make sure I'm not getting myself into a situation where I'm highly invested early on, only to barely make it through Season Three before eventually hearing what happens and shrugging my shoulders in ambivalent skepticism.

One of the things that greatly impacted my adolescent years and helped foster my appetite for reading was the Goosebumps series. I didn't read all of the books, but I was pretty damn close. Then one day R.L. Stein, that literary genius, said, "Fine, you little shits are getting tired of me pumping out poorly-developed sequels like I'm a Hollywood studio draining every last ounce of relevance out of a superhero character?

Try these 'choose your own adventure' books instead and shut up." Although I was not in the room for this statement and can't 100% confirm. My preteen self had all the power, an avenue to determine a story and ending for myself in a way I hadn't really experienced at that point in my life.

With that opportunity, though, came great responsibility. If I made the wrong choice that resulted in the untimely demise of our protagonist, I fucked up the whole reading experience and had to start all over. Feeling the pressure and anxiousness about this newfound sense of control, I would panic and jump to the end, trying to find the route that would get me a win safely out of that haunted house/carnival/day camp.

More on point here, as this open-ended odyssey picks up steam, part of me, a large part, craves to know where this journey's going and how this story comes together, to ensure it was all worth it in the end.

For now, I plop myself and my trusty shoulder bag onto a small private table in the corner of the coffeeshop and decompress over an almond cortado with the fancy milk design on top.

Should I do my consulting work or write?

I want to be able to do it all.

I want to write, and somehow actually make money too. I want a new job every year or two if it has the promise of better pay, a fancy new title, real-life health care, and most importantly, an attractive vacation day policy. I want opportunities that will be better for me at that time, forty-year career and company loyalty be damned. I want to live in places that are warmer, cleaner, more active, more walkable, more eclectic, more likely for me to ride a shared city bike to a craft brewery downtown next to a tapas and wine bar, than the place I was raised and my family still resides. I want to hold out in my dating life, waiting impatiently for the elusive "one" I am convinced I deserve and is just around the corner.

Not only do I want it all, but I get it all. That's my millennial right. Not that I'm entitled to it per se, but that it's all within the realm of possibility, there for the taking, all the best things, all the happiness.

In this jack of all trades, master of none personality of mine, I have envisioned myself in so many different professions: real estate broker, sports agent, film producer, JAG attorney, politician, stay-at-home dad, travel blogger, actor, real estate developer, Instagram celebrity, and most recently, writer. I honestly believe if I devote all time, effort, and passion toward any one of those pursuits, I would be successful at it. I also could see myself living in New York, Chicago, London, San Diego, to name just a few of my realistic residential locations. None of these potential lives for me is out of reach. Yet, when choosing one means saying no to the others, I fear that unknown and unrealized possibility, and maybe go half-assed into it all instead, or move around wildly searching for something to cause me to finally settle on one life for myself.

Which makes things difficult because the anticipation of the emotional pain of choosing something incorrectly and missing out on something else, the valuation of "what might have been" regret again, is a tremendous factor in my decision-making process. It's made all the more anxiety-inducing by an ability to envision that alternate universe in which a different decision was made. Perhaps even another universe where the ending of *How I Met Your Mother* <u>doesn't</u> suck.

The more or easier I can picture myself with the college sweetheart I turned away at a young and dumb age, or of sipping coffee from the balcony of my new condo in Seattle while taking in the morning mist of the marine layer as it begins to fade from the summer air while a bird chirps from the treelined street down below before I head to the new job I just relocated for, the more the possibility of regret will come into play.

The mind fail here is not limited to regret, either, but a general overvaluation or miscalculation of certain probabilities or outcomes, based on emotion. It's why I overpay for insurance (a small and unlikely gamble) and play the Powerball lottery (picturing up until the last number is called, my new house on Lake Tahoe).

Basically, what exists here is a scientifically confirmed if not medically diagnosable case of FOMO: the fear of missing out. The "what if" of it all. It also explains the lack of confidence in making a bold or different decision when the default is safer and less likely to result in a feeling of regret after the fact. In that way, FOMO is always looming overhead, like the dark clouds of parental disapproval or Monday-morning-quarterbacking on a sports radio call-in show.

My phone buzzes, a friend texts about getting drinks later. FOMO plays its villainous role socially for me as well. I pack up my baggage and head north through the tundra for home, my imagination dreaming up vivid scenarios of what could be. If I go out, maybe we'd meet a couple girls and have our "how we met" story, or maybe we'd do shots with a VP at Goldman and end up on the company jet with the Knicks cheerleaders bound for Tahiti.

To go out or not?

I have this weird personality balance where part of me really likes to be scheduled and have a plan, and part of me loves indulging in some "fuck it, let's do it" impulsiveness. I find relatability in the *Yes Man* character of Jim Carrey, who goes from being a stick-in-the-mud hermit to having the pendulum swing to the opposite end as he starts over-committing to everything, before eventually finding the inevitable balance by the end. I also relate to the mantra of Tim Riggins in *Friday Night Lights* about trying things as a way to "create some memories". In fact, just go ahead and imagine me looking like Tim Riggins but with the comedic flare of Jim Carrey from now on, if that helps paint a picture.

Part of that impulsive attitude stems from a FOMO-induced desire to see where the untaken path might lead. The other driving force is probably coming from a need to be liked, my compulsion to avoid confrontation, my distress to not disappoint. To make everyone else happy.

But at this point I'm trying to cut back on drinking in preparation for the beaches of Puerto Rico next month, and I'm slightly skeptical I'm going to end up going to Tahiti tonight, so I choose to be lame.

It's a frigid winter evening anyway, worthy of a night in with a blanket and tea from the comforts of the couch like a proper old. I receive a FaceTime call from my group of friends back in California. It's the annual Christmas party and everyone is there, except for me. They pass me around the room to a steady chorus of "we wish you were here" and "you're really missing out" lines, while Mariah Carey plays in the background and the Netflix fire flickers on the TV.

"Well I would hope I live longer than sixty," I respond dryly to my buddy Achilles on the other end of this FaceTime, who believes this latest harebrained travel idea of mine is the sad display of a midlife cri-... you know what? Let's not use that term, let's call it a readjustment. A midlife readjustment. "But I'll gladly call it a quarter life crisis if it means I live to be 120."

What am I doing right now?
Where do I fit in this world?

I'm not lost, you're lost. I'm not running, you're running. I'm not crazy, you're crazy. It's not me, it's you.

I look up and see friends, family, the people all around me defaulting into the safety life with a herd mentality to the status quo, without explanation or a hankering for objection. A collective conservatism that embraces the adulting traditions that society has established: college, marriage, a family, a career, wearing a tie to the office, working nine to five for five days a week, suburbia, Applebee's and Chili's and Home Depot, living for the weekend, lamenting a case of the Monday's, having ageless feelings of both protection and appreciation for Taylor Swift, eating three meals a day with advice from the food pyramid, an affinity for weekend trips to Target, signing up for a spin class and then not going, complaining about traffic and our bosses, complaining about taxes and mortgage rates, complaining about how our first child was treated unfairly in school by his teacher and how our second child is being screwed over by her soccer coach making her sit on the bench like that.

The FOMO in this space is the fear of being left out by not conforming, generated either by groupthink mentality or peer pressure. So, when I choose what to listen to on Spotify, I note the number of other people who have listened to the song or artist first and choose accordingly. When a presidential candidate wins the primary in Iowa or New Hampshire, I jump on board so as to not miss the bandwagon. I bring my reusable shopping bags to pick up groceries to show how environmentally conscious I am and so that Al Gore doesn't yell at me.

That is what I'm supposed to do, without any second thought about whether or not that life, the life full of 30-year mortgages and coin-flip divorce rates that I'm supposed to lead, is leading me to a place I really want to be.

Would it not be easier to fall into a normal career path, probably at the first company to offer me a job out of college? To marry the person I've been dating for fourteen months, because we're both in our late twenties and not getting any younger and I definitely, maybe think this is the one and we have to start having the kids soon? To move to a place twenty minutes from the parentals?

I probably want to be a part of that world, but I just can't do it. Not now, not yet. To do so would be to give up the power over my own life, to not make a choice for my own happiness, to settle. What I can do for now is use what I can to predict a path that leads to my optimal outcome, even while hamstrung by my natural bias of the "what if?" The unrealized possibility.

I had a picture in the vivid imagination of my mind, of where my life would go and who I would be. Now that I see it not materializing, it makes me want to rebel against all the forces that represent that which I don't or can't have.

Maybe it is just me. Maybe I'm too stubborn to settle for those unconscious defaults, and too excited by opportunity to make the conscious, unemotional decision. To avoid any regret.

I don't know. Maybe it's just me.

THE CHAPTER VERSUS REALITY

chapter four

You know what sucks?

New Year's Eve. And Kanye West. *The Big Bang Theory*. Pumpkin flavored things. Florida. Marathon races. Fantasy football. Coachella. Crossfit. The movie *The Notebook*. IPA beer. Oysters. Most seafood in general. The comic book superhero genre. Eating ice cream from a cone instead of a cup. Snapchat. Reality TV, especially shows that make losers appear more successful than they are, like *The Apprentice*. Or FoxNews. But right now, mostly New Year's Eve sucks.

Any attempt to go out into the public in celebration results in a long, late, pressure-packed night of waiting in endless lines to get your fill of the $150 VIP package you were forced to purchase from this bar that would charge five bucks for a beer on a regular night, all in the attempt to stumble into a random stranger for a drunken kiss at midnight to somehow validate your entire year, almost always ending in letdown by 12:02 one way or another.

My route to Puerto Rico for the next month of workcation is via a New Year's layover in Kansas City. Yes, that Kansas City.

My current bucket list count of states visited is at forty-four, and of the six I'm missing, Kansas is the most random and isolated, essentially requiring a dedicated trip to cross it off the list. Since New Year's is dumb anyway, I might as well try to get something productive out of the holiday. My friends Nestor and Poseidon join me in the most flyover of locations. We spend the last night of 2016 in the Power and Light District, where we have one of those stupidly necessary all-inclusive drink passes. We start at Howl at the Moon for some singalong, before moving over to the country-themed bar with the mechanical bull and the Daisy Dukes for the remainder of the night. Drinks are had, lines are waited in, eye tennis is played, and midnight comes and goes as it always does.

You know what sucks?

No, not Kansas City. Despite having an atrociously designed airport and being described as "the city that sleeps", it's actually kind of sort of cool.

It's Airbnb Customer Service that sucks.

Our experience in K.C. is defined by the worst Airbnb encounter I've had to date, courtesy of our host, this short, mid-thirties douche who, despite the cold December air, looks to have recently emerged from a late night at the worst club on South Beach, dress shirt half buttoned far enough down his pasty chest to reveal his ten or so hairs there, light linen pants with loafers, taking his ratty-looking dog out for a piss on the street corner. In showing us to the unprepared apartment to drop our stuff off early, he ushers us through a loft that surely must double as an active crack den or trash storage facility in addition to an Airbnb unit.

Used Band-Aid on the counter, cool. Rotting brisket in the fridge, yummy. Pile of questionable white powder on the corner of the island, great. Frying pan in the sink with some disgusting liquid morphing and growing tentacles by the hour, awesome. Oh, and more trash than a *jersey shore* beach bar on a weeknight in October. As the dude is walking us around this place with no shame, he has the gall to actually tell us that he rents to hookers on the reg as if it was a point of pride, maybe thinking we were cool with that, or showcasing some Napoleonic false bravado or machismo that befits his meager stature.

After arranging some alternative accommodations, we get into a pissing match, threats are made on both ends, Airbnb Customer Service proves themselves to be as pointless and useless as Daylight Savings Time, and we go our separate ways with a truce not to take any further actions against the other (oops, smirk emoji).

To memorialize the whole Kansas City experience, I post a picture to Instagram of our group of friends from the Boulevard Brewery, using the hashtags #friendship and #whatareyouguysdoinginKC to gloss over the harsher realities of the moment.

You know what else sucks?

The middle seat on an airplane.

In a younger, more impressionable day, I was a consummate window seat person. The rush of takeoff, zooming rapidly over the familiar buildings, landscape, and sightlines below, either well-known from calling that place home or newly-acquainted at the tail end of a successful trip. And on the other end of the flight, returning home safely or to come closer and closer to the start of a new adventure, the exciting allure of an unknown and imminent experience coming clearer into view on landing. My own twelve-inch personal portal to the outside world, offering an altered perspective to it all.

My favorite part, though, is mid-flight, after reaching cruising altitude and mentally cursing out the dick in front of me who throws his seat back automatically and with reckless abandon into my space, when I look up from my book/laptop/crossword-puzzle-in-the-back-of-the-airline-magazine and catch a glimpse of the boundless blue beyond, and imagine how awesome it would be if it were possible to run and bounce across the clouds. As I travel more with age and for work, and attempt to remove my head from the clouds, I find the aisle seat to be much more convenient in avoiding claustrophobia, discomfort, and bathroom trip disturbances.

This morning I'm back in my familiar setting, viewing the unfamiliar below on approach into San Juan, sitting ocean-side out the left window as the January Atlantic shimmers clean, cold, and clear. I smirk to myself at the absurdity of my current situation, in contrast with the regularity I not so long ago left behind. The enormity of what I'm doing has really not hit me yet. My typically instinctive sense of planning and mental preparation has been stowed away in favor of a cavalier attitude to approach this new life on a tropical island for the next month, in a heavily Spanish-speaking location that is basically an international relocation. This becomes blindingly clear as I emerge into the sharp sunshine outside the airport, in equal fashion struggling for half an hour getting my Verizon cell service to work while deciphering the unnecessarily confusing taxi line at the terminal.

My foray back into the Airbnb game takes me to an area of San Juan called Condado, in the northwest corner of the city, located conveniently in between the charmingly authentic Old San Juan and the bustling local scenes of Santurce and Ocean Park. The apartment is perched on a narrow strip of peninsula separating a lagoon to the south and open ocean to the north. From my back bedroom window I get the Atlantic in my face, and from my front living room window, the only thing blocking my views to the lagoon are the pool and the palm trees.

As I unpack the contents of my comically excessive amount of baggage, the excitement of my endeavor finally starts to kick in. This is real, I live here now. The cool ocean breeze shuffling through the tunnel of open windows is a swift reminder we are definitely not in Kansas (City) anymore.

I take a sunset run along the bridge connecting Condado and Old San Juan and splitting the Atlantic and lagoon, reaching the wave-crashing rocks on the ocean wall at Punta Escambron to pause and reflect. And smile again. And to snap a few selfies, obviously, to send to friends not here.

You know what sucks?

Holy humidity, Batman. It's January, relax.

The nasty humidity offers an impolite welcoming back after being estranged in California all those years, providing me the wonderful opportunity to sweat entirely too much through my shirt while also losing total control of the curl in whatever hair I have left.

While drenched from my run, annoyed by a zit that popped up on my selfies, and struggling with the controls for the air conditioner, what I share to the world tonight is a post from my front porch, through the palm trees and over the pool, of my new idyllic lagoon #view.

One of the goals that I set for this trip is to opt for rentals in lieu of hotels, for a few reasons. The most obvious motivation is financial. I've taken the funds I would've spent on pricy monthly rent in Los Angeles, along with utilities, car expenses, and other costs of being a normal adult, and repurposed the funds toward plane flights and accommodations. If I turn around and pour it all into hotels, I'd earn VIP status at Marriott Rewards in short order, but just as quickly be looking under the couch cushions to book a return flight home.

The other, more mental objective is the feeling of being a local, even if temporary resident, in the places I travel and bunker down for the month. There's a different vibe in my daily functions and routine life when I wake up in a house or apartment instead of the fourth floor of the Fairfield Inn. I want to avoid the mindset of a tourist, both internally and how I'm viewed by the locals. I want to try to blend in, and get to know the culture and local hotspots, and maximize the experience of each location, with an eye toward finding a home and the solution to at least one of my adulting dilemmas.

I add a new video to my Story so everyone can see the neighborhood.

My first wild Friday night is a solo stroll through Condado with a cup of fro-yo, side-stepping around the unexpectedly bustling plethora of families that have invaded this relatively quiet corner of San Juan.

You know who sucks?

Tourists, pfft. They ruin everything for us locals.

The humidity decides to take a break in favor of a fast-moving tropical shower from which I have to take cover under a hotel overhang with some other stranded survivors. Maybe I'm just more in tune with these feelings at the moment, but again I'm humorously brought into a moment of clarity, this one being that of a now-resident in a tropical and unpredictable locale. I laugh a little, toss out my empty cup of nutritious dinner, and jog the three blocks home in the rain.

There's something to be said for an early and sober Saturday morning, waking up not feeling like a complete fucking degenerate waste of space. It's nice.

I trek through the same streets this morning, silent and soaking in fresh, cleansing rain water, a stark contrast to the spirited scene from the night before. It's a good day for some exploring, and some golfing, so I grab a very reasonably priced rental car from the nearby Hertz and head east.

You know who sucks?

Drivers in Puerto Rico. Like, all of them.

My first venture into driving in another country, sort of, comes with many... adjustments. The compactness of the cars, the even more pronounced compactness of the parking spaces and alleys and garages and streets, the local driving customs and habits of the roads, trying to figure out what the hell a kilometer is.

It takes all of about fifteen anxious minutes on the road, while crudely converting signs in Spanish and the metric system in my head, before a car comes flying into the highway from the on-ramp, nearly side-swipes me, guns it down the lane in front of me, barely misses another guy, and then decides at the next exit that the best time to take the off-ramp is from the center lane after already passing by it while crashing into the guy next to him who was properly exiting. It's like watching Yoshi cut in front of me with a speed boost mushroom to try to avoid a green shell and a banana peel, and spinning out while taking Mario and Donkey Kong down with him.

Meanwhile, my Wario kart continues on, mouth agape and unsure of what to do exactly in this situation. Am I supposed to stop and talk to the local police officer about the maniac? I feel incredibly out of my element at this point, and begrudgingly proceed in my travels with hands at perfect 10 and 2, eyes darting all over in defensive observation.

The rest of the ride, once I safely and delightedly leave the highway portion, is one for the record books. It's a good thing I've curated extensive skills in the art of texting and driving, because I cannot stop taking notes of the sights and sounds that surround my Toyota Yaris on this scenic northern coastal route. To the left a seedy establishment actually advertising cockfighting, to the right the mountains and lush green forest of El Yunque National Park, back to the immediate left the white sands and palm tree-lined backdrop that I swear I've seen in someone else's Instagram before, over on the right the scattered beachfront bars and small shops of local proprietors. Up ahead, a jungle atmosphere awaits, with an encroaching canopy of trees enveloping the thin "two lane" road shared with cars, bikers, and iguanas alike, darkening out the gorgeous morning sun just for a moment at a time. I abandon my strict schedule to make my tee time at the St. Regis Bahia Beach golf course and pull off instinctively into one of the many partly secluded beaches that adorn the route in unlabeled and unspoiled fashion.

I may have 99 problems but a beach ain't one. Saving that line for use in a hashtag someday.

You know what sucks?

Sitting on the beach all day.

I just can't get into it. I love to be near it, to see it, to drink next to it, to walk on it at night, to know that it's there. But there's a point of diminishing returns for me and it happens after about thirty minutes on the hot, sweaty, salty, sunburning sand, then it's time to go.

I upload a picture to Instagram of the palm trees and ocean and sand, from my appropriate distance away from the beach and safe distance away from the manic streets, with a post that has a peaceful, commercial bliss like it's #sponsored by Corona.

After a too brief moment of exuberance just staring complacently at the beautifully bare beach in front of me, I book it for the course and join up for a round with a random couple from New Jersey. In between attempts at avoiding bunkers, iguanas, the jungle lining this secluded course, the

beach lining the eighteenth hole (which I obviously hit anyway), and another tropical rain shower at the turn, we get to
chatting about life, love, and the love of travel in life.

I'm normally not one to be overly talkative about my
travel experiences with strangers, or ever really, but I find myself feeling completely at ease as I regale the couple with old
stories over beers at the clubhouse: the time my friends and
I visited the Blue Grotto in Capri but it was closed to boats
for the only day we were there, so we jumped in the water
despite the warnings and swam through the portal to have
the famous cave to ourselves; the time Poseidon and I road-
tripped across the country and made a literal last-second
turn to detour to the Four Corners on the way to the Grand
Canyon, and got back on track in just enough time to get to
the South Rim for the last thirty seconds of the sun setting
over the majestic vista; the time my grandfather and I traveled around Sicily together, visiting family in Palermo and
the hills above Agrigento in the tiny Ciancianna town that
my relatives left almost a hundred years prior, to the family
house that still stands today; the time we went to Kansas City
and had a nightmare of an Airbnb experience.

We go back and forth enjoying each other's tales from
the road: me, thirty, and this couple, late fifties, well-traveled
and semi-retired, feeling like I can keep up with their stories
and match them with my own travel bona fides.

My lack of cable brings me out the next night for Sunday football and the Giants game. I post up at the bar of the
aptly named Tacos & Tequila for some tacos and tequila, while
stealing long, soul-satisfying glances through the open wall

of this beachfront restaurant that charmingly frames the sun setting over the ocean not far beyond the bar's televisions. This setting was built for a Boomerang, from the ocean, to the bar TV, back to the sunset, back to the game, all right in front of me. This is the type of experience I imagined, a best of both worlds.

You know who sucks?

The New York Football Giants.

As I take in the ugly playoff loss to the Packers on my right and the pleasing sounds and views of waves crashing to my left, a group of Americans is chatting across the bar about living in San Juan. A few people know each other and are local, and they inform a tourist couple next to them about the tax benefits of living here, and of all the area's recent development. Then, much like my conversation with the New Jersey couple the day before, everyone begins to throw around a laundry list of destinations seen and soon-to-be-seen.

"Oh yeah, India is incredible. I loved Goa."

"Ah, I haven't been to Chile, but I'm supposed to go with my friend in the Fall."

Tonight, rather than interject and join this discussion with my own list of proud travel achievements, I stay in observation mode and just take it all in. Quickly, that old wanderlust question re-emerges, and I'm back to some awkwardly-timed self-reflection on the commotion of my motion, and the motivations thereof.

Why do I like to travel? Is it a means of accomplishment by crossing items off a list, like taking and meeting challenges to prove something to someone? Do I want to be relatable to a broader community, to say, "Yeah, I've been there too" and fit in? To be able to discuss and reference the unique and exotic as a man of interest and sophistication, so I can land my own Dos Equis commercial someday?

I wrestle with these thoughts, then upload the Boomerang of my ocean bar view to Instagram with a #noworries headline to show the masses that I'm doing great.

Perhaps I could become Insta-famous from this experience. After all, Personal Branding is offered as a course in Third grade classrooms these days, right after "Long Division" and before "Six Figure Student Loans: Friend or Foe?" More realistically, maybe I could generate some buzz in smaller, more niche communities of similar nomads that could be useful for any kind of future writing and traveling endeavors.

I started on Instagram late, though, and at this point I have less friends than poor Tom has on MySpace. The first "trade tool" I use to beef up that following is to be a tool and incorporate an abundance of carefully selected hashtags for my photos. Basically, I want to attract people looking for similar or specific photos, with tags as wildly creative as #travel and #views. People scouring the app, either for pleasure or more likely for gain, might see my photo under this "branding", and like it, comment on it, or go so far as to follow my account. I specifically want to attract the digital nomad community, and brand my travel as #remotelife and #workfromanywhere. The strategy seems to be working, as I gain about a dozen or so new followers with each post, and these types of things usually snowball. At this rate, I could be around five figures by May. Look at me now, Mom.

You know what sucks, though?

Instagram games. I'm noticing an annoying pattern of losing about ten of those twelve new followers within a couple of days. After a minute of research, I see that the Insta-famous game is really a pathetic practice of following and unfollowing people with regularity. The hope is that they follow back and stick on your list long-term, even as you're ditching them for a new set of suckers.

This is the way of the world, where hot people influencing others on the internet is entirely more lucrative than teachers influencing the future leaders of America.

I can hate the game, while still being a player, at least for as long as I think I want to be a player. And for now, I do, so I share a new post of a fresh Boomerang from the coastal rocks by Old Town San Juan, my smirk of mixed motivation shining through. The caption that follows is loaded with hashtags, and absent of shame.

You know who sucks?

My friends. Some of them, anyway.

To this point, much of the fuel I've found on this adventure comes from reveling in the praise of friends, family, and followers, and the tequila shot of enthusiasm to my exploits that chases each comment of support and expressed jealousy.

But at the same time, in my isolated state, I'm starting to recognize an oversensitivity in myself to little comments from the peanut gallery in my feed, feeling stigmatized for doing things differently and trying something outside the box. Other "friends" have taken the approach of either unfollowing me and showing the shallowness of our relationship, or purposely not liking or commenting when I post. And as always, it's the losses that sting much more than the intoxicating validation I so desperately crave right now.

I see you there, Menelaus. I know you're watching my story but apparently can't be bothered with supporting a friend in his travels. As if my self-promotion is any more egregious than anyone else's in this online world of over-sharing and inflated importance.

But fine, whatever, here's a new post of an iguana next to my ball on the golf course, with no hashtag spam accompanying it. It's getting forty measly likes. Happy now?

You know what sucks?

Social media.

I don't know why it bothers me so much, that some aren't willing to bend the knee to the glory of my showcased life, but it does.

Part of me feels defiant toward the unsupportive, and I throw a spiffy geotag filter on this photo of my current makeshift workspace at an outdoor picnic table and add it to my Story, intent on rubbing it in the faces of the people back home living the cubicle life.

A different, smaller part of me feels vindicated by my choice to take this show on the road. When a phone and WiFi is all I really need to get my job done, why should I be beholden to a stale office that drains the life out of me on a daily basis? What is stopping me or anyone from doing the exact same work, more even, from a coffee shop counter or this park on the beach, as I do today? The answer to that, as has become clear these last few weeks, is nothing really.

You know what sucks?

The office. Not the TV show, the real life version.

Believe it or not, the monotony of the every-day (waking up early, being overly dependent on coffee, moderately adhering to a gym routine, pretending to be productive most of the day through primary motivations of avoiding the ire of the boss and being able to pay rent, getting irrationally annoyed by emails that just say "Thanks", mentally preparing to do it all over again the next day) is made so much more tolerable when it can be done from a mobile environment. From this new location, I'm able to take advantage of the time difference at my west coast office, getting my day started before California even wakes up. I'm in a groove now, getting accustomed to these exotic surroundings and breaking out of the long-term tourist mindset again in favor of my resident status and new work digs. I feel accomplished and energized, like I've found a lifestyle that is the best fit for my personality.

In my latest battle of Instagram life versus the real world, I post a picture of my laptop from the beach and let the promotional hashtags fly this time. "I don't care what people think," I say.

Luckily for me, or more likely by subconscious design, my work history has generally allowed a certain amount of freedom from the rules. Not as an attorney, though. I ditched that path immediately after law school, so that's a fun $180,000 mistake I'm still paying for and will be even when Tesla is making flying cars. After passing the bar, I fell ass backwards into telecom development, an obscure field I knew as much about as my nonexistent retirement portfolio. Don't get me wrong,

I have the "lounge back and drink a cocktail while wearing a bright floral shirt and planning out my next tee time" mindset down. I just don't know how I'll pay for it yet.

The truth is, I've stalled out a bit professionally. I think it's partially because of this jack of all trades, master of none burden I carry with me. That feeling isn't something new to me, though, starting from the days when I was a kid and could pick up a ball or stick or bat and be very good at whatever the sport was, but never good enough at any one to go anywhere significant with it. But I'll get to that Margaritaville life some day. On my schedule, and my way.

I'm stubborn that way. I get really annoyed at my FitBit wristband anytime I haven't yet walked 250 steps in an hour, and it warns me ten minutes before the hour is up to get off my ass and move around. I have a hard time following my mother's advice or direction the first time, even though nine times out of ten, she is right (as she smiles and nods while reading this). Any time I've been given an assignment by a boss that to me seems inefficient or a waste of my time, I will either express to them as much or find a way to avoid it. Long story short, I'm not so good with the taking of orders.

You know who sucks?

Old people. Especially old people that try to make me do things.

In true millennial form, the setting I aspire to in my work life is very much at odds with the status quo of generations past. I like hands-off management, freedom and independence to operate, California-casual office attire, and an unstructured work schedule. I believe cubicles are the creation of uptight middle management designed to curb innovation and grandiose thoughts of advancement (no matter how many inspirational quotes, Christmas cards, and pictures of the family dog adorn those gray felt walls). I need to feel like I'm not in a perpetual state of stagnation, and will impatiently hold firm to the belief that I can earn and deserve rapid advancement, in contrast to the antiquated and stupid notion of "paying your dues" just because. Despite what the geezers in the office say, that feeling of desired professional progress carries with it an aspiration for personal and team accomplishment, proficiency in my work, and long hours, as long as the long hours are going toward something meaningful and exciting, and not in monotonous and pointless service to the "man". And I can't speak to this personally, but I know working women would prefer an environment where orange blobs with the hair consistency of what comes out of a cotton candy machine aren't using their tiny hands to grab them by the pussy.

There are some millennial stereotypes that are funny and dumb so they don't bother me. Ones like, "You silly millennials and your avocados."

Yeah dude, they taste good and are really healthy. Sorry, not sorry.

The one I love from the olds that actually drives me nuts is the participation trophy meme. "Oh millennials, gotta have their participation trophies."

Let's think about that for a second. Was I in second grade, finishing 8th in a fun run race and asking for an 8th place ribbon, or was there, oh I don't know, an adult who was the one handing that to me at the finish line? You don't want us growing up thinking we deserve a trophy, don't give me a trophy for finishing 5th in a soccer tournament. That's on you, adults in the room. You don't get to complain about how we turned out now.

And in the workplace, I'm sorry lardasses who sexually harassed your way to middle management, but I'm smarter than you. I have $200,000 worth of student loan receipts to show for it. I absolutely wasn't smarter when I was 17 and essentially forced into all that debt by a tuition bubble and culture that requires parents to pop a $1.99 sticker of their child's hundred thousand dollar college on the rear window of their SUV for the whole neighborhood to view and validate. But I did go to college, I went to grad school, I learned some things, and I grew up understanding technology that's changing the world. Sorry I don't have time for your old school bullshit. I've got $1500 in loans to pay every month. And I'm hungry over here.

Hungry for some avocado, too, because now that I'm talking about it, I could go for some guac. And margs. I get a story up on Instagram of my solo dinner, proof that I can live that #basic life wherever I wander.

I emerge bright and early Saturday morning, rental car back in my control, in constant defensive mode against the terribly reckless and wreck-causing drivers that populate the Route 3 highway on the way to El Conquistador Resort Golf Club on the far northeast tip of Puerto Rico.

You know what sucks?

Missing the fairway.

For this round, I have the course to myself though, aside from the copious number of iguanas adorning the fairways of this hilly, oceanfront track. A beautiful and soul-boosting round, followed by a Corona from the restaurant terrace with the awe-inspiring view of crystal-clear ocean waters and pop up islands sitting just off the coast, immediately registers as one of those never-forget type of moments for the memory bank.

I add it to my Instagram with a new post to really drive that point home. I can't stop projecting the beautiful side of this life. The optimistic side. The epoch side.

You know what doesn't suck?

Puerto Rico.

Of all the places on my agenda, past, future, and those yet unknown in this uncertain voyage, this early section of the trip was probably the one I was most apathetic about. Sure, it was always going to be cool to see for a bit, then say I had lived there with a tone of accomplishment. But this early experience has really been surprisingly satisfying, like kicking off the day with unexpected-but-sometimes-more-fun morning sex. The natural and often untouched splendor of the surroundings is stimulating, from the luscious green of the rainforest atmosphere to the pureness of the white sand beaches. There's water everywhere, and elevation changes to go with it, making for some truly exceptional and original perspectives.

Much about the Puerto Rico vibe to me is unsettling, in a way. And not necessarily in a bad way either. Eye-opening with a touch of adaptation.

Many of the TV channels are the same, and the road direction matches the U.S. at least, so that helps with the adjustments. The metric system is dumb, which I am obligated to disclaim as an American before making any other statements about it, but also much better than ours and not difficult to figure out. The dual language nature of the island is sufficiently clear, and predominantly more Spanish-leaning than I would have guessed. The communication barriers are manageable when combining my Junior level understanding of Spanish from high school a million years ago with my innate ability to talk with my hands in describing things. The extensive English understanding of most locals doesn't hurt also, but it showcases an overarching theme of in-betweenness, or split loyalties or identities.

Continuing in my new bold and adventurous mindset, I make my way down to the small city of Fajardo. I pass through areas of uncertain security, rundown and poor on an island that is largely rundown and poor on the whole. And yet, there is little trash on the streets and no graffiti, in sections of this city far removed from the uplifting influences the American dollar is supposed to bring. The sense I get is one of respect for the homes and neighborhood in a place where modern business has failed to appear. The people may lack for money, but not for pride in their home. A glimpse of authenticity in the reality that surrounds the beauty.

I carry on into the hills of Playa de Fajardo, to a picture-perfect view of a quintessential Caribbean backdrop, in terraced houses, expansive beachfront cays, small islands and that vivid unfiltered ocean water that surrounds them. From my hilltop pit stop looking down on the scene, I try for about ten minutes to get a shot worthy of the feeling of the moment and of my profile, before giving up on the idea that my iPhone camera will ever be able to truly capture or display the views my eyes are being #blessed with.

I love it here, and I'm not entirely sure why. Puerto Rico is foreign, but also not. Spanish-speaking, but also not. I use the American dollar to shop in areas of the city that are both touristy, and not. Hole in the wall restaurants in San Juan serving local dishes like Mofongo and Tostones, situated right next to Ben and Jerry's and down the street from Olive Garden and Fogo de Chao. Having everything and nothing, happy and sad, beautiful and rejected.

Back in my new home of Condado, I find a relatable comfort in the confusion, as if the recent development of the area has made it both unsure of its future status and emboldened by its past, in a state of in-betweenness that will find that right balance someday.

It's authentic and unapologetic and real and #nofilter.

THE CHAPTER ON AN ISLAND

chapter five

"Nobody wants to hear that story," my dad half-heartedly protests through that familiar familial smirk.

My family has joined me in San Juan now before our cruise vacation this week. As we sit around at dinner, my sister details the time my dad accidentally left me at the grocery store when I was about seven years old, and I had borrowed a quarter to call the house on a pay phone. When my dad got home, and my sister told him I was on the phone, he yelled back that she was crazy, turned around in the car, saw I wasn't actually there, freaked out, and burned rubber down the road to pick me up, where I was waiting cool, calm, and collected, chatting with one of the soccer moms from my team. I don't really remember the story, but that does sound very on-brand for me: having no problem being out on my own, hitting it off with an older woman.

We are out in Old San Juan, a colorful, cobblestoned bastion of historic Spanish influence in a Caribbean setting, replete with fervent cruise ship day tourists in just-as-historic cargo shorts staring up at long-dormant fortresses of a forgotten time.

The cruise idea is the second iteration of the new family gift-giving policy we adopted recently for our adult selves to replace the boring traditional Christmas morning unwrapping of clothes and necessary (more likely, unnecessary) household supplies. Last year, my parents revealed our vacation destination in a way that is quintessential Restivo gift-giving. Why just hand over a present when you can make a game of it?

I really suck at giving gifts, hate sending (and receiving) cards for holidays and occasions, and am really bad about getting physical presents for friends. I think it's the obligation aspect that I don't like. I'd much rather show it with actions, but if I do get you something, I'm probably going to have fun with the presentation. For my ex, Stella, I booked us a trip to Arizona for baseball spring training and the Grand Canyon one year, but I presented it as a challenge of putting together the not so indecipherable hints I had gotten her for the trip: sunscreen, a baseball, and a travel game. Generally, the siblings and I get a group gift for our parents and present it as a scavenger hunt or game, last year sending them all over the house with clues until they found the new kayaks mounted to their car in the garage.

In divulging the location of our trip for this year, my parents put together a version of the 1980's game show *Clas-

sic Concentration, having us chip away at the answer hidden behind the doors until we matched enough pairs to uncover the Royal Caribbean pictorial representation on the board, to our hesitant but hopeful enthusiasm. I was able to make the correct final guess, after honing my skills over many MS-DOS computer sessions in the early Nineties, popping in my floppy disk version of the game into our old school Apple and solving away. Yes, I'm a nerd.

In search of some post-grub drinks, I consult the universal guide to the food and drink galaxy, Yelp, and sift through reviews that often drive me crazy. There are certainly more egregious ways to provoke my ire, but none come to mind right now more than a snotty and irrational Yelp commenter. "The food was great, but my experience was ruined when the waitress took, like, forever to bring our check... one star. - Sally". Fuck off, Sally. The waitress probably hated you because she kept tripping over the giant stick up your ass.

After some awkward, fish-out-of-water dancing in the streets to Reggaetón music in celebration of who knows what exactly, everyone grabs Ubers to their hotel, but I decide to mosey the two miles back to my apartment to work off some of the booze and take in the enchantment of my neighborhood on the last night at my place. After about ten minutes and bored with the prospect of walking the remaining thirty, I break out a move that I started in college and jog the rest of the way, a habit I developed the winter of freshman year living on the far end of a bitterly cold campus. I know I must put on a decent show for others on the street over the years, watching a drunken guy in regular clothes running down the road late at night, but when faced with the options of walking and getting home in thirty minutes, or jogging and being in bed in ten, I often choose the latter. And yes, I know it's probably one of the weirder things about me, but if that is the main baggage I'm running around with, I am easily outshining most of Congress and will gladly carry that.

But it's not all I'm carrying, and I load up my gear the next morning and bid adios to my surprisingly redeeming Airbnb apartment.

You know the bustling dock scene at the beginning of *Titanic*, when Leo and the Italian extra are running through cargo and past families toward fate and some pretty poor mid-Nineties CGI of a ship? That's how it feels as my taxi rolls up into the port of San Juan into a cruise-controlled chaos. The hubbub is punctuated by a palpable buzz amongst the crowd anxiously gathered at the entrance-level deck to this towering behemoth that will serve as home for the next week. My expectations for my first cruise experience are anchored by the cautionary tales of cruise-skeptic friends, and buoyed by the seasoned veterans who swear by them annually, but mostly I'm swelling with excitement about the excursions on the individual islands. (I'm going to halt the nautical puns now).

My biggest concern as we pass through ship customs is over the frustratingly authoritarian alcohol policy, which I've heard from those seasoned cruise vets is incredibly strict. As a result, the only drinking supplies we're allowed to carry with us are a few Franzia-quality bottles of wine we picked up from CVS the night prior. But as we make it through customs without anyone even checking our bags for booze, I curse the fact that I very easily could have brought a handle of Tito's, or a keg really, on board.

Once cruise-bound, the novelty of the experience is both thrilling and irritating, as my emotions swing over the excitement of the mini golf course and multiple pools on the upper decks, to the annoyingly blatant money-grabbing techniques being shamelessly forced on guests below deck. My fellow shipmates are an interesting cross-section of the American population, trending decidedly lower middle class, seemingly Southern-heavy, older or family-focused, and highly susceptible to the strategically marketed on-board scams that the cruise line has clearly perfected over decades of fleecing practice. Marked-up drink packages, marked-up dining extras, marked-up photo sessions, marked-up luxury jewelry and clothing shops, marked-up WiFi, marked-up breathable air.

It's easy to avoid these promotions, which would make even the executives at Disney blush with envy, with a simple universal "no thanks" policy, yet I watch as so many unsuspecting guests are reeled in hook, line, and sinker to what's made to appear as standard procedure. In a closed off and isolated environment on this floating mega-resort, with no communication to the outside world, people are all "on board" with Royal Caribbean. (I'll see myself out now).

For now, I embrace the dearth of accessible data, refusing to pay the exorbitant WiFi price tag, and explore the better parts of the ship experience with the fam, sans cell phone. I feel a bit lost without it, though. Like I don't know what to do with my hands.

Our first port of call in the morning is St. Maarten, the Dutch portion of this two-country island best known for Maho Beach and its absurdly close airport runway landings. My personal activity of the day is ATV exploration, and I pick up a rental at the shop right off the terminal. Before the cruise, I was resolved at some point to rent a motorized vehicle and drive it all over an island, and I waste no time getting my 4-wheel on. It's an experience from my past that I remember about as fondly as drinking Slush Puppies after Little League games, Pogs, or the Nick at Nite lineup.

Ten years ago in the Greek Isles, my study abroad friends and I took an Easter Sunday and drove all around Corfu on ATV's, over mountain tops and through small towns, the smell of lamb roasting on outdoor spigots overtaking our senses while friendly locals waved happy hellos as we drove by. A few weeks after that in Sorrento we indulged again, with mopeds along the Amalfi Coast, through dangerously winding oceanfront and mountainside roads to the breathtaking Italian hillside beach town of Positano. Two of the best days of my life, and something that I often encourage others to partake in if possible. It's absolutely the best way to take a standard vacation and make something more of it, getting away from the tucked-in-shirt tourists and out into what I really want right now, the authentic sights and sounds of the world. It's the truth, but that seems really douchey as I write it, so I'll happily put a dollar in the douchebag jar.

In lieu of traditional wedding presents and in my typically atypical gift-giving form, I usually opt for a similar type of honeymoon activity, something the couple will never forget when they're tossing away that worn-out Caphalon pot set from Uncle Jimmy. While we're on the subject, we should have a conversation about the antiquity of wedding registries. The whole purpose back in the day was to help kids that were twenty-two, not living together, and getting married start their home. But now we're hitching up much later with jobs, dual incomes, and shared residences already, so let's come up with a new approach to the wedding present. All I'm saying is, you want a shitty fondue set from Macy's? Buy it yourself. From me, you're getting wine tasting and a catamaran ride. You're welcome.

A life goal of mine is to eventually live in a place where I can feasibly drive some kind of ATV around on a daily basis. Maybe the influence of Van Wilder cavalierly riding through campus in a golf cart has just stuck with me. For now, though, my ATV charges down the poorly paved and sometimes cobblestone roads of St. Maarten, bound for Maho Beach with sketchy directions and street signage leading my way in the absence of data and Google Maps. I meet up with the rest of my family, who went the boring taxi route, as we wait on the tiny strip of sand barely separating the Caribbean from the Princess Juliana Airport. Eventually a large KLM Boeing jet comes screaming toward us with fierce and somewhat frightening rapidity, passing overhead at a distance where I feel like if we could jump (or LeBron James could jump) just high enough, we could touch the extended wheels above. I capture a solid Boomerang video and hit the road for more exploration. Light rain in my face does not deter me on my way north into the French side of the now-named St. Martin, where I meet up with some of the family again for lunch in the small harbor town of Marigot.

My afternoon consists of a solo loop around the island, pausing excessively for photo-taking opportunities and basking with bliss in the beauty, and once to let a herd of goats cross the street. Somehow, I take a wrong turn and end up on a residential off-road in what appears to be a ghetto but is actually just a regular housing development for the area. It's an entirely poor island, with no real industry aside from our tourism dollars. The contrast of the abject poverty so close to the untapped and unfiltered majesty of Orient Bay on the north shore, where I crash on the beach for a couple of hours, is tough to shake from my mind and provides more unfiltered perspective.

The sensory overload of so many unique and significant sights and emotions has made me so much more aware, creating this new challenge to feel like I'm appropriately grasping these moments as they occur with such frequent regularity now. So many people, some on this cruise itself, labor for hours, months, years, in order to be able to afford an experience like the one that comes at me on a seemingly daily basis at this point.

It's a weird feeling that I'm not used to, a thought I've never really had before and am not sure what to do with. I don't even know what to call this. Appreciation? Blessed? Buzzed from mimosas at lunch?

With a sense of misplaced guilt, I motor on into the mountains, taking it all in as best as I can with a vow to not take these opportunities for granted. Back on the Dutch side, I ride down the cobblestones of the main Front Street area of capital city Philipsburg, past shops and fellow cruisers with a bit of showing off but also a slight sense of pride in my activity choice of the day. There is no way anyone else on the ship had the full island experience I just had, so I'm feeling accomplished.

Day 3 starts off on the island of St. Kitts, the place I have pegged for my only golf outing of the week. With sharp skepticism that I'm either being totally ripped off or taken to a back room somewhere so someone can try to ransom my release before realizing I'm actually hundreds of thousands in debt so they eventually kick me to the curb, I jump in a taxi with my clubs at the terminal exit and we drive on the wrong side of the road to Royal St. Kitts Golf Club on the eastern shore. I'm apparently a trailblazer out on my own again, because I arrive to a completely empty course. I breathe it in and smile in the exact same way Kevin McCallister does in *Home Alone* when he receives his delivery and declares with unbridled delight, "a lovely cheese pizza, just for me." I obviously say the same thing at every pizza delivery as well, but this time my smile is directed toward the scrumptious green openness that greets me at the first tee box.

The round takes me up and down along the St. Kitts coast, with holes that bring up-close-and-personal views of the Caribbean to the south, and the expansive Half Moon Bay of the Atlantic to the north, tucked strategically in between mountains on one side and open ocean on the other. It's at the elevated 14th green, after finishing off a par putt at the tail end of a surprisingly well-played round, when I pause in place for about ten minutes to take pictures, on my phone and in my mind. There's no one playing behind me, and I'm in absolutely no rush to leave this scene yet. This is the highest point on the course, but also the highest point of true contentment I've had in a minute.

For the first time in my notes, my description of the moment at hand references the word "happy".

Happiness, this elusive emotion, this confusing, mysterious sensation that's been creeping its way into my consciousness and soul recently after years of unknown respite. This feeling of ease that's so damn hard to find.

I created that for myself right now, somewhat by accident, out on my own in a weird part of the world, and it overwhelms me a bit on this mountainside green overlooking crashing waves below and four more holes left to play without distraction or seemingly any care or worry. I don't want to leave this moment, but I return to the clubhouse at the end of the round, jaw sore from smiling at my circumstances so much the last few hours.

Whatever the cause recently and over the last couple of months of travel, whether it's the new year and the accompanying resolutions of being better this time, or the exotic new locations of the nomadic experience creating a fresh start feeling, dabbling in writing and viewing the world through a different angle has me paying attention finally. I notice it in my settings, in interactions with others, and now in myself a bit.

Cut to: motivational poster from a 4th grade classroom of a puppy sprawled out in a flower garden that reads, "Sometimes you have to relax and smell the roses."

This is something I never did in the past, taking the time to actively see the world with focus and an enhanced observational mindset, and more importantly, its whole effect on me. Viewing life through the lens of a "writer" is an entirely different experience for me than that of a "normal", not that there's anything wrong with that. I'm noticing so many things out in the world around me that I never would have before, and taking notes down all day with reflections, ideas, poorly constructed jokes that make me laugh but will probably fall flat to a general audience. (How did that motivational poster joke do?)

It's a deep down, can't explain it kinda feeling of happy, that something's happening here. Something's changing. Something feels good.

Having flipped a 180 on where I was just a few short, long months ago, I have this irrepressible urge to shout from the St. Kitts mountaintops, "Started from the bottom, now I'm here." Wherever that is exactly. And whatever that means.

I find temporary connection in social media, stealing some WiFi time at the clubhouse for a few hours before heading back to the ship. While the last two days cut off from the world back home have been good for me, that compulsive need to depend on my phone, for both social and work-related updates in real time, is not an addiction that can be dropped cold turkey. And right now, sharing my amazing experiences and views with anyone paying attention is a particularly strong desire, despite this lone wolf persona I've constructed in my mind.

Luckily, this week I still have my family on board and can recap everything with them back on the boat. Consistent with cruise legend, the dinner options are plentiful and of the large-scale variety, pun intended. The volume is certainly not helpful when trying to ditch the Dad-bod I've got going on, rivaling many in the crowd around me. Personally, I'd prefer to eat earlier from a grab and go spot and hit the bars, rather than spend the ninety or so minutes on the multicourse meal extravaganza that makes me want to go to bed immediately after. But the latter option does allow for everyone to circle up and discuss their days and the one ahead, and it makes my parents happy to have us all at one table again.

At dinner with the family, we get into a conversation about meeting new people, on the boat and in general. It appears that most of the cruise folk go with preexisting relationships, or leverage their couple status to easily meet and hang out with other couples. When dining in your time slot, you have the choice of eating alone or joining a table with other smaller groups or couples. In our discussion, we opine on which we would choose if we weren't all together, and I side with the dine separately crowd. Small talk generally makes me crazy (should I do my elevator rant again?), and I typically approach a conversation with a stranger with a sense of efficiency calculation, in time, energy, and a sense of "what will I get out of this?" I take that predetermination and usually choose my own agenda, which I control, over the uncertainty of an open-ended conversation or circumstance. But my mind wanders back to last week, to my new friends from New Jersey and our unguarded chats from the golf course, an honest dialogue that wouldn't have happened if I wasn't boxed into that arrangement.

Maybe meeting someone for the first time isn't so bad after all.

My brothers and I give the nightlife a shot after the way-too-long feast, and head out to the handful of bars on board. What we discover right away though is a scene reminiscent of showing up to a party at the scheduled start time and twiddling your thumbs waiting for everyone else to arrive, except on this ship, no one ever comes to the party.

The early night leads to an early morning run around the upper-deck track as the sun rises on our arrival in Antigua and our scheduled group excursion: a catamaran ride with snorkeling that the whole family agrees to do. Unexpectedly, we are transported from the cruise ship equivalent of the no-fun tiny town from *Footloose* to the catamaran equivalent of a frat house party. The music is bumping and the rum punch starts flowing just long enough to provide a solid buzz for the ride, but not too far to make our first snorkeling stop a cautionary tale for cruisegoers everywhere. The water we jump into is the cleanest and clearest blue I've ever witnessed, making the goggles almost a hindrance in pursuit of my colorful marine friends and in avoidance of the coral moon rocks beneath.

After a successful snorkel cherry-popping for me, we continue getting liquored up on our way to a picture-perfect, Instagram-worthy private beach island, continuing the series of seemingly unbelievable events of my last few days and weeks. And we can go ahead and add "snorkeling in the Caribbean off Antigua" to my "this makes me an asshole for doing it here for the first time" bucket list, along with surfing in Maui and skiing in the Swiss Alps.

Before getting back into the internet abyss, I sneak in a few hours of free WiFi at a boardwalk restaurant in Heritage Quay off the port terminal. Have to keep that digital nomad life going and check in on any super emergency telecom consulting emails. But mostly, social media still.

Wednesday morning brings with it a certain level of comfort and familiarity with our floating home on what is now the fifth day on board. I start the morning in the gym at the top front deck of the boat, watching between elliptical motions as we pull into the definingly mountainous island port in St. Lucia. Today we have the second of the two activities everyone in the family could agree on, a full day guided tour of the island and a dip in the natural mineral baths. As vividly blue as the Caribbean has been to my amateur eye the last few days, the green of the St. Lucia interior is just as striking and impressive.

But again, getting out into the countryside and seeing a piece of how the locals live is as eye-opening as the island's beauty. The 25% unemployment rate looms large like a dark cloud over the lush landscape and stilt construction houses, many left unfinished on the ground level until the owners can rustle up enough funds to finally complete them. People are hustling everywhere at each stop we make, praying for a sale and trying to generate something, anything in this part of the world where the contrasts between the tourist haves and the local have-nots is as stark as the poverty of the neighborhoods compared to the rich scenery that surrounds them. It's tough to get mad at the many pestering hustlers, because at least they're trying. I feel overwhelmed, with too many to try to help at once. On the way back to the boat, and for the second time this week, I'm caught in a traffic delay caused by free-ranging animals, this time cattle crossing the street. I'd say I feel like we're even more out of Kansas now, but this scene might actually fit there.

Our last island stop is in Barbados, the proud home of some of the best white sand beaches in the world, wonderfully happy habitants, brilliant turquoise bays that shine bright like a diamond, and most importantly, Rihanna. Barbados also has some history with pirates, one of my absolute favorite subjects. Once this damn book is done, I'm writing a badass pirate movie script, not that Johnny Depp Disney bullshit with the skeleton ghosts. As such, my last excursion on shore had no chance to be anything but the Jolly Roger pirate party boat, combining many of my favorite things: unlimited booze, pirates, incredible beach settings, girls in bikinis, snorkeling (now that I'm an expert), and rope swings from the top plank. All the guys in the family join me, while the girls go the tamer beach-and-shopping route. We play all day in the water again, in between more rum punches and basking in the stunning surroundings, sobered only by the knowledge our trip is wrapping up.

Friday is our last full day on the cruise, and it's entirely at sea as we make our way back up to Puerto Rico. The pause in the action gives me another chance to take a beat and reflect back on the wild and crazy events of the rapid-fire last week in the Caribbean. I'm finding relevance and meaning in small coincidences that may not be so coincidental, and it's been happening a lot more lately as I actually pay attention.

Right on cue, I open the pages of some new reading material from my poolside deck lounger, soaking in the last hours of the Caribbean sun for a while. After months of being compared to the story that defined in the common vernacular the tale of the lost, soul-searching travel experience, I decide it's time to ditch all the mental and emotional avoidance, and steer into the skid by finding out what *Eat, Pray, Love* is really all about.

The first similarity in our stories that gets my attention, aside from the author and I both being from Connecticut, is the concept of being a good traveler, something in which I've always taken pride. Being able to pick up conversational language in new locations, to not get sick or have a limited palate in trying new foods and drink, asserting oneself when necessary, having a strong sense of direction and spatial recognition, but also knowing where and how to get somewhere, being calm under pressure and having an ability to roll with the punches, being prepared and well-researched, and a habit of making friends with anyone. That's the anti-wandering elixir I've been looking for right there. Purpose in the exploration.

The next piece that hits me comes right after taking a break from reading to observe the pool scene around me on the top deck of the ship. I notice a very attractive girl sitting on the edge of the pool, seemingly unattached. Where has she been hiding while we've been running around empty bars all week, or surrounded by couples and families at every stop? I'm way too much of a pussy to just go up and say hello though, and after a few minutes, a single bro (actually, where has he been all week, too?) makes his move and they chat in front of me for about an hour. I turn back to my book of the month just in time to read all about an early theme in the author's travels: loneliness.

One massive, overlooked snag in all these extravagant plans and memory-creating moments, especially notice-able as of late, is that so many of them have been on my own. I'm craving another person to share with so badly that I splurge in the social media game just for that sense of at-tention and camaraderie, while at the same time, also re-minding everyone of what they're missing with an in-your-face-ness of lonely resentment.

The author, Gilbert, prior to leaving her husband, and then boyfriend, and then America, was unable to shake feelings of being alone and missing something, and in the wrong place or with the wrong person, until she found a way to embrace the loneliness in her travel and grow from it. I think back on my Los Angeles mood last year and find com-monality again. Maybe these snarky comparisons to her that I receive are not so far off after all, even if unintentionally so.

Finally back on land, the family says our goodbyes to Puerto Rico and each other. My parents and I are on the same nonstop segment to JFK, where I pass them the overweight baton of my golf bag, packed with my clubs and the leftovers from my first attempt at baggage downsizing, realizing al-ready that I brought too much shit with me.

As much as I want to continue on with my clubs through Europe and Southeast Asia, practicality overcomes my fan-tastical wishes. So I part ways with them, and my parents, at JFK and walk a little lighter to my Virgin flight to London.

Armed with my trusty plane-ride sidekicks of a large SmartWater bottle and pack of almonds, but unable to get more than a few broken hours of rest in my seat because I'm a truly terrible plane sleeper, I break out my *Eat, Pray, Love* guidebook. I pick up with one of the author's early moments of clarity, realizing she habitually exercises the Puritanical American mindset of feeling guilty for not working or for feeling pleasure, a troubling question of, "Did I deserve or earn this?" It's a notion completely antithetical to the Italian mindset around her. The author didn't know how to just be happy. She was so busy thinking about the science of finding pleasure or defining the reason for its absence, she was missing the natural experiences of it and the opportunity to be a "yes woman" and just see where it takes her. It was the letting go aspect that was missing. My natural smirk turns to ponder hands as I close the book for now.

Back in my window seat location, I sneak a peek outside and glimpse London for the first time, bubbling with an unmistakable feeling that I'm on the cusp of something unknown but big, probably requiring many pages of intense action and intrigue. I sure am excited to keep going, aren't you?

THE CHAPTER WITH THE CONFIRMATION BY-US

chapter six

The opening and closing scenes of *Love Actually* (for those that have been living under a rock during Christmas season, or on top of a rock above Whoville) cycle through a collection of unknown characters, embracing with smiles of joy or relief upon arrival into London, in a perfectly cheesy, over the top, roll your eyes, so bad its good message of hope and confirmation that love actually is out there after all. As I exit my arrival gate at Heathrow, fresh off a truly mesmerizing landing approach over the endless switchbacks of the Thames River, pockets of development squished into each crevasse in villages that are as old as... as... well, I can't think of anything right now, but they're really old, I pause to take a picture of the large "Arrivals" sign on the wall. I figure I can force some *Love Actually* allusion in a DM to carefully selected individuals who would appreciate the reference, most likely my female friends. I turn and snap a quick photo, but when I open to view it, I realize in the foreground I unintentionally captured an elderly husband and wife seated on a bench, her arms around him and head on his shoulder in a modest, tired, loving, shared embrace. It's true you guys, love actually is all around us!

My faith restored in the state of the world, I soldier on and find the Tube into central London. The compactness of the train surprises me, and I stand as far to the side as I can, feeling guilty and awkward as the obnoxious American for carrying all this luggage and taking up half the train. For reference, at this point I'm rocking my old school European backpackers backpack from college, a regular schoolyard backpack, my carryon roller suitcase, and my laptop shoulder bag, all packed to the brim and testing the elasticity of each compartment's lining. And somehow this is downsized from when I started. We roll methodically through the London suburbs and the simple note I take on my first impression of the neighborhoods is "so much brick, so much old". So, there you go.

I arrive at the Sloane Square tube station, in the southwest section of the city center, minding the gap on my way outside, only to get smacked in the face with a cricket bat of everything I could have ever pictured in my mind of a quintessential London street scene. A bright red double decker bus is on the left side of the road passing a line of black cabs parked next to a scarlet telephone booth and an old-timey newspaper stand on the corner, while the newspaper vendor shouts down the street in his British accent past a uniformed bobby to a mate outside one of the shops that make up the ground level of this enclosure of three and four story buildings drenched in classic architecture and brick everything, surrounding a public green that is slightly hard to see through the unabashedly grey skies and chilly mist that permeates the late January air. Just for a moment, I am overcome with an out-of-body experience, dazed and confused by London's potent and thorough welcoming shot.

I pick myself up off the proverbial mat and make my way to my accommodations for the next few weeks. I sense a collective confusion on sidewalk protocol, as no one can decide if they want to walk on the left side as the cars go or the standard right side, leaving a constant state of inefficiency in walking pace. These are things that are noticeable and important to a northeasterner, apparently. I had a conversation with my grandmother a few days ago about being safe with the pedestrian directions, and well, funny story Grandma, in the first five minutes I come perilously close to a side-swiping from a cabbie. Despite the very user-friendly directions "Look Right", "Look Left", "Watch out for Buses, Dummy" spray painted at all of the crosswalk entrances, a simple enough request I can comply with, I fail to look left and *behind me* to the turning taxi and narrowly escape certain and immediate death.

And they say our generation is overly dramatic.

My destination and home for the next few weeks is a place called Roam, in the heart of this posh Chelsea community steeped in expensive brick row housing that perfectly fits my unapologetically bougie nature. Roam has a fresh and intriguing concept that I generally describe to others as an "adult luxury hostel with private rooms and shared community spaces, targeted toward remote workers". I've had to explain the unique setup to so many people that I now have the phrasing memorized. This London location is one of a few Roam properties around the world and is designed like a professional *Real World* mansion within this five story row townhouse, with a large work area/living room next to the main entrance, a community kitchen and TV area on the ground level, an office on each floor, and private bed/bath combo rooms spread throughout. It has the personal space and privacy that I love, along with the community feel and ability to mingle as I please, a great balance and interesting design I'm looking forward to testing out. I drop the infamous ole baggage in my cozy and surprisingly large second level bedroom and set out to explore the new neighborhood.

Much like the shock to my senses when first stepping out into Sloane Square, my exploratory stroll down the main street called King's Road leaves me in a trance-like state of wonder that is truly hard to pin down in feeling. The emotion could best be described as assured contentment, like yes, this is right, and I feel good about it. After a few minutes, I stop into a French café, order tea because when in London... and kick back in cheerful delight while listening to the small tables of guests around me conversing in a smorgasbord of English, French, and German. I've seen about ten blocks of this city at this point, and you know what they say about love at first sight. I'm ready to send Christmas cards together and update that Facebook status.

I continue deeper into Chelsea still at peak happiness (which sounds way more sexual than I intended), only breaking my fascination and appreciation when I hear cheers of a small celebration. A newly married couple emerges for the first time from Chelsea Old Hall to a handful of family members and friends tossing the obligatory rice into the crisp afternoon air. Turning off King's Road toward the Thames, a group of six or seven kids of all ethnicities charges down the street past me on scooters to some arbitrary finish line. The odd beep of an ambulance emerges as it tends to the darker realities of life. After my initial crosswalk scare, I feel more comfortable and confident in my crossing aggression, looking left, and behind me, with the determination and casualness of a local.

No sunglasses are required here, a previous staple of my "grab as you leave the house" routine along with keys, watch, wallet, phone. I find a neighborhood salon to get a good haircut for the first time in three months, an unappreciated challenge of the nomadic life. My current hair, left untouched for so long, has gotten obnoxiously curly in a style that is unfashionably undefined and far too poofy for my present hairline position. I go short this round in an attempt to drag out the time needed for the next cut, and I feel refreshed in shedding that mess. My next stop is for groceries, and I take a little extra time sorting through the unusual brands and trying to figure out what the hell a crumpet actually is, before determining it is reminiscent of what we would call an English muffin, ironically enough. Despite all the variances from the comforts I know back in the U.S., the adjustment here feels seamless and natural already, a polar opposite sentiment to the one I had just three months before in California. It kind of feels like home here, if that makes any sense.

Not feeling at home is a funny emotion for me, because as much as I like to travel, I've always been able to adopt and maintain a sense of home wherever my base is, whether a weekend trip at a hotel in Napa or a long-term rental during one of my stints abroad. That feeling of home is one that is unescapably difficult to define, operating in the vicinity of "you know it when you see it" territory, and as annoying for a writer to try to capture as I'm sure it is to read my attempts to do so now. But taking a stab at a meaning here, to me it's that instinctual gut feeling, an internal sense of comfort, happiness, ease-of-mind that where you are is where you're supposed to be. That even when you venture out for however long, it will be there waiting with open arms when you return.

I knew in my gut during my last year in L.A. that when it came down to it, I was simply not where I was supposed to be, I was not in a place I felt home. That realization was actually the easy part. The real challenge then becomes, "okay, well where is that, then?" When you're thirty years old and still refer to your parents' house in Connecticut as home (as in, "I'll be back home for a few weeks this summer"), but have not lived there in almost ten years, you might say you have a bit of an identity issue. However, having moved around as much as I did over my eight plus years in California, basically living twelve-month lease to twelve-month lease, knowing that I never intended on staying to raise a family, the only place that seemed to fit that definition of home was the place I grew up and where Santa still visited every Christmas. And as much as I love where I'm from and glad I was raised there, Connecticut is not a place where I want to live again. That was home for my parents, and for my developing self. The question now is finding one for my future self.

But how does one figure out where to call home? Asking for a friend here, of course.

On the existential plane, I can always turn to fortune cookie wisdom to help define what it means to me: home is where the heart is, home is inside you, etc. Both of which are probably true on some level, but work better in theory than in answering the practical question of where should I park my car and set up my Keurig machine?

Historically, this decision was made by default (throwback alert) based on where families were located, or to a probably lesser extent, where a long-term job and career was centered. I've noticed, especially in the last few months as I started moving around, that my father in particular has developed a bit more of a patriarchal concern for the status and pin locations of his flock, spearheading the new family trip idea and as we parted ways at JFK, making an earnest request for me to check in with them on a daily basis. To my parents, this wandering concept is pushing me further from the home they know, with an open-ended notion of where I might end up and call home going forward.

I come from a generation that has proudly and stubbornly fostered an all-encompassing desire for flexibility and mobility that includes variety and oftentimes spontaneity in where we choose to live. SoCal, NorCal, Seattle, Denver, Nashville, Atlanta, Dallas, even Portland and Austin for the "keep it weird" folks, all house at least one of my friends from home or college who picked everything up and made the move, maybe for a job, possibly for a significant other, most likely to avoid a significant other. My friends and I are going urban en masse in search of eclectic, semi-affordable but probably overpriced, active, up-and-coming cities where everything is new and growing and exciting. And forget about paying for cable when we get there, we'll just stream that shit.

This is all broaching the notion of where I call home in more nebulous, emotional terms. But there are practical implications as well, including choosing and affording a brick and mortar building and all the pains and pleasures of home ownership. It also typically involves that dreaded term, "settling down", as one wants to prepare for the space and setting needed to raise a family. Mortgage payments, fourth bedrooms, kitchen upgrades, property taxes, building equity. All indicative of and required for proper adulthood. But how am I going to buy a place when I have no idea where I want to be in the long run, if that place will include offspring, and if my work life will support it all? I see people around me making that leap seemingly assertively and assuredly, without pause for contemplation or course-correction. Meanwhile, I'm over here staring at this damn fig tree, impatiently waiting for a city to fall into my hand, or me into a city, and put to bed the question of "what's next?" on the geographic front. Well not yet, there's more traveling to be done. But soon.

Back at the Roam house, I grab a snack in the kitchen and drop into a detailed conversation with a couple mid-twenties Turkish guys who are evaluating the co-living concept to potentially bring back to Istanbul. As they report it, there is no socializing amongst young adults because no one wants to leave the house, so this community environment is an appealing idea to them to bring home.

At tonight's house dinner, there's do-it-yourself sushi-making stations, an activity I might have blown off in a prior era, because, and I'm going to say something controversial here, sushi is overrated.

I'm enjoying the company, though, and the topic du jour is of life as a digital nomad, vets and neophytes alike sharing tips and stories of life on the run from city to city. The most noticeable element of adjustment in my first few work days from London is the time differences, and effectively managing daylight hours and time changes. My location now puts my end of workday whistle from the Pacific at 1 A.M., with late-night conference calls ending well past my bedtime on a school night. But despite this initial concern, it's been very manageable to adjust, confirming my belief, and my Instagram games, that you really can #workfromanywhere.

The dinner discussion evolves into a broader conversation about the modern working mindset, and the shift from prior generations. In a lot of ways, we still see work as a means to an end, but the end is not about money and financial security, for better or worse left to be determined. Now, the objective is moving toward overall happiness and striking better balances in life in achieving our ultimate desires. As I sit back and take it all in, offering only timely opinions as a newbie to this type of lifestyle and the dialog surrounding it, it shocks me that although relatively small, this community of remote workers is much larger than I had realized. My previous reference point to this way of life and mindset was limited to the handful of traveling nurses I knew who were doing this sort of thing. But there's an easing, welcome home feeling of comfort in finding this shared philosophy and perspective.

Social weekends are back in play for me now too, after a monthlong hiatus in the Caribbean. As a small group of merry wanderers, we crawl through the streets of Chelsea, stopping at pubs that all seem to be named (Insert random animal) & (Insert other random animal). I'm particularly fond of one uniquely titled pub called The Walrus & The Carpenter. Like, what? Why? We return to the house after a few pints, entertaining the neighborhood along the way with a rendition of *The Fresh Prince of Belair* theme song, for which knowing all the lyrics is a requirement of carrying a millennial card. Back in the kitchen, we break out the British version of Cards Against Humanity, and are treated to charming and confusing new surprises that we sometimes have to research like (warning: may be NSFW, I'm not really sure) Ed Balls, The Hillsborough Disaster, A Chelsea smile, Waking up half-naked in a Little Chef car park, Gentlemen's Relish, Daniel Radcliffe's delicious arsehole, and Queen Elizabeth's immaculate anus. There must be something about the butts and the British. Wait, *bums* and the British.

This is the type of game that to really enjoy and play well requires a thorough understanding of the crowd, knowing each other's personalities and senses of humor. Our group of five, together for only a week at this point, is up until three in the morning acting like we've been old friends for years, cracking each other up until our jaws hurt from laughter as if we had just been given a Chelsea smile (sorry, too soon. And horrifying).

I'm thrilled with the ease in which I'm able to form a genuine connection with the community, a group of people we call our Roamily. Get it? Like family, but instead of fam, you replace it with Roam. Roamily, you see? Oh, and like you're known for your profound wit.

We emerge into the light of late Saturday morning and hit up the Chelsea farmer's market in Duke of York Square, strolling around and searching for some kind of meat concoction to go to work on the mild hangover. A successful refueling trip to the market turns into a random adventure consisting of drinking at the pubs all afternoon while pretending to care about and understand rugby.

Side note: anyone that prefers going out at night to day-drinking is flat out wrong, and I will not listen to an argument otherwise.

We end up back at the house at a reasonable hour, having had a day. Somehow the conversation turns to living arrangements again, and the thought process that goes into our location choice. The idea of the suburbs is put on trial for its premise of finding a balance between city life and country life. Hermes, an Irishman gym owner who splits time between Los Angeles, London, and Dublin, has a particularly strong opinion about suburbia: "It's like Middle Earth. There's no best-of-both-worlds there, just a whole bunch of bland nothing." We share our relatable experiences in Middle Earth and all conclude a similar verdict. Give me an urban life in the concrete jungle, or some time by a lake in the mountains in the middle of nowhere, but keep the T.G.I.Friday's and Lowe's shopping centers adjacent to cookie cutter prefab developments far, far away from me.

This particular city life continues to elicit feelings of contentment and comfort as I develop my daily routine. And as I say that word again, "routine", I'm deciding I dislike the pejorative connotation of it. It is far more pleasant to think of it as getting into a rhythm. So, as part of my daily rhythm, I join a gym again and feel like a real local every morning as I traverse new routes to and from the facility in Victoria. I get bolder every day in my non-Maps directed internal compass, eventually settling on the most aesthetically pleasing paths past my favorite architectural designs. In my unplanned travels through the neighborhood I find hidden gem coffee shops, cool-looking wine bars, and more pubs named The Donkey & The Manatee, or a variation thereof. London speaks to my sensibilities in a way that just seems to work and make sense. The clean, classical architecture, an unmistakable feeling of centuries of history in the air, an old world setting with modern, busy people bustling to and fro. Even the perpetual state of gray that saturates the winter skies, as if living in a filter set to low brightness, does not bother my spoiled California sensitivities.

The personal balance I try to strike is one of participating in the Roam community (or Roamily, if you insist) while finding my time to get out of the house, be productive, and explore this incredible city. This is where I can use the time difference at the home office to my advantage. The schedule I've created now involves a rise-and-shine at a reasonable mid-morning hour, a few hours of reading and writing in my room or one of the office spaces, a late morning walk to the gym while clearing my head along the way, or alternatively, developing more ideas for what you're reading right now, back to shower, and usually lunch with people in the kitchen.

My new friend Anticlea, a beautiful mid-thirties African-American from Philly, joins me in the kitchen and we discuss the concept of wanderlust and how it has affected our progress in adulthood, both good and bad. Her boyfriend, who co-founded Roam and is now one of my closer friends, a mid-twenties dude named Laertes, joins us and we delve into the future of the workplace and housing, what home means to a person, and the practicalities of living in one place versus the nomadic life. I finish my lunch and head upstairs to the conference room, but before I get started on work, I find Persephone taking a break on the couches. We rap about her own wandering journey that led to a period of spiritual fulfillment, all of which started with a brave step toward an unknown destination, and how it was controversial for a Portuguese woman in her late twenties from a predominantly Catholic community to break away from the pressure of conforming to societal norms. Her focus in her consulting work is on the modern workplace and the opportunities available to this generation to find the right type of job for them and to do things differently than the geezers of the past.

Finally starting the work day in the afternoon, I mix in days of longer consulting work and less writing, and vice versa depending on if I'm feeling frisky or not. The timing suits me well, allowing for an appropriate amount of me-time during the day and backloading my working hours until my preferred times later on, obliterating the notion of the nine-to-five requirement and emboldening my feeling that I am really sticking it to the man.

Of course, there are time difference realities that cannot be overcome with my simple intransigence, requiring the occasional late-night session in one of the private offices where I have to load up on my calls for the day. Keeping in touch with my parents back in Connecticut or my friends in California is also a challenge I have to be mindful of, watching the times when it's appropriate to call or text. The Super Bowl kicking off at just short of midnight on a Sunday also makes for a rough start to the work week, especially when the Falcons completely choke away a lead at 3 A.M.

The beauty of being so far away from the office, though, and away from the rigidly formulaic and archaic American mindset about work, is that if I want to take a half day to sleep off an extended Super Bowl party, I can test the belief that the world is going to come crashing to a perilous and fiery death explosion because I failed to respond to Paula within an hour of her "highly important" email. Spoiler alert: we're still here.

Sometimes my always scheduled personality just needs a timeout to have a day of immobility, so I take one now and dig into my *Eat, Pray, Love* studies.

We are currently in India for the Act II "Pray" part of the trilogy, focused on meditation and finding inner peace. I am curiously struck by Gilbert's portrayal of meditation and its calming effects, a general concept I've always rejected out of knee-jerk principle. Yoga and meditation, to my suburban white Catholic male sensibilities, seem so cliché and too obvious as common practices of the exploratory world traveler. Although, I suppose my conservative opinion on these subjects is itself as cliché as my impression of the concepts.

I'm not someone that practices a religion, despite my upbringing of mass every Sunday, and have generally been more of a spiritual person than a member of any formal and organized religion. The spirituality focus is one of the things that brings me close to my mother, who is both religious and heavily spiritual, as we often discuss hidden and deeper meanings in the world around us. She was the one that introduced me to *The Secret*, among other potentially crackpot ideas that still seem more realistic to me than anything I ever found in a church. Yet despite my openness to alternative theology, I remain skeptical about the yogi and meditation world.

Something Gilbert writes catches my attention though, hitting on some of the purposes of meditation. Namely, controlling our thoughts with the ultimate objective of controlling our emotions. When our emotions are tied directly and consequentially to our thoughts, like when we stress out about an upcoming deadline or when Taylor Swift is going to release a new album, or we get angry when we think about how an ex did us wrong or more importantly, when one of Taylor's did her wrong, it creates swings of feelings that disrupt any semblance of inner peace. A wandering mind is chased by the emotions each thought carries, preventing a level of calm stasis as well as a full appreciation for the moments I'm in at the time. It's something I am blessed and cursed with, traveling from past to future and idea to idea with rapid and random succession like a Maui sunset. Meditation, the act of paying attention to breathing in order to quiet the mind and its resultant feelings, comes naturally to some. For others, the type that drop all their shit into storage and mindlessly run around the world because of undiagnosed unhappiness, more practice may be necessary to achieve even a smidgen of Zen.

Part of my hesitation in getting into this kooky meditation practice comes from the same overly sensitive mindset I've been carrying to not be the walking cliché everyone expects. "Oh, you went to Thailand and got a tattoo? Of course you did." "Oh, you went to Bali and are really into yoga and meditation now? Of course you are." "Oh, you ate a lot of pizza while you were gone? Well actually, yeah, you always do that, so that makes sense."

For me, the classic chicken or the egg question is completely applicable to the yogi and the world traveler. Does one beget the other, or do the personality traits just coincidentally match for each? Maybe I should just shut the fuck up, and stop being so judgmental and self-conscious? Yeah, I agree.

There are a handful of people at Roam that I regularly seek out in my day, with Zeus being one of both the most available and enlightening. Zeus is my age from Atlanta, tall with a cleanly shaved head, quite successful running some kind of tech company out of Hungary and coming off a difficult separation from his wife. We hit the pub Chelsea Potter (no relation to Harry, I checked), a few blocks away for fish and chips and a few pints. I pick Zeus' brain on the digital nomad life, something he's been doing for over a year now. We dig into our travel motivations, dating history, future goals, and my writing ideas and progress, and in a way that I've never really been challenged before, he chips away at so many of my preexisting notions, offering an alternative perspective not to be contrarian, but from a place of genuine interest and experience. He's not buying the sundae-with-a-cherry-on-top story I'm selling about how I ended up here, the self-satisfying "oh I just love to travel" and "when else will I get the chance to do something like this" platitudes, and what it all means for me and my writing. With probing questions that force me to open up about the things that were bothering me last year and today, and what I want out of it all, he offers a level of awareness that I appreciate and respect, oftentimes sending me back to the drawing board for a do-over and a deeper dive.

To this point in this venture, I've been in a self-conscious, self-created power struggle over the narrative that surrounds me and what I want to make of it for myself. In an effort to control that narrative, through the fear of some self-perceived stigma as a social pariah, there's a story I've presented to the outside world of taking control of my destiny, of taking charge and living the good life, and that's why I do what I do now. But Zeus smells a rat in the pub that's really holding me back and wants me to keep chipping away for the real story of how I got here.

A few nights later, shooting the shit after a Mexican dinner night in the kitchen, people start talking about what's next for them with a casual assuredness that surprises even my overly spontaneous senses. Zeus is discussing a ten-day meditation retreat in Tokyo he thinks he needs right now, and will know soon if he got in and is hopping on a plane next week to Japan. Laertes and Anticlea are running through the logistics of their upcoming plans that include a wedding in Georgia, a month working in Guatemala, and a trip to visit his sister in Kenya. Another who has just returned from Bali is checking the calendar to see when she will be able to head back, committed to return after a fulfilling, view-altering experience. They're all dealing with stuff, relationships, work, life, but they're all handling it in their own, different ways, without judgment. With purpose, not escape. I throw out my thoughts about possibly joining friends in New Zealand next month, which is met with a chat about logistics, past experiences there, and encouragement.

Here in front of me, amidst these folks, the type of people that don't have an address readily available for Amazon shipments but have their passport numbers memorized from regular use, I feel a quiet calm in the form of a validation I never knew I needed. Not from Instagram likes and new random followers, but from genuine connections and commonality.

Six months ago, I'm struggling to get friends to agree to happy hour on a Thursday. Now, wild thoughts of hopping on a plane to the other side of the world next week are supported and treated like standard and completely appropriate conversation material.

Since I have to sort out my upcoming agenda post-London, I open a Google Flights map and gaze with anxiousness and excitement as if staring at the blank page of a piece of paper waiting to fill with prose. All of a sudden, the prospect of an open-ended ticket to the world feels totally natural. And yet, I close the map and settle on my next course of action for the coming months with unchecked delight: I'm going to stay ten extra days in London, giving me a full month here. Then I'll do a month in my old stomping grounds of Florence, followed by a remote work program in Bali for April. I'm especially excited for the opportunity to bunker down and spend the extra time in London and at Roam, to continue this period of heightened development, and work on my British accent.

Each day, multiple times a day, I'm challenging myself and challenged by Zeus and others to address questions lying dormant and ignored for far too long, lost in the commotion and chaos of the dubiously named "real world". What are my relationship goals? What makes me happy about my job? What makes me happy? I need to continue with this progression before the clock strikes midnight on my time in London and I turn back into a jet-setting pumpkin.

Valentine's Day is approaching and the majority of us here, obviously, do not have a significant other to waste money on in the form of roses and dark chocolates. Instead, we waste money on ourselves in the form of whiskey drinks in the hipster-ific area of Shoreditch. We start at a unique place called Boxpark, which is a bunch of small popup bars and food stalls built within repurposed shipping containers, because hipster. Eventually we make our way to a small dive bar playing music too loud for my aging ears, where everyone around us, literally everyone, is making out. Here seems as appropriate a spot as any to have a conversation about love and other drugs, digging into personal history like meeting the parents and broken hearts, birth order and sibling differences, amongst a group of people with diverse backgrounds and ages from Houston, Philadelphia, Belgium, Munich, and Connecticut/California, yet despite the distinctness, all sharing the trials and privileges of this life in collective camaraderie.

It's been an eye-opening, game-changing couple of weeks, in the same way that Backstreet Boys' "I Want it That Way" got me to re-evaluate my opinion on boy bands, or like when I discovered that chopping up hot dogs and putting them in my mac and cheese made for a fantastic meal.

It's the sharing aspect, the open vulnerability that is the most consequential for me, and completely out of my ordinary character. Conversations of elevated and heavy discourse seem to flow naturally and frequently throughout the course of the day. And that is absolutely not a knock on any friends or family back in the States, but when you put a collection of like-minded and similarly-situated individuals who picked to live in a house like this, you see what happens when people stop being polite and start getting real. The Roam World: London.

I no longer feel out of place, or an outcast in my own home. I feel home.

I find something special and uplifting about making connections like these from the small things in life, ones that hit home in unsuspected ways and open my eyes to the commonality of our realities. It's the reason why some shows, or movies, or books, or friends, or family, can come into or grow larger in life at certain non-coincidental points in time and uproot the foundations of some deeply entrenched perspectives. These come from a place of mutual understanding, a kind of "I got you" feeling that the things that unite us are far more frequent than the things that make me go "WTF am I doing right now?" It's that feeling of connectedness that tells me I'm saner than what my own mind often tells me.

Who among us hasn't struggled with a breakup (or two) and wanted to drop everything to explore the world and oneself, as in *Eat, Pray, Love*? Who hasn't struggled with weight loss, or sibling dynamics, or the massive responsibility of raising children, or dealing with death, as in *This is Us*? Who out there has never struggled with first dates, or knowing if someone is the one, or how to handle feelings for a friend who's dating someone else, or how to find the best taco in our neighborhood, as in *Master of None*?

I have a hard time convincing my friend Perimedes to watch the latter, because the way I've sold it to him, he thinks it will be too real, too on the nose for its portrayal of life and love, particularly the bits about lovesick heartbreak, for him to handle. But for me, it's in the authenticity of a story, whether from Netflix or a friend here in London, that I personally find comfort right now, a solemn yet reassuring construct that stands in opposition to the belief that I'm doing things wrong, or am out on a ledge on my own.

Sometimes we can escape into the mundaneness of ESPN or Bravo, depending on personal preference (you do you, boo), to avoid a bit of the real life that storms around us. But there are times when I look to find reality in these mediums and others that rocks the world I thought I knew, and offers a hand in comfort.

In honor of the pending high holiday on the 14th, I fire up some *How I Met Your Mother* on The Netflix. My friend Helios and I, in our innocent immaturity, would often complain while the show was running about how long it was taking to meet the damn mother. Helios wanted to see her right now, I was more patient to a point before I began raging irrationally for that storyline as well, sick of so much love triangle. It wasn't until the third or fourth show binge, and some advanced aging, that I came to appreciate that the overarching lesson those wily writers were trying to teach me was that the true story is not about the "mother", but how we get to that point, all the development along the way that leads to him finally being "ready" to meet that elusive one. Great title, lots of meaning in those few words.

THE CHAPTER WONDERING: IS IT TOO LATE NOW TO SAY SORRY?

chapter seven

"It's just not the right time for me." "It's not you, it's me." "I'm in a different place right now." "I just really need to focus on myself and figure out what I want." Stop me if you've heard that before. Or used one of those gems before.

I have been on the losing end of the timing excuse a number of times and always passed it off as a lame but non-complicated and mutually understood breakup device. An easy out to avoid a relationship, or a defense mechanism to prevent someone from eventually getting hurt. A nod to social decency in collectively navigating rocky dating waters, a lesson learned since I first entered that arena in middle school.

There is a decent and depressingly real possibility that, much like Pokémon cards and Tara Reid, I peaked in 1999. Class President, captain of the soccer and championship-winning basketball teams, voted most likely to succeed, multiple girlfriends throughout the year that I would makeout with at recess, owner of some rad Billabong T-shirts, I was killing it. My foray into the good life, steeped in imagined power and novel social prominence, may be the only period, as short as it was, into any consistent semblance of self-confidence in my relations with the opposite sex. Throughout the remainder of my dating misadventures are recurring themes of awkward confusion, missed opportunities, inflated expectations, and over-the-top gestures pulled from the so-predictable playbooks of romantic comedies. The overwhelming consistency across the board is an utter lack of any ability to appropriately read signals, or even figure out if there was any signal at all.

This is not a new development. From the days in elementary school when I was loading up my Trapper Keeper and throwing my backpack over one shoulder of my fresh Starter jacket, I've been lost romantically. On Valentine's Day when we would bring in those generic little cards for our classmates with the Looney Tunes or Ninja Turtles on them, I would find a way to both 1.) make an effort beyond what was a standard and routine activity, trying to write or do something special with my card for the girl I was crushing on, and 2.) read way too much into the cards I received, holding onto the ones in my desk where I felt I was getting some coded message of attraction that might mean I would have to take my cootie shot off for someone soon. "She gave me a card of Patty Mayonnaise asking Doug to be her valentine, but gave Jake one that just said he, like Porkchop, was a super friend! What does that mean?? Is this going down? Should I share my Gushers with her at lunch now?"

The overanalyzing has sadly not improved over time. She sat next to me on the bus for a field trip to the science museum. She picked me first for her Red Rover team during gym class today. She handed me an invitation to her birthday party before the rest of the class. Yeah, really, that bad. Even the signals that probably were significant in actuality, like Penny holding my hand in Fourth grade as we skated around the roller rink to R.E.M.'s "Five Hundred Miles", I still couldn't make sense of: does she like me or is she just trying to survive the death arena out here on four wheel shoes?

In high school, fresh off trading in Green Day CD's and Billabong for Nelly MP3's and Abercrombie (while avoiding Connecticut's Double Polo Popped Collar Travesty of 2003), it was the notes during class, folded up into impossibly tight little squares with a flap to open a world of more implication confusion. By the way, I love that we used to refer to this time period in the adolescent dating sequence as "talking", as in "yeah Danny and Rachel are talking now, so it's getting pretty serious."

We might even share phone numbers for brief conversations on the landline, resulting in having to call the girl's house, as the gentleman taking charge, and asking her dad meekly, "Is Nicole there?" I mean, she gave me her home number, plus she sat next to me on the couch at the party last Friday, that has to mean something right? Then there was the formal dance clusterfuck, trying to decipher the meaning of Homecoming and Prom dates, and messing that up too.

The progression online added so much more intrigue and stress, as I took my awkward social experience into the world of AIM screen names and MySpace pages. (I wonder what Tom is up to these days? He was a good friend, always there.) The deterioration of interpersonal skills, particularly in relation to relations of the dating persuasion, began with instant messaging and flip phones with texting capability. Deciphering meaning from response time and message length and more recently, emoji use, let alone the actual words coming across the screen, added a whole new fun carnival game of things to overreact to. Is that AIM away message with the Destiny's Child lyrics aimed at me? What does it mean that she used "ha" instead of "LOL" in her response? To use a smiley face or not to use a smiley face, that is the question.

Facebook came along and changed the game by not changing the game at all, exacerbating the degree to which we, or at least I, interact and overanalyze everything with the calculation of a Third-grader on February 14. The friend add, the direct message, and for too short of a time of relevance, the hilarious poke, all a digital form of potential meaning and more opportunity to submerge into a cloudy pool of likely nothing. Today there's the added blessing of being able to monitor and obsess over social media activity: top friends and consecutive day streaks on Snapchat; follows, likes, comments, and tagging on Instagram and the 'Book; read/seen receipts; seeing the little bubbles pop up that the other end is typing, and seeing them disappear without response; public birthday messages; LinkedIn follows. Just kidding, nobody gives a fuck about LinkedIn.

The good part, if you can call it that, about dating apps is the ability in most circumstances to be notified that someone on the other end liked me first, and at least has some modicum of initial attraction based on a carefully selected and strategic collection of five of my photos. It's the real-world confirmation equivalence of meeting a girl at a bar and having her find me remotely attractive enough to not throw up when I say hello, so at least I've got that going for me. Of course, that's just getting step one out of the way, with an abundance of opportunities to screw things up from there. Open with a joke, give a standard pickup line, say "Big plans this weekend?" And with that I'm right back into the dating dance, searching for meaning in the search for the one that makes it all go away.

While I've never had a bad first date requiring the sitcom staple "emergency call from the restaurant", that doesn't exclude the presence of some certainly inept encounters, particularly in the goodbye scene. There are clear-as-day moments, rare and welcome as they are, and then there's the perpetual onslaught of mixed signals making up the overwhelming majority of the remainder of dating life.

I had this conversation with a female friend the other day, about the very strange and confusing position I feel like I'm in for a lot of these types of situations.

Culturally, socially, I've been engrained with the notion that as the man, I need to make the first move, from asking someone out, planning a date, driving (for the non-urban folks), paying the check, and initiating physical contact, with various degrees of the latter being on the table depending on the situation, from hugging, hand-holding, kiss on the cheek, kiss on the lips, full on solid makeout, to all manner of more sexual, sock-on-the-doorknob type activities. There is an incredible pressure, even more so today in the continued and necessary progression of gender role equality, to find a balance between being confident, assured, and willing to take charge, qualities typically found to be attractive and desired by women, but also being respectful and deferential while avoiding what might be perceived as crossing the line from assertive to aggressive. I've joked here of my poor ability to read certain signals, but this one in particular is a serious cultural imbalance issue and stresses me out more than anything else in dating, and may never be a trickier standard to strive to uphold than it is today. Just to add another challenge to the dreaded dating scene.

At least in the "first date" scenario, there's an element of at least some mutual understanding, that there's the potential that dinner or drinks with someone we are attracted to could lead to something more.

What about being out with a friend, one I might be interested in or with whom I could at least see potential, and not even knowing if we're on a "date", or have any indication of their thinking, expectations, attraction, or interest level, with the added consequence of completely fucking up a friendship if a move is made and the feeling is not mutual? Aside from determining why the Kardashians are popular or how a sexting app like Snapchat can be worth billions of dollars, both of which I will never understand, breaking out of the friend zone may be the single greatest unresolvable mystery humankind has ever faced, unanswered from the time Adam met Eve, or when Harry met Sally.

For a non-dude perspective, I asked some of my closest female friends about their experience and thoughts, if any, on the friend zone designation. One said that she makes the determination early on whether a guy is friend, fuckboy, or boy she wants to fuck, and is then fairly locked in after that point. A quick game of Marry, Bang, Kill, all in her head. Another wasn't so quick to drop the hammer, but agreed with the fairly quick calculation with little chance for movement in another direction. As expected, the distinction between the genders in this approach generally comes down to which part of the body they're thinking with, the head, the heart, or the other thing.

Somehow, my parents were able to make the transition, although I'm honestly scared to ask the question of how, fearing I may never recover from the trauma of hearing about their relationship in college. For a less personal example of the friends-to-relationship progression, I look to *Friends* training videos for reference. The most famous of these in probably all of the sitcom genre is the Ross and Rachel rodeo, starting as a one-sided school-age infatuation that eventually turns to more when Rachel finds out explicitly about Ross's crush, views him in a different light, and decides to go for it. Some back and forth ensues with poor timing, perfect little Julie, a cat, a kiss, a list, a fight, a not-Ross named Russ, and finally a prom video to hook those crazy kids up. Not sure we can take much of a lesson out of these two, aside from the idea of putting your feelings on the table and taking a chance. How about Monica and Chandler? Good buddies, closer in friendship than Ross and Rachel ever were, they embody more of the partnership, marrying your best friend type of relationship. So how did they break through the friends barrier? Getting drunk in London. Is that the key here?

Because I'm out in London with my new friend Athena from the Roam house and cannot tell what the situation is. We're running around Chelsea and South Kensington all day, starting at a pub for some beers and a football match (U.K. version), continuing on to a cozy oyster bar for dinner and wine, and then on to another pub for more beers and a football game (U.S. version), all the while the thought is running through my head of "gee, this seems an awful lot like a date". The ill-defined setting of this scene from the offset, a single guy and girl who are friendly but have known each other less than a month, out on their own all day with alcohol and close quarters being the recurring characters, a series of uncertain signals being sent, both ways I'm sure, serious and real conversations mixed with laughter and a possible hint in the eyes, leading to a classic conundrum that every sitcom requires in an episode. The tension of the will they or won't they, the one party putting it out there and being rebuffed, the missed signal. I decide I can't pick up a good enough read one way or the other and default to the no harm, no foul approach, thinking we may be better off as just friends. And judging by her vibe all day, the "uncertainty, landing on inaction" play is probably a mutual decision.

Making the move in any situation like that is scary, no matter the gender taking the minor leap of faith. The vulnerability of being out there exposed in expression of a risky sentiment is nerve-racking. Are you operating in the territory of Jim and Pam on *The Office*, or acting out the classic tale of she's just not that into you? Athena and I are new friends with less on the line, especially considering both of our intentions of moving on from London soon to our own international residencies, i.e. no real future and most likely limited to a weeks-long fling. Still though, the anxiety exists on any level of potential "relationship" and is only multiplied exponentially when the attraction is for a long-term friend. Outside of the drunken hookup and a serious conversation in response, the world may forever be stumped on how to seamlessly move from friends to more, along with how many licks it takes to get to the center of a tootsie pop. No sexual undertones there, I promise, just an old-fashioned head-scratcher.

It may be necessary at this point to put out a disclaimer and cover my ass. My interest in the friend zone dilemma is not with the intention of figuring out how to hook up with my female friends. Let's clear that up in case anyone out there is getting an unintentional creepy vibe. I'm just saying, in the past there have been a handful of longtime friends that 1.) I was attracted to, and 2.) based on our history, think there was a possible future relationship with legitimate potential. I mean, we all want to "marry our best friend", right? I've read that on enough dating profiles to know it's a universal sentiment. My question is, how do we, as a society, get to that point and make things easier on humanity? Like, for real.

I'm left to wonder: is there a point when we catch feelings, beyond a general attraction and interest level, where the risk is worth the potential reward? Like a rule or a scale of relative weighted factors that we could quantify in some internal test of feasibility that would dictate the degree to which we should say "fuck it, let's do this". Something that tells us that the juice is worth the squeeze. Maybe we call it the Juice Test? Play around with that idea and get back to me, I think we might have something here.

Back on the online stranger front, I've yet to fool around much with the dating apps in London, having taken an unofficial break. But I match with one girl on Bumble named Queen Elizabeth (no, not really, come on) that intrigues me. We exchange a bunch of messages, but I'm working on an exciting head cold and not feeling up for a date at the moment, at least that's my weak excuse to myself. We both deploy the Fizzle Out stratagem, a practice that has apparently made its way across the pond. Later in the week, our Roam crew heads for a night out in SoHo, London's most lounge-centric semi-wealthy drinking scene. We pop around to a few hot spots, ending up in the basement of a bar that is club-lite, and bust out some white person moves on the dance floor. I make my way through the dimly lit club to the bar to grab drinks for our group. I turn to my right after placing my order of a vodka soda-heavy round, and there directly next to me, with a bloke ordering a drink for her, is Queen Elizabeth on a date.

Of all the gin joints in all the world, am I right? I turn away quickly, shaking my head in conceded amusement, hastily grab our basic bitch drinks, and scatter.

It's later in the night and the majority of our group has made the trek back to Chelsea, but one of the girls and I decide to stay out and try another bar. After about an hour together throwing back drinks, we end up in one of those characteristically questionable situations on the dance floor.

At this point, not feeling great about the events of the night or my overall relationship status, and a bit erotically charged, I lean in somewhat slightly for a kiss that I'm not even really excited about or sure why I'm making the move. It was more that it was there in front of me after dancing for so long, it seemed like the time was right, and I'm drunk. She's not really excited about the idea either, catching my slow deliberateness in time to turn her cheek to the side, at which point I immediately apologize in her ear. That was just dumb, I know it, and she knows it. We laugh it off a bit, dance a few more songs together with boundaries appropriately established, and call it a night, hoofing back casually to the house on an otherwise great night.

I just have no game right now. Although as I think we've fully established by this point, I've never really had any. I know that I'm incredibly picky, and have a pretty solid idea of what I *think* I want in a partner. I've also developed a type, that oddly seems to be a very specific "bubbly, witty, athletic, successful, five foot five-ish blonde from Northern California". And Sir Mix-a-lot, I love you and respect your opinion on the back, but I'm definitely a boobs man. I've dated or had a crush on too many women of this whole description for it to not be a thing. Though lately I've been trending more toward the dark-haired, possibly Italian-looking type of the same personality, from Kristen Bell to Minka Kelly. The only exception to the rule being Isla Fisher, who tops them all. Boy, I'd love to just, you know, take her out for a steak dinner.

Also weird, I have a completely inappropriate habit of developing crushes on girls in relationships. Not that I've acted on it, as far as I know, outside of one time in Florence during college. But it still weirds me out as something happening too frequently to not be a pattern. I'm in a perpetual state of the Rick Springfield classic "Jessie's Girl", or if I'm feeling more sinister, Old Dominion's "Break Up with Him".

I know the easy diagnosis would be to say it's about me wanting what I can't have, which may be a piece of it. But honestly, I think it speaks to my reserved nature, and feeling comfortable enough around someone to be more open and carefree, knowing that the sexual tension of an "is this happening?" is out of the picture. Of course it's that very sense of security, and self-confidence, that leads to the chemistry and unfortunate attraction, resulting in a cycle of unhealthy emotions on par with harboring unreciprocated feelings for a friend. So basically, I find attraction when I can be my most natural self and develop something through a friendship, but within a framework that is typically off-limits to anything beyond what exists. And outside of those dead-end scenarios, I am a Pandora's box of reservation and dating faux pas providing very little by way of emotional investment and no escape to something normal. Is it any wonder why I'm single?

Luckily Roam is filled with other lonely hearts this Valentine's Day, and although we opt out of the card-giving tradition, we join up in solidarity for an Italian dinner in the butler's kitchen downstairs, red wine and carb overload to comfort us. During dinner, we discuss the holiday of record and dive into some relationship history. After we have made a sufficient dent in the pasta, we break out one of the house card games called "Who Should I Be With?", a topical question for the night. In a series of either/or card options, I have to choose which of the two opposite features I'd prefer in a partner. It could be something like "Very rich parents or Very poor parents", "Very confident on the dance floor or would say no if you asked them to dance", and "Sporty or Bookish". It becomes a question of wanting to find balance in a partner, and knowing yourself and what works and doesn't work for you. It's dumb, but pretty fun, and surprisingly accurate, as the embodiment of my final card selections is basically a slightly younger and nerdy lady-on-the-street-but-freak-in-the-sheets, who is also friendly and likes cuddling and being loving. I am excited to meet this person, wherever you are.

Eventually the crowd retires to their respective rooms, but Zeus and I linger with new friend Polycaste over red wine at the table, chatting about her current relationship status of "It's Complicated". Long story short, there's an element in play of the infamous "long distance" nature, two words that make the hair on the back of my neck stand up. The only real relationships I've had have all involved some form of trying to make it work from afar, and failing unceremoniously and unsurprisingly. I have long cursed the long-distance name, an easy target to blame for the shortcomings and ultimate demise of what might have otherwise been forever ever. But now as I look back honestly, the main thing I can glean from this boulevard of broken romances, even my elementary first love with Penny, I suppose, is that I was just not ready at the time. As much as I'd want to throw the liability of the breakup at my significant other of choice, I have to believe most were on me. For not knowing myself and my needs, or what I was looking for, or how to be in a relationship. An all of the above type of answer.

With my law school ex Stella, I was just too young. I had a confidence issue that stemmed from both my lack of real dating experience (at the age of twenty-four) and the juxtaposition of my ballooning law school debt compared to her father's very well-established wealth. That feeling of financial insecurity in general is still a hindrance to the ole self-confidence meter. But ultimately, we wanted different things and in different locations, a conclusion we both knew was hanging over us ready to drop, but she was brave enough to make the call for us. I blamed long-distance forever, for breaking us up twice, but really the experience just expedited the inevitable result.

With Calypso, I also lacked a certain amount of self-confidence, a trait she said she was initially attracted to, an outgoing nature I embodied that balanced out her more reserved qualities. It was a funny observation to me, because I'm typically not that way in social settings with new people, as has been well-established by now. But since we met at a party I hosted with friends all around, I was more relaxed and sociable. What killed me, and our relationship (I think, having no confirmation of this, insert winking emoji), was my fear over the seriousness of it all. I fell for Calypso, and fell hard, and in doing so became scared to show my true personality, the one she initially found attractive, out of fear of driving her away somehow. So I was milquetoast and lame instead. Along with a whirlwind romance that all became too much too soon, and my inability to handle the situation and dial it back, a pressure bubble built up until it burst all over The Bahamas.

Outside of those experiences, my trending story carries an unfortunate tag of #hesjustnotthatintoyou. It's not something I take pride in or feel good about, but an honest assessment of my historical sentiments. I subscribe to the notion that when you know you know, and you know it pretty much right away. There is something that happens inside that could best be equated to how I feel seeing a Bernese Mountain puppy chasing a tennis ball. Or seeing pizza. If I don't get that feeling right away, or even an inkling of it, I have a hard time believing it will ever grow into any kind of raging fire necessary for relationship sustainability. And it's so rare that I've tried to give it a shot to be there despite my initial read, but without the energy from that initial bolt of lightning, the possibility typically fades away. The part I struggle with now is wondering if the moment is so rare for me because of something I'm doing, something I'm blocking from happening because of an unrecognized condition in myself, and that really sucks.

When a situation hasn't worked out, whether it was the serious relationship I cared deeply about or the girl across the bar I never talked to, typically I feel like I lost. But it's not an ego thing like you might think. I'll use a sports analogy here to explain: at the end of a game, if I lost but I left it all out on the field/court/rink, I could feel okay with myself knowing I did my best and it didn't work out the way I wanted. On the other hand, if I fail and know I could have been better, done things differently, or if I didn't even make an effort, that's when the loss is tough for me to swallow. Potentially missing out on forever love because I just didn't have my shit together in time breaks my heart more than any failed Empire State Building rooftop or Brooklyn Bridge meetup ever could.

I have always believed that "the one" is a factor of two overarching elements: chemistry and timing. The right kind of chemistry, including communication ability and matching values, can be had with more than one person. In fact, it can be had with many people, including good long-term friends (and thus, the reason for my frequent mentions). The key variable in the whole equation seems to be timing. Being in the right place at the right time. Knowing enough about myself, and my wants, my needs, my future, and having another person in the same headspace at that same time. Having the ability to spot what I'm looking for in another and how to share all aspects of life with that person.

Sure, I know I'm looking for someone who is kind, and smart, and passionate about life, and fun, and keeps me on my toes, and challenges me, and has great conversation, and loves to travel, and makes me laugh with witty banter, and is close to her family but not too close, and attractive in a way that is the perfect balance of sexy and cute. And according to my dating history, is apparently six inches shorter than me, light-haired and from the Bay Area.

But maybe it's not about what I'm looking for in someone else, maybe it's me. Maybe _my_ timing has just never been right. Maybe it's me again...

I'm not sure what just happened, but as I lie in my comfy bed with my tea fueling this morning motivation, something clicks and I actually say out loud to myself, "Hmm, I think I just got over Calypso." Finally. After fifteen months that were way longer than anything like that should have taken to get past. I opened Instagram, and for the first time, checked to see who viewed my story and realized I had done so without subconsciously looking to see if her name popped up. There's something about seeing an ex still checking out your shit, or maybe even liking a photo, that provides some level of reassurance, a confirmation that they still care even in the most minor of ways to press a button that involves you. I go so far as to search for her name, having unfollowed her a year ago, only to see that she has been dating someone new for a little while now. The reaction I have is a meh-like shoulder shrug, and further confirmation that I think I've finally let it go. Maybe it's the feeling that I'm currently accomplishing something of note, or the distance, but the feelings of anger and loss are gone, almost bordering on happiness for her. Well, not quite yet, but I am willing to cede custody to her of our shared Spotify playlists that were left parentless in the breakup.

It's a few days after Valentine's, but I open my newly arrived copy of *The 5 Love Languages*, which Polycaste suggested to me the other night. I can already tell I'm going to like this book, which has the page quantity of an instruction manual from Ikea. The author, a marriage consultant, has simplified love into elements, a technique and learning style I thrive in from my younger math-centric days to my more recent legal training. To summarize an already brief subject into further condensed form: every individual has a unique love language that we speak, and are spoken to, fitting into one of five categories. In a relationship, when our partner is speaking our language, our "love bucket" gets filled and we feel higher emotions for our partner than if that person was speaking a different language, even if their acts were entirely benevolent and loving. Most problems in relationships can be traced to partners being on different pages in terms of how they show love, and how the other receives it.

I pause in my reading to send a birthday text to Stella, pretty much the extent of communication we have at this point, five plus years after breaking up. A few years ago, I hid her from my Facebook feed, too chickenshit to deal with seeing her moving on and happy in her life. We chat a little bit via text, catching up on where we are in life, and eventually the conversation gets serious and brings me to tears.

Because Stella was the one to be the stronger person and call the relationship off, she has always borne the burden of the breakup. My immaturity in being able to deal with what was clearly a heart-breaking but inevitable end to our time together caused me to go dark on her for the most part, and I never stepped up to let her off the hook, left lingering after all these years. I'm incredibly ashamed that until today, I never let her know I understood, agreed, and that everything was okay, with not even an ounce of hard feelings. She reveals a crushing personal story that I missed while being a bad friend, and I express how truly terrible I feel. In an intense and necessary exchange, I apologize for it all, breaking down at the release and hoping it would relieve her as well.

I end the day, one that could be considered watershed and heavily emotional, back in bed and thoroughly covered, happy to have discovered the coziness of down comforters in my life to go along with my insistence on sheets that hit four figures on the thread count. I quickly finish the love languages book (it really is that short), and in one of those coincidental moments that if it happened in a movie you'd say, "Come on man, no way", I read the last words of the book about falling in love at exactly midnight on Stella's birthday and receive a text at the same time from my mom, completely out of the blue. We were talking earlier in the day about my recent personal growth, but I hadn't said anything to my mom about relationship stuff or Stella. But that spiritual synergy we seem to have must have kicked into gear, because she makes an unsolicited point connecting my development to dealing with Stella, someone we haven't talked about in years. I have no idea what it means, but there's something going on here.

The next day, fresh off an emotional roller coaster, I test out the love language questionnaire for myself. It comes out that my primary language is Quality Time, with secondary appreciation for Physical Touch and Words of Affirmation, which backs up my stance that I'm not about the game-playing, and I like girls that like me. So primarily, I'm happiest just spending time with my partner, whether its cuddling on the couch for a Netflix binge session, having an intelligent debate about politics or how great *Friday Night Lights* is, or taking a road trip or vacation, location mattering little. Gift giving is absolutely not my thing, as I already knew. Even looking back on previous presents I've given in relationships, I have doubled and tripled up on the Quality Time aspect, making the actual gift-giving an experience to share together and generally giving a present that involves doing something with each other. Quality Time is definitely my relationship drug.

I really appreciate this love language concept, and certainly think there's merit to the idea of tapping into that which makes us feel love. As I'm going through this wave of development specifically related to happiness, I contemplate its application to an individual as a sort of personal "happiness bucket". Knowing the specific languages and events, actions, choices that make me the happiest, whether that be professionally, socially, or whatever. And it could apply in the big picture or on everyday happenings. Maybe I don't need a specific theory or pamphlet-sized book to confirm the belief, but just a general awareness to what that means for me. And how it relates to those around me.

It's Wednesday night and we're all hanging around the kitchen after a group dinner, with some rumblings about going out in Chelsea. I'm really not a fan of the weeknight drinking adventure beyond a glass or two of wine, a statement that if my twenty-two-year-old-self heard my thirty-year-old-self say just now, he would punch me right in the throat. But thus is life as a semi-responsible adult.

I employ some classic stalling techniques, pouring more wine in the kitchen for folks under the premise that if we stay in drinking for long enough, I can avoid going out. But eleven o'clock rolls around, and somehow there's still an uncontrollable tailwind behind the movement to the pubs. This is where being a "Yes Man" with elevated levels of FOMO can be a really terrible trait to have. The momentum gets started, people start laying down the guilt trip, and in very short order I'm saying, "Fuck it, sure I'll do some lines with you and go out." Cut to a blur of multiple bars and lounges, too many vodka sodas in an attempt to play catchup on the night, ending in our group of six being the only ones on the dance floor at Prince Harry's favorite club, sometime around two in the morning. Again, on a Wednesday.

It should be noted that one of the people peer-pressuring me to head out is the Australian community manager for the house, someone who I think is cute as hell, get along with swimmingly, and have slowly developed a crush on despite, get this, her having a boyfriend. When I knew she was going out and she asked me to come, of course I began my tried and true practice of reading too much into a completely innocuous gesture. Getting a little jiggy with it together on the dance floor pushes me over the edge to partake in my other patented pastime of overly bold performances, this time in the form of a late-night confession at her door: that the only reason I went out tonight was for her. I'm not sure what I'm looking to accomplish with this move, and the old axiom that nothing goods happen after 2 A.M. holds true, especially ninety minutes past the deadline. I think I had some notion in my misguided mind that it would come out like the poster board confession to Keira Knightley in *Love Actually*. My foolhardy and poorly planned attempt at a romantic showing of course falls flat, as she kind of oscillates between surprise and pity, hugging me with maybe a touch of "if I didn't have a boyfriend...", but the latter is surely just in my head.

I wake up the next morning, fresh off a night of snoring and grinding my clenched teeth, my typical drunk and/or anxious overnight tells (To My Future Wife: good luck), and decide that I'm just going to stay in bed. Forever. My forehead hurts from the massive face palm of pain enduring from the shame of the night before. As much as I've developed emotionally and mentally in the last month, it's never more abundantly clear to me than right now that this is a process, a few steps forward and one step back type of progression. The other plainly obvious conclusion to reach is that I belong nowhere near a female of interest, and have no business being anywhere near anything resembling dating or a relationship right now. There's way too much work left to do.

So in conclusion, my time is not now. Not yet. I'm just not ready. I'm doing something wrong in my dating life, in my approach to the whole scene that isn't working, especially right now given my fluctuating location and mental makeup. I have a sneaking suspicion that the nervous, unsure energy I've exhibited in the past is preventing me from being myself, and myself from being ultimately lovable. I'm just not confident in what I'm bringing to the table at the moment, and I know girls can sense that. It's time to take a legitimate break from the whole idea of female connection and go back to school with myself as the subject, the objectives being to not be such a mess and to figure my shit out for real.

Basically what I'm trying to say is, I'm sorry but it's just not the right time for me, it's not her, it's me, I'm in a different place right now, and I just really need to focus on myself and figure out what I want. Classic.

HOW I CONFRONTED MYSELF

chapter eight

Pizza. Tacos. My mom's mashed potatoes and gravy. A quality charcuterie board with stinky cheeses and Italian meats. Somehow losing weight despite a clear food obsession. White wine in the summer. Rosé every day (no, not really every day). Puppies playing. Or sleeping. Or doing anything, really. Writing. Making myself laugh. Making other people laugh. Nineties throwbacks like *Legends of the Hidden Temple* and the Olsen twins. Fall weather. Leaves changing color. *Friday Night Lights*. Tailgating a football game. The feeling at the end of an intense gym session. The feeling at the end of a focused meditation session. Christmas at my family's house. Lakes. Campfires on lakes. Day-drinking outside. Patios with string lights overhead. A book that makes me think. A show that makes me think. A person that makes me think. Being a nerd. Traveling to a new place. Traveling to an old place I love. Great sex that makes you go "wow" at the end. NBC sitcoms. Oxford commas. A medium rare steak. Seeing Snapchat fail. Hiking. Kayaking. Mountains. Well-designed cities. When no one sits next to me on an airplane. When my sports teams win things. When my niece and nephew do things. When a coffee shop has an open table with just a pinch of sunlight hitting my back. A good, strong cortado. Italian things. Tiny horses. Golfing. The movie *Casablanca*. Broadway shows. Trivia nights. Drinking beer in the bleachers of Yankee Stadium. Yankee candles. Classic Disney movies. Disney theme parks. Country music. Snapbacks and beanies. Banana Republic. A fresh, new hotel room. Bro dinners consisting of meat and scotch. Winning kickball games. Spending the entire first two days of March Madness watching college basketball on multiple screens all at once. Driving with the windows down. Perfect airport arrival timing. A solid suit-shirt-tie combo. Being able to do most of my work in a T-shirt and gym shorts. Afternoon naps. Being location independent. Making lists. Checking things off lists.

That may be the first time in my life that I took the time to write down some of the things that make me happy. Being happy should not be difficult, but that might be the struggle of adulting that consumes the everyday more than anything else. I am far too prone to getting distracted and lost in the pursuit of happiness.

This is easily the hardest I've worked on anything.

My conclusion in London is tracking closely with the completion of my *Eat, Pray, Love* homework, as the final takeaway thoughts from the author's story are reinforced. One of those points is finding your heart, finding love inside and the joy that exists there and tapping into that in everything you do and in your own way. Sounds nice.

The other, more practical and enduring message I pull for use in my own male millennial take on the *Eat, Pray, Love* travel and writing experience is particularly apt for my current circumstances: happiness is not luck. Pause, read that back. Happiness is not luck.

Shit, well that explains a lot.

As I've seen in these last few weeks, it's the conscious effort to find and recognize happiness that has generated all of this momentum and development. I can confirm with my crisscrossing colleague here, this pursuit is not something that just happens. It's something you fight for, strive for, insist upon, even travel around the world in search of. And in the end, Sisyphus may get that boulder to the top of the mountain after all.

The challenge I set out for myself in the first stage of this journey, the initial inquiry into my wandering mindset and the story and writing that emanated therefrom, has been the catalyst and setup for this recent reckoning. The writing piece in particular, the process of going from thought to words, words to screen, screen to paper, paper to something anyone is going to give a shit about, is completely new to me and soul-consuming. Putting this all together, while still living and acting it out on a daily basis, in a way that might make sense, has forced me to clarify and hone in on what exactly is going on upstairs in the noggin.

Downstairs in the house, it's time to say goodbye to Zeus, the one who has pushed me along in that process more annoyingly, invasively, encouragingly, kick-me-in-the-ass-and-out-of-my-comfort-zone appropriately than I ever expected. The one who opened the vault to a buried past I was afraid to acknowledge or release.

Zeus is on his way to Japan for his retreat, a meditation marathon where he won't be allowed to talk for ten days. Sometimes, when I think about having to converse at a networking event, or Twitter mentions, I wish I could not talk to people for ten days, too.

I still have a few more days left in London, but I'm getting a bit antsy for the next steps. Much of the initial Roam crew has left for their next adventures, and I'm getting ready for mine. That's not before another Saturday morning market stroll, accompanied by the customary order of some meat delivery device, a kebab today, and afternoon beers at the pub. This fantastic tradition takes us to the Portobello Market this week, followed by a search for Hugh Grant in Notting Hill, a pitstop at the famous and very Instagrammable Churchill Arms pub, and more of the Six Nations Rugby tournament, though for a billion pounds I still couldn't tell you who was winning.

The next morning is a venture out to Fulham, my first chance to see a Premier League soccer match in person. We jump on the double decker bus to get there, picking the prime seats at the front of the second level to get the best bang for our quid out of the harrowing experience. On the way back to the house, we stop at a pub to partake in the English custom of a Sunday roast. Traditionally, the mid-afternoon meal consisting of some kind of roast meat, potato, veggies, and Yorkshire pudding is the family gathering event, either at the home or the local pub, and seems an appropriate way to go out with my Roamily (is that catching on yet?).

In addition to the writing process, the social engagement, at this level and with people I've known for less time than a Britney Spears marriage, has been my other driving force on this expedition. Meeting the right people at the right time, a perfect storm of mostly American late-twenties modern drifters with a bit of a rebel heart and an eye for Asian food.

The openness and abundance of sharing comes through consistently, with everyone showing their own vulnerabilities, fears, struggles, and skepticism with adulting in their own not-so-unique way. This level of discourse is something I never would have expected in L.A. as I organized weekend day-drinking excursions to Cabo Cantina for two-for-one margaritas, but maybe I should have. I get the profound sense that this may be a bigger matter than just my challenge. Sure, we have a lot of similar people here with personalities that might be kindling for lighting this sort of conversation, coming from people who have all actively chosen this path of wander and wonder. But what if my peers back in the U.S., distracted by any manner of attention-grabbing interruption or YouTube comment section, have these same kinds of thoughts and feelings, and no outlet or forum to voice them properly or reassuringly?

This example of self-understanding and assuredness, even in the face of significant uncertainty in all manner of future endeavors and locations, is motivating. But the part

I find most inspiring in the people I've met recently is the willingness to be open and honest, and to share on an emotional level with, for all intents and purposes, strangers. Persephone's story of breaking out of a conservative social structure to pursue her passion. Zeus's story of heartbreaking separation while managing a multinational company. Laertes' story of his come-to-Jesus moment, fresh off a night in Vegas living the finance life with bottle service, a booth next to Tiesto, and a "douchebox of bros" as he calls it, driving home after to the tune of "life doesn't get any better than that", when he realized he hated that life. He left to happily help start this co-living movement and empower a new community, sacrificing his financial stability in the process. Everyone is dealing with adulting adversity, some are just more willing to admit it than others. And do something about it.

That honesty begets my honesty, firstly and most importantly, with myself. I can picture Zeus nodding his bald head approvingly from his seated zen-like position somewhere in Japan right now.

It's hard to pinpoint the exact moment that the loud "click" sound goes off, but if I had to score the sequence of events that leads to my first truly genuine moments of self-assessment and realization in montage form, it would definitely be set to "Let it Go" from *Frozen* as the background track. It's an acceptance that the struggle is real, and not mine alone, allowing me to ditch the defensive pretext that defined so much of my outcast attitude over these last few months and just embrace the story. I am keenly aware that everything that happens from here radiates from this moment of admitting the insecurity and letting go.

The short-sighted and indeterminate nature of my initial steps on this path are directly correlated to just about every emotion, particularly the negative ones, that I've carried up to this point. Every ounce of guilt, of embarrassment, of confusion, of disorientation, of isolation, of failing in some way, stems from my inability, until now, to admit and accept the precariousness of my previous positions without judgment. That the conquering hero of this epoch may not be as flawless and carefree as I might portray or envision, with an origin story that comes from a place of negativity instead.

When I set out from L.A. back in November, I was relying heavily on fate to intervene in a way that would resolve my unresolved and unaddressed shortcomings and unhappiness. My only expectation was to have some fun and lead an interesting life in a completely shook-up environment from very social media-worthy locales. The menacing, threatening, impending cloud of conventional adulthood was casting a dark shadow over even the flawless Southern California skies above me. Removing myself from the storm, fleeing the scene entirely, I ran scared.

I admit it. And I am okay with it.

The challenge for me, now that I can finally move forward having slayed the motivations of my past and confirmed the "what's done is done" portion of my "what's next" mantra, is to figure out how to deal with what's to come in a way that doesn't send me anxiously searching for the next flight to Hawaii or ditching my new membership in the Do What Makes You Happy and Fuck All the Rest Club to rejoin the League of Extraordinarily Bitter Gentlemen again.

I can start to brush off any lingering comments from the peanut gallery that may poke fun, or question my entire purpose, as a distraction, not narcissistic injury. A defense mechanism borne out of misplaced misunderstanding, and adeptly similar to the self-defenses I've employed to this point on my end.

Now, as I talk to more people back home and they get wind of what I'm up to, I feel considerably more support than I initially realized. The gains begin to outshine the losses in my psyche. This confirmation found from friends in London is now also coming through from friends at home who were unaware of the extent of my endeavor. So many have begun to express benevolent respect for my opportunity, appreciate the value in the experience, and as I start to open up more with the people I've known for much longer than a Britney Spears marriage, recognize a similarity in the sentiments about the traditional way we "grow up" and function as adults in the modern world. While kicking back on the living room couch, another DM slides in from an old friend, inquiring about my latest post, my travels, and the purpose of it all. We share stories on life and encouragement in both directions, a genuine validation of our joint challenge.

My anxiety, in so many ways, was and is not unique. My feelings of confusion and aimlessness in L.A. may not have been as original and personal as initially imagined, a sensitivity that caused me a great deal of internal grief and guilt. That reflection personified in the mirror of an oddball staring back at me with judgment for having these feelings and acting on them in this way. The uncertainty about so much of what I wanted in life, and how to make myself happy, and what to do next, was, as it turns out, as completely normal as collectively despising Donald Trump. The confirmation that we're all in the same boat, perhaps universally in our shared misery and glory, is transcendent and liberating. I knew in many ways we were probably all the same, struggling with balancing loan budgeting with avocado expenditures, but not on this level. I'm just dealing with it all a little differently, and that's okay.

So, it's not just me after all. Well, it's me.

But also, it's us.

Abandoning all that negative frees me up to focus on the other side of that equation, to pay attention to myself with honesty, find that happy, and chase it.

And that, my friends, is how I met myself.

Wait, no, I jumped the gun again. There's no way in hell I'm "ready" right now, we can't meet me yet.

It's a new concept that's going to take me some time. The truly remarkable notion in my mind now is how simple this all really should be. I'm writing of this personal awakening as if it rivals the discovery of electricity, or the polio vaccine, or things made with kale. But really, it's not that revolutionary. Maybe this is a bit of an extrapolation, based on a personal sample size of one and applying it to the entire population (okay, maybe a massive extrapolation), but who today really takes the time to pause in our everyday lives and ask ourselves one question: is this what I want? Or put another way, will this or does this make me happy?

So much of my angst over the last year plus, so much of my feeling of discontent, can be blamed on not knowing what I want. Maybe I want kids, maybe I don't. Maybe I'll just get a dog. I mean, dogs are better than people, right? I honestly just don't know what I want right now. But how could I possibly know that, or what I want in a job, or place to live, or family and social life, if I never ask the damn questions of myself?

Contemplating and evaluating the impact of so many of adulthood's pain-in-the-ass challenges, especially within that FOMO context that defines the millennial life, I've certainly not settled on anything yet, but feel like I'm collecting the tools to build something. And at least asking the right questions now. Or the right person.

No longer worried about what the town Elders might think, I decide it's time to dabble more in this meditation craze all the kids are talking about.

At the Roam house, Laertes runs an early morning group session twice a week, an activity I blew off even when I first moved here and was participating in everything. But now at the tail end of my stay, open in so many more ways, I decide to break the seal. My first experience is quite enjoyable, and the seemingly painful process of sitting in silence for thirty minutes goes quicker than I imagined. I definitely have some work to do on my breathing, which is a really odd thing to say, but I can feel myself going deep, into the back of my mind and body in unfamiliar waves of consciousness. I sit down for my second round and feel like I'm traveling much deeper this time. I see a vision, swimming through the waves of the ocean, then on the beach at dusk, the sun set but the sky a plum purple, script written into the emerging stars, and bam. Just as I'm trying to decipher the writing, I become self-aware and snap out of my trance. This is some good shit, this meditation fix.

Again, I have no idea what it all means and how this will be important to me in the end, but I'm going to have to keep at this because I really like it, a surprising development on the same lines as my discovery of and now fondness for feta cheese.

Zeus was always pushing me to try to this, talking about the balancing, stabilizing effect it has on the mind. He will meditate for an hour or more at different times during the day, and since he is one of the most in-tune and stable minds I've come across, he must be doing something right. He suggested to me an introductory level book on meditation, written by a Google employee with a ridiculous job title like "VP of Happiness" called *Search Inside Yourself*. I put it on the Amazon Prime delivery list and head out to the coffee shop down the street to write some more.

The idea of finding balance in life, in my emotions, in my approach to dealing with the unexpected as well as the everyday, is another emerging theme of recent note, though something I've found intriguing going back to high school but never gave enough attention. One of my favorite books back then was *Siddhartha*, and no, it's not because it's so brief you could read the whole story while waiting at a traffic light.

I always enjoyed Siddhartha's tale of indulging wholly in the spiritual life and wholly in the secular life, and then finding happiness somewhere in the middle of the extremes. I'm not sure how it all comes together simply by closing my eyes and focusing my attention on my breath, but the timing of the introduction to this world while all the other self-reflection hits is too conspicuous to be coincidental. I'm long overdue for some roll up my sleeves and sit cross legged on the floor hard-working introspection. It's further confirmation to me that I'm in the right place right now.

But the sun is setting on that time and place, as I emerge from the Roam house into the fading mid-afternoon sunlight and tube over to the West End in an attempt to win lottery tickets to see *The Book of Mormon*. I was supposed to see this play last December with a certain ex on her first trip to New York who bailed on the plan, and me, after the tickets were already bought. Not naming names though. My parents enjoyed the show in my stead, despite the fact that neither of them uses swear words. Like ever. Which is funny, considering. In any event, the active decision to see the show right now is just another minor data point in the mounting evidence for my case that I can "let it go, the past is in the past".

Not discouraged by my lottery strikeouts in New York to see *Hamilton*, I line up outside the Prince of Wales Theatre to attempt to win Ten-Pound tickets the old school way, with someone pulling pieces of paper out of a steel wheel. About thirty names are called off as I'm waiting, watching while people from all over London, Europe, and the U.S. eat up all the golden tickets until we get down to the last chance. Of course. I never win these sorts of things. Tonight though, karma is doing its thing, and I'm shocked when I'm the final one called to the chocolate factory. I text a Roam friend to join me, the one of the "late-night dance floor confusion" fame from last week, still on good terms after our little moment, and enjoy laughing at religion for the rest of the night.

You know those random memories of moments from early childhood that really make no sense as to why you can still recall them? One of mine from when I must have been about five or six is of playing wiffleball in the backyard with my uncle, who would have been only slightly older than I am now. It came right after dinner at my parents' house, and not a particularly important dinner or event at all. Certainly not worthy of a lifelong memory. But as I was running around, being an appropriately active and annoying kid, my uncle had to pause for a minute, and I asked him why. He told me that he was an adult, and it takes longer to digest as you get older. An incredibly forgettable and unmeaningful exchange otherwise, but for some reason stands out in my mind right now for a couple of reasons. One, this past month of heavy consumption, fed with a steady diet of emotional breakthroughs, with a side of challenges to the psyche and mind, have me feeling a bit like Thanksgiving evening stuffed up with turkey and those aforementioned mashed potatoes. I'm in desperate need for some digestion, some time to take it all in and really process, before I head back out on the wiffleball field.

The other relevant feature of that story is that it speaks to my lifelong inability to show any kind of patience, ever. My mom likes to tell the story (and I clearly don't mind) of when I was three years old and anxious to start reading, so she taught me a few letters, then sounds, then words, trying to break me in slowly. Instead, she would catch me sneaking away with a book to continue learning on the side, impatient with her slow-rolling me, to the point that I was reading on my own within a week.

My current reading, the last few pages of *Eat, Pray, Love*, detail another relatable story applicable to this notion about patience. Without giving the story away, the author, in a frenzy to complete an Act III task in Bali and cleanly wrap up her year-long journey, begins feeling over-eager and pressing the issue with her friend to get something done on the author's timeline, blaming it on a New York mentality. If we call it a "Tri-state mentality", I can also place the blame for my own rushed timelines on this trait, though I suspect for both of us the flaw is more personality than geography. In prior relationships that I really cared about, I pushed my partner to get to where I was emotionally, signing my own death warrant in the process. In this journey, one of particularly ambiguous ends, I still struggle with wondering where this all ends up, both personally and in this writing, and am anxious to get there.

Throwing up my hands and letting the process take hold is incredibly antagonistic to my natural tendencies, but I'm learning the value of digestion and letting things come to me as they are "supposed to". The "everything happens for a reason" mantra is a lot easier said (as I have, a lot), than done. But I'm getting there.

At this point, I can't go an hour without some measure of connection or application of an important lesson and means of self-analysis entering my mind. I'm taking notes down constantly. Being able to confirm that the past is in the past and let it go, while realizing aspects about my personality and needs by taking the time, finally, to actually devote to these prospects, has changed everything and opened up so much excitement and possible paths to happiness. Or at the very least, less anxiety in the future. It's like a gigantic hole has blown open in that vault and riches of acceptance and purpose have come flowing out.

It's time to move on now though, and Roam sends me on my way with a pancake breakfast in the kitchen before my Uber arrives for the trek to London City Airport, and on to my long-anticipated return to my study abroad home, Florence.

Flying as much as I do, I make a concerted effort to minimize my airport down time, pushing the limits of any scheduled departure. If I can walk through security (and passport control here) and onto the plane exactly when my boarding group is called with a medium-sized water in my hand without delay or hurry in my step, then I have won some imaginary victory over something.

The ride out of town hits the major talking points: Buckingham Palace, Westminster Abbey, Big Ben, London Eye. A rare bit of late-February sunshine peaks through the morning majesty, glimmering even brighter as it reflects off the golden features of the iconic clock tower.

We cross the Thames and there is no turning back now. Aptly, I give a buzz to my parents, who are looking forward on my behalf, most likely to my anticipated June return back to the States so they can sleep easier at night. By the way, I very much enjoy the ability while abroad to refer to it as "the States". I give my parents the Cliff Notes version of the last few pages, and then our attention focuses on what's next. Sure, there are the locations, and flights, and hotels, and dates to sort out, and that will come in due time. That's the easy part. The more revolutionary thought is something my dad says, after I detail all the development I packed into my excessive baggage for this next portion of the trip: "You can't go back again."

The view out of the rearview mirror has an unintelligible glare to it. That old life, and any negativity that came with it, is being left behind. In so many ways, I can't see myself returning to the past. Any question marks I might have had about returning to L.A. as home are gone. Any chance I might have had to return to my old job, show up in an office every day, and waste time at the water cooler is gone. Any lingering resentment and hurt in love I might have been holding onto is gone. To go to the *Frozen* well one more time, this stuff can't hold me back anymore.

So what's next, then, as my Uber weaves purposefully through the choppy streets of east London? Who knows? We'll continue to look forward though, and keep progressing into the unbounded and unknown. To a place I've never been.

Oh, wait... where's this plane heading?

INTERMISSION

This is an Act Break. Grab a drink, visit the restroom. The story will begin again shortly.

A CHAPTER WHERE WE AIN'T EVER GETTING OLDER

chapter nine

There's a reason Florida is called God's waiting room. The elderly reach a point where their old bones just can't handle the cold anymore and fly south. For me, it's not so much the chilly weather that makes me hate winter, but the shortness of the days, an extended darkness that discourages and depresses action and positive momentum like a tamer to a Marching lion. Arriving into Florence in the rapidly encompassing dusk tempers my excitement of touching down in Italy. The homeland. History.

I pop out into the winter scene and pass my apartment information to the taxi driver in broken and strained Italian, then sit back in wonder at the sites that surround me. We roll up to an old building on an old street in an old section of the city. The driver shouts something back at me and points, and I respond with some amount of Euro bills that I think are sufficient for the fare. I unload my abundant cargo onto the irregular cobblestone street and close the trunk door, and before I can collect myself to make a move for the house, my taxi has sped off and left me a bit dazed in the dark. I stare keyless at the door to the apartment building with that age-old feeling of, "Oh hey, I probably should've done a better job of making sure I was prepared for my nighttime arrival into a new housing situation in a foreign country."

Unsure of my entry directions, having been provided incomplete and shoddy instructions from my point of con-tact, I stare at the door feeling about as useless as the car alarm going off down the street.

What's the point of a car alarm anyway? Who's ever heard that sound and said, "Well, I guess I better alert the po-lice, someone is obviously robbing that Fiat", instead of what we actually say, "Ugh that's so annoying. SHUT UP!"?

After about ten minutes of street-side confusion, look-ing completely ridiculous just standing outside this building with huge suitcases while being annoyed by a car alarm, eventually a woman exits through the door to walk her dog. "Grazie," I say, as if that's sufficient explanation for the absur-dity of this random American with too much baggage just waiting in the dark for her to leave the building. She is not phased though, as I lumber into the foyer. The door shuts behind me and I turn to face what's next. My relief at being inside quickly turns back to helplessness, the complete dark-ness of the ancient atrium before me stalling any positive movement I just accomplished.

My eyes adjust slightly to the darkness of my setting and it becomes clear there are no apartments on this floor, and my next step is up. I shuffle my way to the stairs, laboring slowly from both the dubiousness of my path and the tonnage of luggage in my tow. Dressed in heavy winter clothing, stuffed Eurotrip backpack over my shoulders and a suitcase in each hand, I start my ascent up the deep, stone steps in this black, cavernous, antiquated corridor, ascending each stair one by one, plodding along. About three hours later, give or take, I make it to the first level, pause to listen outside the door, hear a local broadcast on the television and some fast-talking Italians conversing, and realize this is not my destination. Onward and upward we go, employing the same monotonous approach up each level of the building, striking out on finding my designated apartment all the way up to the top floor, somewhere around five flights up. As I finally reach the end, unsure of what will happen if this last unit is not my place, someone enters the building downstairs, and shouts up, "Palazzo Rucellai?"

"Yes!" I scream down the stairway in excitement at the announcement of my new Florence program, and "Oh thank God!" my mind screams to itself in excitement that one way or another, I made it. The man runs up the stairs with much more impressive fleetness of foot than I just displayed, tells me the power is out in the common areas of the building, and I should have waited for him downstairs and he would have helped me up. Well thanks, buddy, my time machine is almost fully functional now, so when I get that up and running, I'll redo it right the next time. I can't stay mad at him though, as he is the gatekeeper to the official start of my Italian experience, and he lets me into the apartment I will share for the foreseeable future with my roommates from UConn. My first time in Florence is off to an interesting and stressful start, but it doesn't matter because 2007 is going to be incredible for me, I can feel it.

Plot twist!

The sudden jolt of the plane wheels smacking harshly into the Florence runway is a jump cut for me back into the present, ten years removed from that initial Italian entrance.

This arrival is not as dark or mired in the same kind of apprehension and confusion. The bumpy landing today is into gray skies and pesky drizzle, though, as I exit onto the tarmac on the first day of March into a thick fog of vague familiarity. The sentiment in the air overtaking the moment stands in stark contrast to my gut reaction just one month ago on my entry into London. Something just felt right there. Something feels... off now. But I can't put my finger on it yet.

You know that impression you get right away on a first date? Like okay we have a little spark going here, or in the alternative, there's no chance in hell this is going to a second. Well, I feel like I just walked into a sushi restaurant to meet this girl for the first time and she's wearing a red MAGA hat. But at least you can get out of that disaster scenario. If things don't change, I have a whole month in front of me of feeling like something is out of place here. Or I am.

It's weird to have this emotion, because Florence holds such a profound spot in my heart and has for a decade now. Since the moment I left Florence at the conclusion of my study abroad semester in May of 2007, I've been clamoring to get back, telling anyone who would feign interest, or just be located next to me at the time, about how incredible my experience was and how I ached to return. And so I'm here hosting a personal ten year reunion for myself in desperate celebration, returning to the scene as a way to recreate or relive that life-altering story of a younger age.

As soon as I exited that taxi cab ten years ago onto Via Ferdinando Zannetti in the heart of Florence, lost but with all of the world in front of me, nothing would be the same. After a week in our fifth-floor apartment, where the electricity would shut off multiple times a day requiring us to hike all the way downstairs to flip the breaker back on, our school managers relocated us to an upgraded apartment that would end up defining our experience. 7 Via del Corso was a three-story townhouse that seamlessly fit the five of us, with three kitchens, three living rooms, three bed/baths, and most importantly, a rooftop terrace that looked straight out at the Duomo two blocks away. Our central location and mind-blowing digs, not just for a twenty-year-old, but for anyone really, made our spot the main meeting location and social center for our entire program at Palazzo Rucellai.

Five or six nights a week, we were up on the terrace drinking, whether it was a Montepulciano red and a pasta dinner, Chianti and chess, or beer pong with the crew to pre-game a night out, ending most by grabbing a doner kebab for the walk home and a nightcap with our domed neighbor. We made very close friends with a couple groups of girls from UConn and others from Penn State, and much like the party that started when one of our many cans of Pringles was popped that semester, the fun didn't stop.

We drank champagne on the famous bridge triangles, we drank champagne at Piazzale Michelangelo at sunset, we drank an entire bottle of champagne as a sidearm while playing beer pong at dive bars like Faces and Red Garter. We took in art and culture and dinner and gelato all over the city of lilies. We saw a gypsy fight from our balcony involving some domestic abuse, but it was the woman who beat the shit out of the guy before the cops eventually came. We climbed the tiny steps to the top of the Duomo and waved back at our apartment terrace from the apex. And we played more beer pong.

The other fantastic part about the city was its central location as a jumping off point to the rest of Italy and Europe. From day trips to weekend excursions, our group of five, ten, sometimes thirty friends ventured out to get lost in the canals of Venice, hike the hills of Cinque Terre, and roam the ruins of Rome. We spent a weekend in a beachside cabin in Sorrento, renting scooters to drive the Amalfi Coast, executed our Blue Grotto caper, and ran through Pompeii right before it closed (for the day, not because of volcanic activity). I took a trip to Milan and hunted for George Clooney on Lake Como. We skied the Swiss Alps and paraglided over Interlaken, we outdrank our bar crawl guides before ending up at a strip club in Prague, we partied Easter weekend in togas in Greece, we absorbed all the history and beer we could in Berlin and I broke a new land speed record running away from hookers in the park.

To be back in this place that launched it all, a source of so much joy at the time and in recalled memories over the years, is a completely surreal experience.

I have a little time to kill before my Airbnb is ready to move in for the month, so I stroll through the city center in a state of internal upheaval, overwhelmed by the emotion encompassing me. There's a pronounced level of excitement that pushes a subtle, serene smile onto my face as I reminisce in real time at the recognizable spots around me, while still confused by the entire weight of the moment. Considering the significance of this place, a leading actor now in the two defining travel and development experiences I've undertaken, the return to Florence and this moment standing in front of the Duomo's ancient visage again is undoubtedly one of my pinnacle moments.

I turn toward the San Lorenzo neighborhood in search of my favorite old pizza restaurant. On our first night in Florence a decade ago, we met a restaurant bouncer named Kenny G who enticed us into his place with a very convincing Bronx-native sounding "How you doinnnnn'?" and it was there that I found my all-time favorite four-cheese pizza. I'm disappointed but not totally surprised that it has closed during my absence. I pause for less than a second wondering if I might ever be able to find another good pizza joint anywhere in the city, before stopping in the place right next door for a Quattro Formaggi that holds up just as well. Imagine that.

While waiting for my lunch, I tap into the WiFi and allow myself to finally do something that I've avoided in all the years that I've been gone. I pull up Yelp and search for my favorite kebab place, a spot I went to probably twice a week and I still rave about as the best late-night drunk food of all time. I haven't allowed myself to see if it was still open out of fear of some kind of Schrodinger's cat situation, hoping I will be pleasantly surprised now that it's in practical reach again. My effusive reaction when I see on Yelp that it's active and open surprises me, as the emotion of these first few hours really is fucking me up in an inexplicable fashion. I'm bordering on tears at this pizza place over a kebab shop being open down the street. Shit is so weird right now. Also, did I mention I love food?

Sufficiently satisfied with my first Italian pizza experience back at the source, I ditch my New York stride for a Florentine shuffle on the slow walk back to the Airbnb, passing through the Piazza del Duomo again. Still lingering after a few hours in town is the unshakably pervasive impression that everything is different this time around. The eyes with which I view this familiar setting are changed now, older, more seasoned, more traveled, from wide-eyed and impressionable to proficient and focused. Everything about Florence seems so much more manageable and smaller in my mind than the memories I carry with me. I remember the walks taking longer, roads being wider, buildings being taller, places of interest being farther apart. Even the Duomo, the quintessence of this city, a monumental beacon standing tall and massive as the focal point of a region, people, and the entire Renaissance era, looks so tiny to me. The tourists who have made their way to the cupola surrounding the outside of the dome are close enough to hear their conversations and reach out to give a high five.

The more things stay the same, the more they change. Or something like that.

In my mind and for such a long period of "holding on", I put this place and the whole study abroad trip on a pedestal as the best thing I ever did. The realization almost immediately hits me as to why it feels so weird being back here. I'm in the middle of something right now that is even better, topping that experience and leaving it behind in the dust. My time in Florence in college was a little over four months. As of right now, I've been on a new global travel adventure for about three and a half. By the time I leave here at the end of March, I'll have surpassed the amount of time committed to the experience, with at least a few more months to go after this. The feeling that I have is clearly coming from a fear of going backward, almost as if I've already moved beyond this, into more and better and different, with no need to romanticize the past anymore. The letting go theme has been especially prevalent of late, and it appears I've quickly stumbled upon another aspect from the past that needs closure in symbolic form. Not that the period had some debilitating hold on me, but more as a test of my progress, in the interest of realizing that returning to the safe space of a past love or the comfort of a memory is no way to move forward and grow.

These are the exact kind of emotions and thoughts you hope to have about a place a few hours into a month-long stay there.

In the interest of powering through and enjoying Florence 2.0 for what it is and will be, I settle into my wonderful new apartment in the city center. The Duomo's omnipresence is a stabilizing and reassuring site, just a block away from my door. Inside the apartment is a huge, loft-style design with a galley kitchen, cathedral ceilings with exposed wood beams, two fully stocked floor-to-ceiling bookshelves sandwiching large French doors to a small patio peeking at the Duomo, and an upstairs bedroom, bath, and office looking down quaintly over it all.

I seek out the same grocery store for supplies that I used to frequent, excited by a chance to return to the home-cooking habit and perfect my specialty for dinners-in: pasta out of a box and sauce out of a jar. Perfetto!

The feeling that initially permeated my thoughts of a super small city comes back to bite me in the ass in the fifteen-minute walk home from the store, sweating and laboring while carrying bags in one hand and a heavy case of water on my other shoulder down cobblestone streets. Maybe that's what actually made me feel like Florence was bigger before?

Market life is one of the best parts of living here, and a fun aspect to work into the daily tasks, as I do during my first week of establishing myself. A gym is out of the question, no Italian has ever lifted a weight before, but the space in my apartment is prime for in-home remedies. I carry with me and can now utilize my trusty Shaun T Max 30 DVD's, without fear of disturbing the neighbors while I'm bouncing all around the floor like a madman. I also have the space to set up my agility ladder for plyometric moves, and I bounce around that like a madman on alternative days, while working some steps up to the loft into the equation. The apartment's conversion to a makeshift fitness center is a happy surprise. I fill the rest of my days with reading, writing, and working, with a slight increase in meditation frequency as well. Trips to the Conad grocery store or Central Market to keep things fresh are becoming an every-other-day-excursion, restocking on water, pasta of course, and whatever kind of protein meat source I can get my hands on. I develop a delightful lunchtime habit of popping into the Oil Shoppe, a favorite of my past, an American college-student-friendly sandwich spot with the best meatball sub in the world, and now selling avocado iced coffee (insert heart eyes emoji). I grab one of each to-go and return home to stream some *Lost* on Netflix while I mangia. I figure I need to study up in case my plane goes down over the South Pacific when I head to Asia next month.

After scarfing down the sandwich in less time than it takes to be confused by who The Others are (that's to say, really quickly), I pull out a deck of cards I've carried somewhere in the luggage this whole time. When I'm working from home and not out at a café or restaurant, I need something to serve the purpose of momentarily distracting my attention the way people-watching does for me when I'm in public. The cards are now my distraction, giving my hands something to do while they're waiting for my brain's next move. Sometimes it's when I pause in my writing, sometimes when I'm bored on the phone talking to a client, but I can reset and think about the next thing I want to say while shuffling the cards in my hands. When my brain catches up and I've sorted through my task at-hand, I put the cards down and begin again.

Saturday arrives and although I need to break the streak of outdoor market strolling I started in London, I endeavor to do something daunting that I avoided last time: cross the Arno. That's an exaggeration, of course, since I had to ford the river to get to the Michelangelo viewpoint and to Faces bar for the 10-euro-all-you-can-drink deal of the millennium. But my opinion of crossing the Arno is similar to that of my beliefs on crossing the 405 in L.A.: no.

I always wanted to check out the Boboli Gardens though, so I swing by the Oil Shoppe for a sandwich and avocado iced to go, and cross to the other side to see if the grass really is greener. I route my path over the river via the Ponte Vecchio, which means "old bridge" in Italian, fittingly named considering it's, you know, an old bridge. After wandering the gardens for the afternoon, stocking up on the story-worthy pictures aided by this cloudless canvass, I pull up at the main lawn area and settle under a tree for lunch and some writing on my equally well-traveled laptop. I lean against the back of the tree, soaking up the sun and crunching on an apple with the coolness, at least in my head, of my favorite literary character, Tom Sawyer. Surrounding me are pockets of Italian teenagers and study abroad sorority squads lounging in the grass and enjoying the almost-Spring day. While I feel the profound air of solitude in my current state, I'm comfortably at peace with it for the moment, a small reprieve from the mentally and emotionally turbulent last few weeks.

As the sun starts to set on this pretty nice little Saturday that involved no time at Home Depot or Bed, Bath, and Beyond, I exploit my position across the river to bounce over to

Piazzale Michelangelo for the stunning view again, an experience that should be on the bucket list of any world traveler. I have no champagne with me this time, and no one to join a selfie set against the backdrop of the entire Florentine skyline, but the setting never disappoints, no matter the company or amenities. As I work on my perfect panoramic, I pause to snap a few photos for people who request my clearly keen eye for framing, or just to take advantage of my solo status as an easy sucker for the task. I'm hoping one of the inquiries is from an attractive single girl roughly my age, who also likes ramen and reading narrative non-fiction, but alas, my magical meet-cute story and resultant film production starring Bradley Cooper and Rachel McAdams is denied by fate this time.

Returning back to the house and feeling pretty good about things, something drives me to check Instagram and engage in a little ex-stalking. Maybe a test of myself? Maybe some masochistic desire to self-correct into unhappy? I'm going to go with the test theory for now.

I just so happen to stumble onto Calypso's page (weird, right?) and see her with the current boyfriend. She seems genuinely happy and pure in her smile, and I accidentally catch myself smiling back. I'm legitimately glad for her in a way that would have made me sick a few months ago. I think there's something in the acknowledgment that we are never, ever, getting back together. Like, ever.

The oddly delayed but finally arrived feeling of closure in my mind is therapeutic, and at least I have one thing I can release from its imprisoning hold on me. I kick back for the night, play a little Solitaire on the couch, and unwind with *Lost*.

Back in the school week, I decide to check out the old class building and see if any unfamiliar faces are still there. Believe it or not, sometimes we would actually go to class when I studied abroad here. Although to be fair, that was very much a joke.

My Art History course was set up so that Mondays were in the classroom, and Wednesdays were a tour of one of Florence's incredible, world-famous museums, a blessing I certainly did not appreciate at the time. My History and Culture of Food in Italy class (yes, it was actually called that and it was awesome) took two field trips to wineries in Tuscany, and one to a villa for a cooking class where we prepped our own lunch of gnocchi, ravioli, salad, chicken cacciatore, and tiramisu. We drank wine while we waited for it to cook, then feasted with an A+ level work ethic. My end of semester paper for that class was on the differences between classic Italian cuisine and the American version. Spoiler alert, in case you ever get around to reading it: the dishes we know in the U.S. as quintessential Italian (chicken parmesan, spaghetti and meatballs, pepperoni pizza, fettuccini alfredo) all have something in common, meat and cheese, two products in abundance in America that previously alluded the peasant, pasta-eating class in the majority of the homeland, and that's why you fail to find them in Italy. That hard-hitting and critical analysis got me an A.

I saunter by as the cool alumnus that I am, but the program has apparently moved on and elsewhere. Foiled in my plans for some interaction, I walk around the corner and set up shop at a café with an authentic espresso. I open my notepad to a blank page and sit back to take in the bizarre notion of working from the same place I used to work when I went to school a couple hundred feet from here. My stomach turns a little, either from the espresso or from the thought that all this time has passed, and yet I'm now back in the same position.

I return home through the impossibly narrow streets and sidewalks, barely squeezing space enough for one car and one person wide. I travel past huge arched wooden entry doors, guarding in ancient purpose the expansive atriums and hallways, stone steps, stone everything, that wait quietly on the other side. The buildings of massive blocks stacked high in medieval glory rise abruptly from the street below, casting a shade of darkness and a concrete jungle atmosphere the skyscrapers of New York can't touch. It was through this dated setting ten years ago that my friends and I joined a St. Patrick's Day pub crawl that started with sangria and ended with a few dozen of us chanting "Ole, ole ole ole" through the timeless Renaissance streets.

Church bells ring with imprecise and seemingly uncoordinated regularity, at all times and all locations I might find myself in the city, which isn't very many. There are people in the middle of the streets in perpetuity, walking everywhere and anywhere like a Bourbon Street, without the hurricane in hand or the smell of vomit and piss everywhere. It's off-putting to see people this time taking selfies in front of the David statue and walking these streets with their heads buried in their smart phones. I don't know how things would have changed if we had apps like Google Maps, Yelp, Tinder, even basic text messaging ability to play with at any time. When I was last here, a $200 per month flip phone was standard protocol, while using an actual Kodak digital camera for my pictures. And we had to walk barefoot fifteen miles uphill in the snow to school. Both ways.

I'm finding that Florence is not well-suited for my non-suited work attire. My daily getup, pretty much wherever I go, is a T-Shirt and gym shorts, preferably with flip flops, although as I mature, and more aptly, as I moved out of California, I realize I can probably leave the sandals out of the luggage next time. Still, in comparison to Florence, proper and stylish in a way that rivals Paris fashion, my khaki shorts and snapback hat style draws some derisive attention. You can take the boy out of California, but...

Now home, my cozy apartment extends its arms of welcome, the walls wrapping me in safe embrace. As crazy as it sounds, given my propensity for the road, I honestly think I'm a homebody at heart. I like to venture out, get my fill, return to comfort, and repeat the equation with a new destination. The calmness of my solo ride through each day now gives me a chance to catch up on establishing a bit of stasis in mind and movement. My love affair with this apartment causes me to spend more time inside than I probably should, but the design inspires a creative energy that feeds this fragile ego, broken down over months of self-sledgehammering, and is just starting to possibly rebuild. Something about sitting outside on my patio as the birds chirp and the bells of the Campanile next to the Duomo holler back at me that spurs me on. The same goes for my loft desk perched above the downstairs scene, staring at the bookshelves full of tomes that I hope to join one day.

I toss some cards around and set my sites on a quiet night in, when what to my wandering ears should appear, but "No Scrubs" by TLC blasting through the windows clear. I poke my head out of my second-floor bedroom and realize there's a group of American college girls living upstairs and across from me. Well, this is a welcome development.

I battle back with my own playlist reverberating through the open windows and inner garden area of the building's rear, skipping "No Scrubs" on the Spotify sequence since the girls already covered that one. It's not a big deal to skip, that's just one of the many jams I feature in my infamous party play-list called the Hangge Uppe (named after a legendary bar in Chicago), a source of pride that I never miss an opportunity to throw into conversation. Hey, look at that, I did it again. The night turns into later that night and they don't take the bait, apparently in the midst of a wine and flowy pants session at home. Just guessing. I suppose I could go up and introduce myself, but do I really want to be the weird (or charmingly mysterious?) solo dude living downstairs hitting on the girls ten years his junior? I'm going to opt for no, and hope I natu-rally run into them in the hall. Even just as people that speak English and have impeccable taste in music, it would be nice to have someone around with something in common.

Ten years ago, I know those girls. I'm close friends with them, they're from UConn, too. One of them we called "Mama", since she was the mom of the group. I got the moniker of "Dad" because, well, you can figure it out. It's a nickname that has stuck with me, through various locations and friend groups and without any kind of initiation on my end. Maybe it's the

Dad bod, the Dad jokes I tell (So a pirate walks into a bar and he has the wooden steering wheel of the ship hanging out of his pants. Bartender says, "Hey, you've got a steering wheel in your pants." Pirate goes, "Arrrghh, I know, it's drivin' me nuts."), or just a general watchdog, caretaker, planner, decision-maker personality that I bring to the friends table, but somehow I give off a dad vibe. I even wrote my terribly ill-advised sitcom pilot about it last year, with "Dad" as the title.

My dilemma is that I'm not sure it's a trait I necessarily want to engage or a role I want to have in the future. Dads can be fun and goofy and always dependable, but can also be serious in a real buzzkill kind of fashion. I was told by Stella once that I acted that way at times, overly serious in a way that caused me to lose the lighter personality that's my more natural, likable, desired state. A word used in *How I Met Your Mother* to describe Ted, who very much embodies the Dad personality in everything he does, sticks with me: Anhedonic, the inability to enjoy things. It's a word that hits a little close to home and scares the crap out of me, a mindset on life I want to avoid entirely and likely a strong contributing cause of where I'm at right now.

In response, I've been thrown taglines like "immature" and "acting my age", as if my lack of wanting to be a boring, basic adult is about maturity. In some ways, I'm always going to be immature. I'm not going to stop enjoying taking Wario around the track in Mario Kart, or filling with glee at Splash Mountain, or basking in the Saturday sun watching football in the Fall with my friends, or being overly selective with the women I date to the point where my casual attitude toward it all makes people rumble about "getting on in years". I'll figure out how to bring it all together eventually. I just don't want to have to cash out my fun account to restock my hypothetical IRA while I do so.

As I lay down for bed, the sound of music upstairs has been replaced by the sound of baby next door. The new parents seem to be local, as they shout in Italian past each other in an effort to silence the constant crying, an endeavor I fully support. The dichotomy of sounds from my different neighbors makes me laugh, as my gut response to one right now is a clear "yes, please" and the other a "ha, no thank you". The image I have in my head is something like that from a TV show, where the angel is on one shoulder and the devil on the other, jostling for influence over the character's soul and decisions. On one hand, partying to 90's jams. The other, adulting. And since I'm over here not adulting and being basic, my choice is clear. I fall asleep content with my status.

I really do need to get out of the house, though. My weird, attention-divided quirk with the cards has turned into something more lately as my alone time increases in my den of solitude. Instead of just shuffling cards while thinking, my boredom is causing me to do it mindlessly while sitting around or watching TV, as an incredibly insignificant form of at least some sort of activity. Now, that has turned into me playing a lot of Solitaire on the coffee table. I always play the classic way, with three cards down, so I don't win very often. Since I'm stubborn and hate to lose, I'll go on thirty, forty, sixty-minute streaks of games until I can end on a high note, wasting time in a struggle against myself.

I really don't like the idea of heading out at night to par-take in the Florence bar scene, something I always would've despised if not for the group of friends around me during college, but I try it alone tonight anyway. Desperate for that divine moment. I drink my vodka soda slowly, unremarkably, looking around pitifully, begging for connection with a touch of earnestness that accompanies the so-called good guy's plight in surviving the modern love experience.

Sometime around midnight, the bouncers finally start letting in the thirty-year-old overly aggressive Italian douche-bags, who all have leather jackets, the same Ronaldo haircut, live with their mothers, and have been waiting outside the bar for hours to get in and prey on American college girls with their played out "Ciao Bella" catcalls. I spent many a night in college playing that Dad role and beating these guys back with a stick for my female friends, and apparently ten years has not changed their game at all. If I hate the bar meeting under normal circumstances, this scene annoys me to a whole new level. I leave for a kebab and a frustrated early stroll home.

The silent rejection, the outsider's lament is a feeling I'm unfortunately used to as the commensurate third wheel, the perpetually single. There's a tragic poignancy to this sort of insignificant experience, a familiar longing that accentu-ates a night of the truly uneventful and unconnected. The non-story. When all is futile and sinking and sad, and yet the band plays on.

I'm nose diving, time for bed.

Back up and at it on a Saturday morning, I'm determined and feeling productive on another gorgeous early Spring day.

I grab my Oil Shoppe sandwich and head for Piazza della Repubblica to fend off pigeons and writer's block. On my way back to the apartment, a UConn girl walking the opposite direction notices my shirt and shouts "Go Huskies!" Startled from my daydreaming haze by the exclamation, rusty from a lack of any real human interaction for weeks, I barely muster a response as she passes, something along the lines of "You too!" in a moment of pure face palm action. However, buoyed by this new exchange, such as it was, I decide to put my Solitaire game on hold and meander into the world of social drinking, trying my luck at a memory-worthy venture again.

As we know, my preferred drinking scene is a daytime affair, but generally that's only socially acceptable if accompanied by a group of friends. Or at least one other person. Literally, just one other. Otherwise you're bordering on alcoholic territory. So, I wait until moderately appropriate tonight, with the hopes of avoiding the Italian invasion to come later. Going to the bar solo is generally not my cup of Long Island Iced Tea, especially in a bizarre back to the future-like feeling at my favorite old spot, Red Garter, where a majority of the crowd is American college students.

This situation has actually worked out for me in the past, though, on a work trip to Baton Rouge a few years ago. On advice from a friend who attended LSU, I posted up at the counter of Bogie's on a Thursday night, a college dive bar serving drinks for about a dollar a round. I went into the night knowing I was entirely out of place at twenty-seven, surrounded by a room full of twenty-one-year olds (at best), but thought it might be a funny story to tell someday... and here we are. About an hour in, having not really talked to anyone but the bartender the handful of times she comes to refuel me, it was about 10 P.M. and I was getting ready to pack it in, the consistent smirk on my face getting sore from laughing internally at myself in this scene.

I was getting my six cold hard American dollars ready to pay the tab when a beautiful girl pulls up next to me to order. I sneak a quick peek and turn to face forward, in my usual hard-to-get, playing-it-cool, really-just-too-scared-to-make-a-move move. Out of the corner of my eye I see her look at me, look up at the early stages of my receding hairline, look back at me, and in as playful a cutthroat manner as she could, asks, "How old are YOU?" I crack up at the question I've been anticipating the entire time and acknowledge her frankness. We chat for a while about being old, her interest in me piqued because of her status as the cougar of the crowd, twenty-three and a grad student, feeling out of place herself. After an hour or so, I announce my intention to head back to my hotel with an early start in the morning. She announces her intention to sneak away from her friends to come back with me. I go to get my car, but by the time she meets me outside, she comes to her senses about the dangers of going home with an old Yankee she just met, so we makeout for a while instead and go our separate ways.

I'll never forget the inflection and tone of her voice with that biting, frisky opening line, and disarming charm. I could use some more of that now with college kids surrounding me again. I throw on my trusty snapback tonight, partly to look younger and partly because my hair is at a really awkward in-between phase that just does not look good no matter how I style it. I've always hated my hair, in its curly, stringy, thin, never-quite-right quality. The most fun I had with it was when I grew it out really long for hockey in high school and it resulted in a big mop-head 70's look similar to something you might see in *Dazed and Confused*. The thinning out of late, just another point in a growing theme of unstoppable aging, I'm honestly having a hard time dealing with or embracing. In that vein, I've decided to grow it out one more time for as long as possible before it really looks dumb, and then finally shave it for good. But for now, I deal with the awkward.

I claim my post at a tabletop near the bar and make a request for the college basketball games to be on, as it is March after all. After about half an hour of signal searching, the manager sets it up via some shady stream. My eyes split focus between the games and the crowd around me, just biding my time as I wait for this beard fad to die off. If there's one other thing helping the look of youth on my part tonight it's my baby face surrounded by fully bearded twenty-year-old kids looking much older. Despite my being Italian and French-Canadian, two very hairy sets of people, any beard I've tried to grow just comes in patchy and weak, looking the same on day five as it does on day fifty. I curse the day someone at the top of the mountain deciding things said beards should become en vogue again.

As expected, the crowd around me sticks to themselves in their small pockets of friends, enjoying the once in a lifetime opportunity they have this semester. What I wouldn't give to be back in those shoes, with all the worldly wisdom

I have now. These kids don't know how good they have it. It really is true what they say, that youth is wasted on the young. Shit, I'm nose diving again. And with those rambling thoughts, drunken and sentimental as they may be, I'm going to go ahead and cut myself off for the night, grabbing a kebab again for the reminiscent walk home.

The Sunday scaries swirl around me the next day, and I abandon my workout plans, my back aching with all the pain one might expect from someone as ancient as me. I'm not sure if it's the hard mattress or the extended workouts of late, but I have a constant pain to remind me in no uncertain terms that I'm getting older, especially in comparison to the whippersnappers all around me in this city. Like, I get it, ease up a bit.

Instead, I seize the opportunity to stream *Modern Family*, Europe being the only place I've been able to find it on Netflix. I get weirdly emotional at the episode where they drop Haley off at college, flashing back in my mind to my own sendoff freshman year, tears forming in my eyes as my parents drove off for the first time, knowing what a seminal moment that was and still is. And I play more Solitaire.

I head out for my typical lunch, but today at the Oil Shoppe feels different, my isolation and self-consciousness even more pronounced. As I wait for my sandwich, I look around the store and everyone is twenty. Everyone. I can't help but wonder what these kids are thinking.

"Did he get lost?", "Is he stuck in a time warp?", "Should we call his family to come pick him up and bring him back to the nursing home?"

Everyone in this city is an American college student, or Italian, or coupled up on vacation. I don't have a lot of money, but I would put all of it on a bet that I'm the only single, thirty-year-old American male in the entire city. Everywhere I seem to go, I feel unapproachable, out of place, not wanted. Like the honeydew melon in a fruit salad. Or the Three Musketeers bar in a Halloween haul. Or the yellow Starburst. Or an old-fashioned donut.

I slink back to my apartment in a cloud of shame.

WHAT AM I DOING HERE?

I'm being challenged and failing again, and I know it. It's bugging the shit out of me more than the polar bears on the island in *Lost*.

It's my fault. I put myself in this scenario where in the middle of so much progress, letting go of past hindrances and facing forward, I dropped myself into a scene I had no business being in. Like Michael Jordan on a baseball field. Or Trump interacting with a child in *Home Alone 2*.

I knew it right away too on that first day, in my gut. And confronted with the chance to figure out how to deal with real world things, like coping with letting something go when it's shoved in my face constantly, with not being able to connect or communicate with someone, with being the older single person in a crowd, with creating or chasing my happy in different places and scenarios, with being somewhere or having to do things I don't want to do, I turtled.

And not in the good way like Leonardo or Donatello.

I take a nighttime stroll through the neighborhood, fresh off a disappointing conversation with Poseidon who was looking to come visit me at the end of my stay but can't make it happen. As I walk past all these fantastic-looking dinner spots, places we used to go to and ones I probably would have tried if I wasn't flying solo, I see conversation and wine and happy faces filling with pasta, and I feel even more disappointed in this part of my experience. I picture myself as Kevin in *Home Alone*, walking back to his house on Christmas Eve, a puppy-eye look of yearning at the people together and celebrating.

I avoid the sandwich shop the next day and opt for one of my allotted pizza splurges. I try to limit my pizza exposure to just once or twice a week, in the interest of the sturdiness of the old wooden chair beneath me. Choosing to come to the carb capital of the world before spending the coming months on the beaches of the south Pacific may not have been the most thought-out strategy.

As I await my lunch, I get way more excited than anyone should to hear Bon Jovi, Pearl Jam, and Billy Joel playing on the radio, music I'm pretty sure they turned on specifically for me since I'm the only one in the restaurant. A little taste of Americana to placate the foreigner. My pie arrives, a whole cheese pizza just for me, but I can't smile this time. Or even smirk. Something's just not right with all of this.

That feeling when you realize you're the Other here.

Chapter Ten

SCENES FROM AN ITALIAN RESTAURANT

Written by

Jonathan Restivo

Based on Life

ACT ONE

FADE IN:

INT. FLORENCE LOFT - EARLY EVENING

Male, 30, looking sort of like Tim Riggins from Friday Night Lights (but really not), who gives off this vibe of comedic flare ala Jim Carrey, shuffles cards and deals a round of Solitaire on the living room coffee table. He sits on the couch in his expansive, still loft. The large balcony doors are open, permitting an intrusion of light and Spring-time air into the otherwise dark environment. The laptop on the coffee table sputters through a broken stream of college basketball games. The TV on the far wall is on an Italian network. Our hero, at peak loneliness, pauses from his card game only to change channels with the TV remote and fiddle with the computer to try to fix the buffering.

                    ME
          Seriously? There's no
          basketball games? But don't
          worry, they've got According to
          Jim in syndication, so we're
          all set on the entertainment.

                    ALSO ME
               I mean, that show makes
          sense I guess. How else are they
          going to break up the monotony
          of the oh, I don't know, 200 home
          shopping channels I'm surfing
          through here.

                    ME
     Damnit,   my March Madness
command center is a complete
failure this year. This must
be what it feels like to be a
Syracuse basketball fan on a
regular basis.

               ALSO ME
It's especially disappointing
after last year. Remember
that? That was probably my
best creation yet. St. Patty's
weekend, four screens all set
up on my outside patio in the
Santa Monica sunshine. UConn
winning. Sonny McLean's to
celebrate with the crew over
Irish car bombs.

                    ME
Oh Sonny McLeans is an Irish
place? Who would have guessed?

               ALSO ME
I really love Fall, but there's
no better weekend than the
opening days of the tournament.

                    ME
We're all just looking for that
special someone that cares
about us the way I feel about
March Madness.

               ALSO ME
I wonder if anyone else in
Florence is trying to watch the
games tonight. I guess I could
go out and try to find a sports
bar.

                    ME
          What if they don't have the
          games though? Which is likely
          given the hassle I'm having
          with Italian TV right now. Then
          I'm stuck out at a bar on my
          own again. I'll have no choice
          but to order all of the Tito's
          and get weird.

                    ALSO ME
          And then get more drunk food
          tonight. And kill my day
          tomorrow. Ugh, I'll just throw
          some pasta on and keep trying
          to stream something here.

Puts down cards and goes to kitchen to
cook some pasta on the stove.

                    ALSO ME (CONT'D)
          I guess that's the one positive
          to all this isolation. The
          weight loss feels pretty good.

                    ME
          Even with the onslaught of
          carbs this month.

                    ALSO ME
          Same thing that happened last
          time I was here. It's the
          portion sizes and natural
          food. Plus the meal plans, the
          workout plans, the non-drinking
          plans since there's no friends
          around and I'm not missing
          anything. That's how I lost
          those 30 pounds after college
          too.

                    ME
          True, I guess that does make me
          feel a little better about this
          month. The weight situation's
          just so hard to manage. I
          fluctuate almost as much as
          Jonah Hill.

                    ALSO ME
          Or Jonah Hill's acting career.

Playing cards again, playing with the TV
and laptop stream again.

                    ME
          Fucking A. This is so annoying.
          This internet blows.

                    ALSO ME
          At least there's not any
          Cinderella stories I'm missing.
          These games are pretty boring
          so far.

                    ME
          Although how can I even tell? I
          watch the games in six second
          clips before it all freezes.

                    ALSO ME
          Seriously, this is really
          frustrating. I'm starting to
          boil over. Kinda like that
          ravioli over in the kitchen.

                    ME
          Shit, I forgot about that.

Runs over to kitchen to see most of the
ravioli having burst, cheese lining the
pot and floating around in the water.

                    ME (CONT'D)
          Of fucking course.

                    ALSO ME
          If this were a CBS sitcom, I
          couldn't get away with saying
          that. But this is where the
          punchline joke would be.

                    ME
               (sarcastically, over the
               top)
          Dinner for NONE, am I right?
          Cue laugh track.

                    ALSO ME
          This story kinda sucks, doesn't
          it? Is anyone watching really
          going to care about me sitting
          at home, in one of the greatest
          cities in the world, over-
          cooking pasta and complaining
          about a college basketball
          stream being spotty?

                    ME
          This whole Florence section is
          not what I anticipated. In many
          ways.

                    ALSO ME
          A Laptop, a Pizza, and an
          Espresso. That's what I thought
          I'd call this part. A fun dive
          into a romanticized life of
          wining and writing.

                    ME
          Instead it's just a lot of
          whining.

                    ALSO ME
          So let's get back to that.
          Let's get back on track. Maybe
          I can save this whole story
          after all.

                    ME
          Pizza?

                    ALSO ME
          Pizza.

Runs upstairs, changes out of gym shorts
and T-shirt for adult clothes.

                    ALSO ME (CONT'D)
          I feel like there's a joke here
          how Michelangelo from the Ninja
          Turtles liked pizza, somehow
          related to the Michelangelo
          here in Florence.

                    ME
          Definitely, I'll keep working
          on that and come up with
          something really funny to put
          here, probably.

Grabs shoulder bag and leaves the house.

                                   FADE OUT.

          END OF ACT ONE

ACT TWO

FADE IN:

INT. RESTAURANT - NIGHT

Sitting in a crowded, intimate restaurant alone, a laptop is open at the place setting across the table. A waiter waits for the order.

>   ME
>   Red or white?

>   ALSO ME
>   Could just do a bottle of one
>   too?

>   ME
>   (to the waiter)
>   Una bottiglia di rose, per
>   favore.

The waiter retreats. The menu is left unopened.

>   ALSO ME
>   No need to check the menu, I
>   already know what I'm getting.

>   ME
>   Most people think they know
>   pizza.

>   ALSO ME
>   Most people are wrong.

>   ME
>   The Neapolitan style here is
>   phenomenal, but the best in the

                    ME (CONT'D)
world comes from New Haven.
That's not debatable.

              ALSO ME
And that's not hometown bias
either.

              ME
The only debate is which New
Haven spot is best, personally
I say Modern, then Pepe's, then
all the rest.

              ALSO ME
Definitely.

              ME
It's the closest to the O.G.
from here, but improved with a
modern take on the old world
classic.

              ALSO ME
It's even got a twist on the
name to go with it: "apizza."

              ME
They leave it in that brick
oven a little longer, creating
a perfectly charred, thin,
still chewy and foldable crust
having me reaching for the
napkins after almost every
bite.

              ALSO ME
And the tangy, crushed tomato
base is simple as sauce should
be. Seen, but not really heard.

                    ME
          Mmm, I love that gooey,
          glistening mozzarella, coming
          out piping hot and a little
          charred too in decadent
          delight.

                    ALSO ME
          I really should be sponsored by
          someone for all this.

                    ME
          I have to admit, though, I'm
          not sure why the white clam
          pie at Pepe's is always rated
          the best pizza in the world.
          It definitely goes against my
          conservative tendencies.

                    ALSO ME
          Give me cheese...

                    ME
          ...and pepperoni or sausage...

                    ALSO ME
          Or give me death. After New
          Haven, though, everyone else is
          just battling it out for second
          best.

                    ME
          It's certainly not Chicago-
          style, that's for sure.

                    ALSO ME
          My Chicago friends, I love you,
          but what you've got going on
          there is not pizza.

                    ME
Listen, I can support a good
deep dish. Giordano's and Lou's
in particular. But don't piss
on my leg and try to tell me
it's pizza.

                 ALSO ME
I don't really like the idea of
putting red pepper flakes on
pizza either.

                    ME
Far be it for me to criticize
someone for spicing up their
life, but it's just doing it
wrong.

                 ALSO ME
Hey, I like my buffalo wings
as hot as they come and put
tabasco on my eggs, but the
only thing you should be
putting on pizza is more
cheese, via the parmesan
shaker.

                    ME
Amen. And don't even get me
started on putting pineapple on
pizza.

                 ALSO ME
Hawaiian pizza is a travesty.

                    ME
How about the people that dab
their pizza with napkins to get
the grease off?

                    ALSO ME
          That's one of the best parts!
          That's like people who get low-
          fat cream cheese or fat-free
          mayonnaise.

                    ME
          Just don't eat it if you're
          gonna use the knockoff stuff!

                    ALSO ME
          While I'm over here complaining
          about pizza things, I think
          there should be criminal fines
          associated with living in New
          York, Boston, or the entire
          state of Connecticut and
          ordering from a Domino's or
          Pizza Hut.

                    ME
          And everyone everywhere should
          be barred from ordering Papa
          John's.

                    ALSO ME
               (in an indignant, oldtimey
               politician's voice)
          Let it be known, here and
          now: We must demand that our
          city zoning laws preclude the
          construction of these so-called
          pizza franchises as a safeguard
          by the people, for the people,
          to prevent drunken late-night
          decisions to violate this
          viable social contract.

                    ME
          Affirmed.

                    ALSO ME
If I had to go with a second
place pizza between New York
and the average Neapolitan
style found all around Italy,
I'd say it's basically a toss-
up.

                    ME
Pun intended.

                    ALSO ME
Duh.

                    ME
I think I have to go with the
Neapolitan style. Just like
in New Haven, it's sold as a
whole, while the New York style
is typically by the individual
slice.

                    ALSO ME
And happiness is best shared.

                    ME
It certainly is.

                    ALSO ME
The only caveat to this whole
conversation is the pizza that
does the square cut option.

                    ME
There is no slice better than
the center square.

                    ALSO ME
I gotta appreciate that pizza's
dedication to no-crust

                    ALSO ME (CONT'D)
          principles, far away from that
          overly-bready edge.

                    ME
          It's all about the cheese,
          baby.

                    ALSO ME
          That's why I'm going with a
          four cheese pizza tonight.

The waiter arrives with wine, ready to
take the rest of the order.

                    ALSO ME (CONT'D)
          Una quattro formaggi pizza, per
          favore.

                    WAITER
          Mi dispiace, non abbiamo pizza
          qui.

Dejected, looking at the pizza-less menu.

                    ME
          Penne alla Vodka.

                                        CUT TO:

INT. FLORENCE LOFT - THE NEXT MORNING

Packing a day bag in the office area of
the apartment.

                    ME
          Well, I'm getting some fucking
          pizza in Venice today.

ALSO ME
Damn, it feels good to be
hitting the road again.
Finally. I love me some Venice.

ME
I just hope it's not that whole
"me running away from things"
thing again, you know?

ALSO ME
I think we've established,
as long as it's with the
right motivations it's not
running, right? I need a little
inspiration right now, a little
kick in the ass.

ME
I'm okay with it. Let's break
out of this apartment. Out of
this city. Out of this funk.
Just take my mind off things.

ALSO ME
And let's write some more about
pizza.

                              CUT TO:

EXT. VENICE STREETS - DAY

From Florence across the northern skirt
hem of the Boot, into the train station
in Venice and onto a water taxi bound for
Ponte Rialto. "That's Amore" plays over
the scene, because that's like the only
Italian song I can think of.

ME
Venice is so fucking cool.

                    ALSO ME
          Look at all these canals. And
          bridges. And birds. And boats.

                    ME
          Saturdays are for the buoys,
          after all.

                    ALSO ME
              (exasperated, smirking)
          Even I have to shake my head at
          that one.

                    ME
          Whatever. There's just
          something about travel that
          gets me excited. Makes my socks
          roll up and down. To borrow a
          phrase from a Baby Boomer, I
          think.

                    ALSO ME
          I really am simultaneously 65
          and 22 years old.

                    ME
              (getting off the taxi boat)
          I think it's this way to St.
          Mark's Square.

                    ALSO ME
          Perfect, then I'll get
          purposely lost in the canals
          for a bit and find a hole in
          the wall place for a pizza and
          Bellini.

                    ME
          Here's an idea: let's check the
          menu first this time.

From St. Mark's Square, fending off
pigeons and tourist over-saturation,
the camera follows into the canals, with
consistently-overpriced, occasionally-
passing gondola ferries accentuating
the authenticity of the storybook scene.
Pausing for a moment on the edge of
the river wall outside the pink façade
and uniquely Middle Eastern Gothic
features of Doge's Palace, absorbing
the flow of water traffic and waves as
the Grand Canal empties into the basin,
a spattering of random islands nestled
offshore. Continuing back into the
canals of the floating city to a random
restaurant with sidewalk-side tables
looking onto one of the medieval canals,
pausing briefly outside to check the menu
board before perching for a late lunch.

                                    CUT TO:

EXT. RESTAURANT - AFTERNOON

The waiter returns with a bottle of still
mineral water and a quattro formaggi
pizza.

                ME
          Cool, they put sauce on this
          one. Sometimes they don't.

                ALSO ME
          It's basically a 50-50
          proposition with the quattro
          formaggi style. And believe it
          or not, I don't think I have a
          preference.

                    ME
          You mean I don't have an overly
          strong opinion on something??

                    ALSO ME
          That's preposterous!

                    ME
          I like to be surprised by the
          chef's choice in complementing
          the cheeses. The mozzarella,
          the pecorino, the parmesan,
          and most importantly, that
          gorgonzola.

                    ALSO ME
          This is some solidly authentic
          Naples style here. How the
          crust pops up fluffy, airy, and
          charred, surrounding a cheesy
          concoction, oil flowing down
          into the center to a single
          basil leaf.

                    ME
          A red, white, and green
          representation of all that is
          Italian.

                    ALSO ME
          A masterpiece, presented
          uncut, leaving the artistry
          undisturbed out of respect for
          the work.

                    ME
          Alright, shut up and eat.

Digging in now.

                    ME (CONT'D)
This is some fresh Buffalo
mozzarella.

                    ALSO ME
Probably plucked from the
Buffalo tree just this morning.

                    ME
Mmm, it stands strong, but
swirls together in pleasant
harmony with the other cheeses.

                    ALSO ME
Those melted gorgonzola chunks
are a real kick to the mouth.

                    ME
The chef made the right
call here. This is a good
sauce that pairs well. The
ripeness and sweetness of the
tomatoes, properly sautéed for
smoothness.

                    ALSO ME
Get that chunky shit out of here.

                    ME
It's the right combination to
match the distinctness of the
cheeses and that teasing aroma
of basil in the center.

                    ALSO ME
You know, this Neapolitan style
is a great case study in the
proper way to eat a pizza.
First of all, it's designed in
a personal size so I can finish
it all in one sitting.

                    ME
          A whole cheese pizza just for
          me, indeed.

                    ALSO ME
          I really need to chill with the
          Home Alone references.

                    ME
          It's easy to eat the whole
          thing here because look at the
          paper-thin density of that
          bottom crust.

                    ALSO ME
          It's great, it puts the focus
          on the items that matter most:
          the cheese, and secondarily:
          the sauce, without filling up
          on the empty carbs and glutens.

                    ME
          The crust is there to help
          shovel the more important items
          in, and that's it.

                    ALSO ME
          I'm gonna go ahead and set the
          crusts to the side as I finish
          each piece.

                    ME
          Otherwise, it's filling up on
          breadsticks and that's just
          silly.

                    ALSO ME
          Amateur move.

                    ME
          I might eat one or two crusts

                    ME (CONT'D)
          as I move through this pizza,
          but no more.

                    ALSO ME
          I gotta knock the good stuff
          out first, and then if I'm
          still feeling it, I've got a
          little breadstick dessert here.

                    ME
          Then pour some olive oil
          down on the plate and mop it
          up until fully stuffed and
          satisfied.

                    ALSO ME
          And I gotta save the best
          looking slice for last.

                    ME
          Of course. The one with the
          heaviest cheese content, the
          best distribution and balance
          of cheese and sauce with the
          smallest crust ratio.

                    ALSO ME
          That's the winner slice, and if
          I do my job right, I won't be
          too full to get there and enjoy
          it wholly.

                    ME
          And that's how you eat a damn
          pizza.

The waiter clears the table as the
afternoon turns later. Laptop is out,
espresso in hand, gondolas gondola-ing
by.

                    ALSO ME
          I'm full.

                    ME
          But happy. I really needed
          that. I'm not sure why.

                    ALSO ME
          It's been a tough month. It
          shouldn't be, but it has been.
          And I thought it would be all
          sunshine and rainbows and
          pizza.

                    ME
          I know I'm progressing and
          figuring shit out, but this
          part of the trip has been a
          real setback.

                    ALSO ME
          Why do I think that is?

                    ME
          Well we've been fighting a
          lot lately. You've been really
          inquisitive and critical, so
          it's tough sometimes.

                    ALSO ME
          We still agree on pizza at
          least.

                    ME
          Be serious for a second.

                    ALSO ME
          Okay well that's true, we
          usually don't battle like this.

                    ME
We haven't really been in sync
lately. In the past, we're
always on the same page, always
finishing each other's...

                    ALSO ME
Sandwiches.

                    ME
Well yeah, usually the meatball
ones. But I was thinking
sentences.

                    ALSO ME
I need this though, don't I?
The whole point of writing, of
challenging myself and being
honest in this journey, is to
figure out how to weather the
storms as they come. And to
enjoy life.

                    ME
Even if it means there's ebbs
and flows along the way. Kinda
like the waves of the canals
here below me.

                    ALSO ME
Talk about a cheesy metaphor.

                    ME
I'm just in a lull right now,
that's all.

                    ALSO ME
If you want to call it that.
Honestly, I think I'm looking
more like a tattered Ron
Burgundy in Anchorman, carton

                    ALSO ME (CONT'D)
of milk in hand complaining
about the San Diego heat,
wailing over all that was lost
recently: girlfriend, job, dog
punted off the Coronado Bridge.
In a glass case of emotion,
struggling to find a story to
report to the masses in the
pursuit of redemption.

                    ME
Great, I feel a lot better now.

                    ALSO ME
Alright, well let's say I'm
Luke in Star Wars, fresh off
the death of Obi-Wan at the
hands of Darth Vader, forced
to rally mentor-less and band
together in ultimate rebellion
against the Empire.

                    ME
Spoiler alert. That does sound
better, though. Like all felt
lost, but then it got better.
So maybe like in Goonies,
feeling hopeless and I'm gonna
have to walk the plank, before
Chunk and Sloth show up and
save the day.

                    ALSO ME
How about when my boy Ryan
Reynolds gets runaway brided by
Sandra Bullock in The Proposal
because she has too much
respect for him and his family
to go through with the fake
wedding, and he realizes their

                    ALSO ME (CONT'D)
          feelings are mutual and chases
          her down in New York?

                    ME
          While we're talking about Ryan
          Reynolds, how about Definitely,
          Maybe, does that story compare?

                    ALSO ME
          I dunno, that arch seems pretty
          complex. But he does get Isla
          Fisher at the end, so maybe
          there is a little hope after
          all.

                    ME
          Alright, time to get back to
          Florence.

                    ALSO ME
          This was a good, sorely-needed
          field trip. A little reset.

                    ME
          It's all gonna turn out okay,
          right? I'm gonna figure this
          adulting thing out in the end?

                    ALSO ME
          Definitely. Maybe.

                                        CUT TO:

INT. TRAIN - NIGHT

The train back to Florence cuts through
the Italian countryside. After awhile,
it passes a high school with lights on a
football field and a practice going on.

                    ME
          (staring out the window)
     Holy shit, wait a minute, where
     am I?

                    ALSO ME
     I'm confused because there's
     Italians playing American
     football?

                    ME
     Well, yeah, but seriously,
     I just had a mini-freakout
     and forgot where I was for a
     second.

                    ALSO ME
     Was I day dreaming that whole
     setting?

                    ME
     No, dream sequences are
     cheating, and stupid. It's a
     cheap trick to drive a point
     home to the audience.

                    ALSO ME
     Kind of like using flashbacks
     and flash forwards. Remind me
     to never use those.

                    ME
     Looking out at that field,
     though, I literally just forgot
     where in the world I was. That
     was weird.

                    ALSO ME
     Man, I might be more lost than
     I realized.

CUT TO:

INT. FLORENCE LOFT - THE NEXT MORNING

Gray skies and damp overcast air envelop
the windows and vibe of the apartment
downstairs.

> ALSO ME
> I should get out of bed if
> I'm going to make it to Cinque
> Terre today.

> ME
> (checking phone)
> It does say it's supposed to
> rain this afternoon.

> ALSO ME
> Can I hike the trails in the
> rain, or is it too muddy?

> ME
> (checking phone)
> Actually it says the main trail
> is closed for the season, and
> one of the other four is too.

> ALSO ME
> Well, I could do what I always
> do, say fuck it and hope for
> the best. Then be pleasantly
> unsurprised when it all works
> out in the end, the skies
> clear, and I bust through a
> Trails Closed sign and walk the
> path anyway.

> ME
> I just don't know if my

                    ME (CONT'D)
          adventure libido can get it up
          for that today.

                    ALSO ME
          I'm too young to be using that
          excuse already. It's only 10
          A.M. If I get going now, I'll
          be out there by like lunchtime.
          I just gotta shake it off.
          Shake it off.

                    ME
          Sorry Taylor, but what if it
          does rain and I'm stuck there
          on my own? That would suck.

                    ALSO ME
          This is why I'm fighting with
          you right now. This piss poor
          attitude.

                    ME
          Whatever. I'll just fire up an
          episode of Lost and see if the
          forecast changes.

The struggle bus rolls on, as a time
lapse sequences over another lazy Sunday
around the apartment, struggling to
understand the latest season of Lost, and
more Solitaire.

                              FADE OUT.

                    END OF ACT TWO

ACT THREE

FADE IN:

INT. LAUNDROMAT - DAY

Theoretical storm clouds overhead dampen
an otherwise majestic spring sunshine
over Tuscany. Inside, the dark abyss
of suds forms cleansing bubbles on the
glass of the door, the industrial machine
tossing to and fro a finite set of travel
attire, sometimes forming a team spinning
in joint and rapid unison in a tight
spiral of emerging freshness.

> ME
> This is poetic.

> ALSO ME
> Go on.

> ME
> (staring at the washing
> machine)
> It's so symbolic right now.
> Like the cycle of life,
> always moving, sometimes one
> direction, sometimes back
> the other way, but always
> toward its objective. Or
> like, something with cleansing
> and rebirth and a fresh new
> beginning with each cycle.

> ALSO ME
> I got all that from a load of
> laundry?

> ME
> That's how my mind works.

                    ALSO ME
          Oh, I know. But the machine
          also makes me think of
          something I could use in a
          future stand-up routine about
          sitcom clichés.

                    ME
          The red sock trope?

                    ALSO ME
          The red sock trope. Making all
          the other clothes in the washer
          pink. I see it all the time in
          TV and film. First of all, who
          the hell has red socks?

                    ME
          I think I had some once in
          Little League baseball when I
          played for the Cardinals.

                    ALSO ME
          But even if you were in the
          incredibly rare scenario of
          having to wash those ever-
          elusive red socks, and you're
          at a public laundromat ALSO
          washing all your whites,
          wouldn't you take that small
          extra step of saying, "hey
          where are those pesky red socks
          I inexplicably wear and am
          washing right now that somehow
          always end up in the load of
          whites despite being in blatant
          contrast to everything else in
          the load?"

                    ME
          (nodding head and smirking)
How about the choking in a
restaurant scene that requires
the timely Heimlich maneuver
from our nearby hero, who never
seems to release the object on
the first two moves but always
gets it on the third?

                  ALSO ME
And the old Thanks Dave, way
to ruin the surprise party by
showing up late so we waste our
turn-the-lights-on-and-shout-
surprise move on you, only to
have the guest of honor show
up as we're still resetting and
miss the moment.

                    ME
I hate that Oh my God, I can't
believe I waited until my
water broke at a completely
inconvenient time and now I
need to rush to the hospital
in the back of a taxi but oh
damn, look at this traffic,
I'll never make it in time so
I'm going to welcome my kid
into the world in a completely
irresponsible way in the back
of the cab. Or on the side
of the highway. Or inside
a Denny's. Of course with
the help of my best friend,
arch enemy, or drunk husband
coaching me through it.

                  ALSO ME
Or the "everything that could
possibly go wrong does go

                    ALSO ME (CONT'D)
          wrong" wedding, so the solution
          is a small intimate affair on
          the side that makes everyone
          happier anyway.

                    ME
          I grew up in Connecticut. I
          skated on pond ice. I don't
          know a single person who fell
          through. But apparently they
          think it's an epidemic on
          Burbank studio lots.

                    ALSO ME
          I think the thing that annoys
          me the most, or at least
          frustrates me the most right
          now, is the fact that there
          always has to be a definitive
          resolution by the end. And it
          seems to come so easy, when
          it's often not.

                    ME
          Is that maybe why I feel like
          I'm flailing? Because I've been
          trained to expect the happy
          ending? And everything seems to
          be out of my control right now,
          not all coming together like I
          planned?

                    ALSO ME
          Could be. This is new for
          me, and I'm learning how to
          handle it all still. This
          whole chasing happy thing,
          and maintaining it with the
          choices I make. Even the facing
          adversity part.

                    ME
          What adversity? Feeling old and
          out of place? Being lonely? Is
          that really adversity?

                    ALSO ME
          For my story it is. Apparently
          it matters to me, and says
          something about me that I need
          to evaluate. It's an ongoing
          challenge.

                    ME
          And what happens if a story
          like that doesn't have a clear,
          neatly constructed ending?

                    ALSO ME
          Well, it probably wouldn't
          make for a good movie. Maybe
          an edgy new TV show, though.
          Something on Netflix. They'll
          make anything these days.

                                        CUT TO:

INT. FLORENCE LOFT - DAY

Suitcases are being packed again in
preparation for leaving Florence in a few
days.

                    ME
          I don't know why people hate
          on doing laundry. These
          clothes smell awesome. And
          they're still warm. I love that
          feeling.

                    ALSO ME
          Hey, so I know I left things a
          little open-ended before, but I
          hope its understood I'm on the
          same team here. If I'm throwing
          down a challenge, it's for my
          own good. I need to keep going
          deeper, and just be honest with
          myself. And maybe ditch the
          subjects that are easier to
          talk about.

                    ME
          But I love pizza.

                    ALSO ME
          I know.

                    ME
          It's just really confusing
          sometimes. I'm not used to
          this, but I'm getting there I
          think.

                    ALSO ME
          Bro hug it out?

                    ME
          No, weirdo. Damn, I really need
          to meet some new people.

                              FADE TO:
          To be continued...

                              FADE OUT.

THE SOCIAL CHAPTER

chapter eleven

It really feels good to be back in Florence again, ten years removed from the last time I was here. It's been a long wait, and even after a little hesitation at first, I've been clamoring to get back and settle my internal score here, once and for all. This sunny spring day, a slight bite in the air from a lingering winter chill that isn't ready to let go, is just as I remember. Sitting at the Piazzale Michelangelo as the sun turns down, the view is even better this time around, the iconic, towering pinnacles of Palazzo Vecchio, the Duomo, and Santa Croce poke out of the cityscape and into the landscape of the surrounding mountains. There's no scaffolding surrounding the Duomo this time, and its restoration work looks complete. I wonder if that's why that Instagram post I made of this scene back in 2017 never got the credit it truly deserved at the time.

I take a few snaps from that same spot with my iPhone 26. The picture quality on this version is just as good as a long-lens professional camera now. I'll play with the filters later tonight to make sure I get them just right. I don't want to screw up this hard-earned status by posting something that would harm my official InstaRating. Ever since President Winfrey and VP Zuckerberg instituted that controversial travel policy a few years ago, a response to the European nations for limiting entry to Americans after the disastrous Trump regime, it's been all about driving up that InstaRating to be able to apply for a visa to properly represent America on the world stage. It's a score driven by a combination of follower power and influene, picture likability and comment ratios, hashtag creativity, hotness level/swipability, Uber rating, tendency to litter feeds with uninformed political opinions, susceptibility to fake news and email chain distribution scams, and quality of public reviews provided. It's taken years of dedicated work to bring my score up to the 4.7 required for Italian visa entry, and being back here now, I feel like I finally made it in this world.

"When are you coming back?"

The text pops up on my phone as I update my Instagram feed, checking the latest like-count on that no-filter "sunset over Florence" post, back in the present moment after a bit of harmless and not at all exploitative day dreaming/flash forwarding.

That seems to be the question I get asked most these days, followed by the generic "how's it going over there?" and the more acerbic "where the hell are you now anyways?" It's a question I'm particularly sensitive to at the moment, second guessing and self-doubt conspicuously creeping in again, with a string of missed opportunities piling up on the FOMO ledger.

Whatever mental recovery I needed after London was done within a week. The isolation was good, but enough. Way more than enough. The only real conversation I've had recently, beyond the occasional broken-Italian order at a restaurant, is with my Airbnb host, when she comes to repair the toilet I busted and am too dumb to fix on my own. Not exactly a riveting or conducive moment. Come si dice "plunger" in Italiano?

Having struck out entirely on any kind of social connection anywhere, I finally get a Bumble match from a woman I swiped on a few days ago. We go back and forth a bit in banter, establishing her vacation status in Florence from Philadelphia for just one more night. She's apparently in hookup mode, taking charge to ask me out for a late drink by my place, the implication far from subtle in her messaging to the point where even I can read the signal. Even though I could use the "connection", as surface level as it may be, it's just not the kind I'm in the mood for right now. So, I choose sleeping over sleeping with.

I'm really disappointed at this person subsequently deleting the remainder of the dating apps from my phone with a defeated admission of insecurity and insincerity in the effort.

I wake up the next morning to a FaceTime from a friend in San Diego (who I'm not going to put on blast right now), still out for the night nine hours in the past and about to hook up with a one-night stand who wants confirmation from me to my friend's worthiness of her time, and other things. I wingman from afar, feeling somewhat jealous and somewhat not, considering my actions from the night before, eventually saying goodnight and good luck to them on the rowdy streets of Gaslamp from the deafening silence in my apartment this morning.

I habitually turn my attention to what's next, as motivation and with the intention of finding renewal of purpose, or something like that. If I'm going to have the attitude of what's done is done, and there's no use crying over spilled latte this month, then it's time to think about the future.

As I'm making my upcoming plans, I realize that I inadvertently established an interesting pattern for my location scenarios. Generally, I'm spending a month in each spot, and now with the last months of this journey laid out, I naturally, subconsciously, established an every-other routine of social immersion followed by independent travel. So, I started in NYC with a bunch of friends and family around, then went to Puerto Rico on my own, did London in a social setting, then Florence all by my lonesome. Now I'll be in Bali next month with a group of similar remote work travelers, pop around Thailand by myself, followed by a stay at the Roam co-living house in Tokyo to put a tidy bow on this whole journey. The balance is oddly striking, but if Florence is any indication, maybe that me-time side of the scale needs a bit of tweaking. Or full reconstructive surgery.

Next, I contemplate that recurring question of "when are you coming back?" and start game planning for the summer on my return to the States. I open up a blank map and calendar of events and with a freeing sense of flexibility and authority, plot what I want to do and where I want to be, arranging my life accordingly. But the recurring theme in all the plans is a strong desire to be around family and friends. All of a sudden, things are looking up again.

One of the more complex and enigmatic pieces about me has to be my seemingly antithetical place on the introversion-extroversion scale. During a group discussion on the subject back in California, Nestor, a classic and undebatable introvert, almost seemed offended when I self-identified as one, too. "You're one of the most extroverted people I know!" That might not be saying much, considering Nestor, ever the introvert, is a computer scientist working for Google and hanging around with not the most social of characters in his nine-to-five. The outcry surprised me, though, in his assurance of my personality.

How could someone who was a teacher's pet and bookworm in school, who really dislikes public speaking, and couldn't pick up a girl at the bar to save his life, be considered an extrovert?

I always just assumed I knew my place on the scale, mainly because I dislike everyone. Well not everyone, just mostly everyone. I've never been one to strike up a conversation with the stranger on the train, and always found the tendency of my grandmother to become best friends with everyone she meets quite amusing. Growing up, especially, I was shy in that regard. My grandmother, though, in going out to eat at a restaurant, would know before the meal was over the waitresses' name, what her parents did for a living, and her favorite subject from back in middle school. Personally, I'm happy with my dining experience if she just brings me my chicken parm sub in a reasonable amount of time and I never actually find out that Megan liked studying French in seventh grade.

Coming out of high school, I undoubtedly possessed more of the introverted traits. Or at least what I thought were traits that meant I was introverted. I enjoyed my alone time and buried my nose in books to do well in school. My friend group was smaller, but very close. I tended to be shy or uncomfortable in large gatherings and social situations that I wasn't familiar with, although I very much enjoyed the idea of being active and social. When it came time to be listening or speaking, there was no question where I would land on that choice. I was the strong, silent type. I fully embraced a joke my grandmother told me one time about President Calvin Coolidge, nicknamed Silent Cal. As the story goes, a woman came up to the president and said, "I bet a friend that I could get you to say more than two words," to which Coolidge responded, "You lose." My kind of man.

The mistake I made, though, in my understanding of this personality spectrum, is the common one most people make: assuming at its base level that all shy, quiet people are introverted and all outgoing, social people are extroverted. While there's obviously a strong correlation between the two and often heavy crossover, the root of the distinction is apparently in energy consumption and where one finds it. Introverts gain energy from being alone, while extroverts receive it from being around other people, with a whole mess of variation on the margins to keep me confused and on my toes.

Rewinding the tape back to high school, I took great pleasure in attending basketball games and sitting in the heart of the "Mean Girls" popular crowd. I enjoyed going to parties when someone's parents would be away for the weekend, and if that failed, somewhere random in the woods of eastern Connecticut, Lyme disease-carrying ticks be damned. I lacked many of the interpersonal skills necessary to feel comfortable and thrive in that environment, but I still had found a real source of energy. I just didn't know what it meant yet.

Deep down, though, I knew I wanted to get there. To a place where I could feel at ease and at home in large crowds and new social scenes, because I enjoyed it so much. I remember making an active decision entering college, and again going into an even more unfamiliar setting in law school, to push myself to be more outgoing and open. I did this having no conscious idea what that meant about my personality type other than I wanted to not be so shy. Now looking back, I can see I was subconsciously embracing my extroversion and trying to learn how to cope with and support it. I was, and am still, just socially anxious or awkward, even while remaining a social butterfly.

Hi, my name is Jonathan, and I'm an extrovert.

Phew, feels good to get that off my chest. They say acceptance is the first step.

I decide to take a Myers-Briggs test to confirm with more precision just how confused I should feel about my personality. My results show that I'm a walking, sometimes talking, diplomatic, socially-engaging ENFJ, with an extrovert rating of 60%, which makes sense in that middle range. But certainly surprising for someone who until recently thought the opposite. And like so many other things, it's important to view this whole distinction not in terms of black and white, either/or, but with a healthy dose of gray in there representing a full spectrum of varying levels. Still too, my evaluation comes with a few more qualifications to factor in.

First off, the social anxiety part. While we are dabbling in self-diagnosis, I'll caution myself and my lovely reader that my understanding of this area is minimal, but I believe thorough enough to get a decent idea of what we're dealing with here. Plus, who has money for a real psychiatrist anyway? Not with these law school loans to pay back.

My main source of anxiety when it comes to social situations is being on the spot with all eyes on me, when those eyes belong to someone whom I don't know. So, whether it's public speaking in front of a class, or starting a conversation with a new person as the initiator and having the full attention of said audience, that is when I get the feels. Granted, that feeling for me is only mild to medium (as if I was a salsa flavor) depending on the circumstances, but it does cause me to stress out. I tend to choke up and get dry-mouthed, sweat, look down and evade eye contact, worry about what people are thinking or how they're reacting, take a position that's neutral or non-controversial, and avoid conflict or taking a side. It never gets to the point where I think I'm going to shit my pants or anything, that feeling is pretty much reserved for the drive home after an In-N-Out visit. But, at the very least it causes me to be out of my comfort zone, has prevented me from meeting a lot more people, and is something I'm working to be better at, for my own well-being.

In most cases, social anxiety comes from a natural distrust of other people. Someone with a more serious case of the disorder would fear greatly the judgment of others while in public, and thus try to avoid those situations. For an extroverted person, you can see how this would be a problem. Someone who gets their energy in life from being around other people, but is also terrified of that very idea.

Thus, how I can go from "DON'T talk to me on the elevator" to "Oh my God, I'm so lonely and bored I'm playing hours of Solitaire because I have no one to talk to" without flinching.

That understanding of a visceral need to be around others drives my desire for social situations with the people I love and trust in particular. In that type of scenario, I feel free to do what comes natural without fear of judgment. Just ask my friends about a rant I've gone on about politics, or when I yell at the TV after a referee makes a bad call while we're watching a game, or more pleasantly, when I tell a joke or an old story to the whole crew at one of the many parties or events I've hosted. Around the people I trust, I feel free to be as obnoxious and engaged as ever, and they find it so charming and lovable. You don't need to ask them about that last part, just believe me, they do.

Another aspect of the distrust of others may be familial and genetic too, though this assumption requires some wild typecasting. Despite my split heritage, I've always identified more with the paternal Italian side. The food, the family traditions, the extensive knowledge of our family's history dating back to the pre-Renaissance days, the culture, the pop culture, I embrace it all with pride. And in that stereotypical way that an Italian patriarch tries to protect his family and is cautious of outsiders, I too have adopted that cliché role of the Godfather in my immediate circles.

I noticed the territorial trait might run in the family for the first time when I introduced my ex Stella to my parents. My mother took to her immediately, probably out of sheer excitement that I was finally introducing someone to her, really for the first time. My father is absolutely not an intimidating figure by the looks of him, standing five-foot-nine and Italian skinny. And to me, he's always been a softie, pushing and motivating in his own ways, but at the end of the day, always taking care of us with that overwhelming paternal instinct and devotion. In preparation for meeting the parents, Stella wanted to know more about what to expect and how to act, and being the casual first-timer to the situation as well as being generally poor at understanding others, I told her she had nothing to worry about, my parents would be easy. Needless to say, we had a pretty interesting talk in the car after my dad engaged his protective shield a bit, to Stella's surprise and my lack of recognition or expectation of it.

There's a certain "Circle of Trust" aspect to his, and my, opening up process. It takes a lot to get into the place of trust, but once you're in, you're golden. Not having a family of my own to preside over, I've generally treated my friendships this way. I am closed off to you until I'm satisfied that there is mutual respect and value in the friendship, and then I'm an open book and open invitation to all manner of experiences together. And although I never set out for this to happen, while I've traveled and moved around, creating friendships all over the world, that circle has expanded both geographically and by number. Now I have my best friend from high school hanging out in Boston with my brother and my friends from freshman year of college. My Florence roommate meets up regularly in Los Angeles with my law school friends from Pepperdine. Nestor moved out to Southern California, and after I left, still has a crew in Newport Beach made up of a bunch of my friends from law school, and now they all hang out with a couple friends from my old company. This is the circle I trust, my happiest creation.

There's one other qualification to the personality characterization to touch on, and that's the roughly 40% introversion piece of my internal puzzle. To be an introverted extrovert means I generally gain the most energy from an outside environment (lean extrovert), but also require and appreciate independent time through selective detachment in order to recover from the stress that's also felt in that setting (minor introvert). It's the reason I prefer to live alone now instead of with a roommate, and why the Roam experience was so on-brand, because I can pick my spots. The amount of recovery time each of us requires dictates where on the scale we fall.

In classic ambivert form, I accidentally set up a life of balancing energy levels, one month and location at a time. In my engaged months, I've been active and enjoying great interactions with new and different people, trying new restaurants, bars, and weekend markets. In my detached stretches, I'm focusing more on work, reading, writing, and introspection and me-time. Apparently, the key is finding that right balance on the scale. Shout out to my Florence apartment for the hot tip on that front.

Part of the reason I'm a heavy planner, particularly when it comes to social activities, is so that I can control the experience. Sure, part of that is the type-A personality I carry around in my shoulder bag, but much of it is making sure that I'm doing the things I want to do with the people I want to be around, otherwise I'm generally content just staying in and using Nestor's HBOGo password to re-watch episodes of *The Wire* on a Friday night. I can find happiness in both settings. This philosophy is true of travel as well. I generally like to have control over the where and especially the when, and if that means I have to travel independently because no one can go with me, I'm okay going it alone, obviously. But my natural instinct and wish would be to share those experiences. The biggest regret I have for this trip (even though it would have completely changed and ruined everything entirely, so there's that to consider) is that my family and friends couldn't be there to actively partake in the adventure with me.

I guess I really am an extrovert after all. Just an entirely territorial, guarded, socially anxious introverted extrovert, if you want to pin me down and get technical.

And thus, the culprit behind an overwhelming piece of my pre-trip consternation. I was, in a word, afraid.

Afraid of the future, it's my social anxiety that's the ultimate source of so much of that adulting anxiety. It's seeing my friends changing and embracing a certain lifestyle, one that involves me having a fridge so full of save-the-dates that it physically weighs down the freezer door when trying to access the ice cubes to drop into my whiskey after work. I know now I'm not cut out for either a life of complacent traditionalism and conformity like that, nor complete isolationism and independence like this, as I toss the cards around the coffee table. My sweet spot is probably somewhere in the middle, and what that means exactly isn't settled yet, but one way or another, I need my squad around me. Even if it means "Uncle Jon" needs to be spending some time dropping in for multiple missions to suburbia.

The phone-centric life that dominates today, a feeling of being closer to the world I know no matter my place in that world, is not enough for me. My mom certainly appreciates the modern trend, providing her more opportunity to be a "mom on social media" and like/comment on every post that hits her screen. And while I'm happy to keep my parents up to speed on my whereabouts with minimal effort, and collect an automatic like in return, the false sense of proximity and importance of my efforts creates only a surface level sense of security.

The world I'm sharing, that we all are, is the one that I want to show, a crafted life, filtered and framed in a way that is equal parts attention-seeking and worth-defining. It's partly how I got here, FOMO'ed into the prospect of the peachy keen life I was missing amongst the unbound and adventurous, the views of a carefree travel profile depressing a self-value that was doing just fine depressing itself, thank you very much. Now a part of that world, I project an equally fulfilling life from the crushing comforts of my empty apartment.

And the irony is not lost on me now of my inclination to live in the digital world, while professing a desire to live like a local in the places I travel.

In the end, there's no app to replicate authentic connections of the human condition, even if we're really bad at the interpersonal thing these days. Sharing pics of a fun-looking salad at lunch is easy. Sharing heavy emotions with people who may or may not understand takes effort, and honesty.

In a way, this work is my fight song, my social media reckoning, the counterargument to that authenticity-lacking world. A chance to show unfiltered reality. As ugly as it can be sometimes.

I say my goodbyes to my best friends in Florence, the chef and cashier at the Oil Shoppe, while ordering my last meatball sub of theirs for possibly the next ten years (until that Oprah Visa is approved). Ironically, it's this trip, before I announce my departure, that the owner asks me if I'd like to sign up for their reward card since I'm here so much. I just have to smirk.

Fresh clothes all packed, I say goodbye to the other significant actor in my Florentine life, my beloved apartment that became my home. Even if that home was a bit confining, I blame myself more than anything else for the negative air. As I trudge down the stone steps of the building for the last time, I'm sad, but if there was ever a sign that I've been ready to go for a while and in need of a serious reshuffling of the cards, it's the almost ambivalence I have toward leaving a city that means so much to me.

In an earnest attempt at putting this all in the past, I leave that infamous Solitaire deck on the counter, along with a winter jacket I no longer need in my upcoming destinations of a warmer persuasion. All the looking back has been dragging me down, and all my fretting about the dragging bringing me even deeper. It's absolutely time to take the next step and get back on the upswing. My pack sits a little lighter on my back for my route to the train station and the first leg of this long week of travel: twenty-four hours in Rome.

Now in the former capital of the world, I do as the Romans do, which I assume is regularly tour all of the ancient historical sites, so I drop my stuff at the hotel and walk to the Coliseum. I reach this place that I stood inside of a decade ago in absolute awe, slightly more jaded by experience today but still shook by its age and awesomeness, only mildly distracted by the couple next to me hardcore making out in this scene. I'm across from the venue, taking pictures for about five minutes to get the framing just right, and these lovebirds don't come up for air once. Serious tonsil hockey.

Returning to the hotel late-night after my last authentic Neapolitan-style pizza for a while, I plop onto the bed and admire both my ridiculously high step count for the day and the quality of this last-minute Hotel Tonight purchase. I'm more pumped than I should be for the next few nights in a hotel again, a thing I'm weirdly passionate about. There's an odd excitement I get checking into a new place, new city, new room, new sheets, new towels, new views. Dropping luggage on the ground in a defiant act of "this is mine now, I live here" is oddly empowering. A heightened energy level in the whole of the building, buzzing with both business and pleasure.

My too-brief adventure in Rome is over, and I emerge into the morning air for the short walk to the train station, on to the airport and my eventual destination awaiting me many, many hours away in Bali. This portion of the journey is via Emirates Airlines (insert humble brag emoji, there should be a humble brag emoji). Even on this carrier, in another part of the world, people are still dicks about leaning back in their seats on non-overnight flights. Someday, someone is going to solve this global crisis.

Here's my note on flying into the Middle East for the first time: there's too much sand. I hate sand.

My biggest state of disillusionment on arrival is trying to figure out what fucking time it is. In my world this week, I'm tracking the pacific coast, east coast, whatever Italy's time is, my current status in Dubai for a few hours, my next destination in Bangkok, and my final stop in Bali. My head is spinning more than a freshman lying down in bed after their first college party, not speaking from experience of course.

My next day arrival (I think, who the hell knows what day it is now) is into Bangkok for another twenty-four-hour swing through a major international city. This venture into a novel part of the world carries with it all the different feels, smells, air, vibes of a uniquely foreign experience, and I haven't even left the airport yet. On the train ride into the city, which I think just cost me only two bucks, the scene out the window is flat, hazy, industrial, a gray lingering in the air like suspended... something. Time, maybe? This trip, after all, is a bit of a false start for me. I was supposed to be in Thailand in April, but will be here next month instead, so the overnight escapade into the devil's

Asian playground, especially while operating on about forty minutes of sleep, makes it a bit hard to enjoy the moment and appreciate this for the mild absurdity that it is.

Hey reader, you have space or touch issues? Take a train in Asia and you can get to second base with about thirty people in a five-minute span. That should get you past the anxiety of it. I may not regret my excessive baggage more than I do right now as every stop is an episode of "there's no way anyone else is getting on this train, we're completely full… we're stopping anyway?… oh my God, where do all these people think they're going?… how are they still getting on here?… there's no way the doors can close… wow, well still, there's no way we can do that at the next station… oh my God, we're doing it again."

I burst from the sardine can out onto the streets of Bangkok and oh, hello humidity, it's been awhile. After a triumphant entrance into my top floor hotel digs and a well-deserved nap, I head out to explore this fascinatingly weird city as my limited hours tick away. I pass a Jazzercise class of old women doing calisthenics in a park and stop to video this very Instagrammable moment. I love the Asian use of outdoor spaces, gardens in particular. Things are just better outside, though there's a bit of sensory overload for me with the unstoppable action, noise, and smells in this central neighborhood of Phra Nakhon.

Squeezing in as many sights as possible is the agenda for today, so I make my way to Sathorn Pier and find a couple of old ladies at a makeshift table, as if they were volunteering at a church raffle or bake sale, and fork over the fifteen baht (about fifty cents) for a ferry ticket on the river. The whole operation seems so quaint and simplistic, I love it. The ferry takes me north to the Chang Pier, where I jump off and switch aquatic transports to make the short trip from east to west across the river on basically an enhanced raft, costing me a whole four baht. Seriously, that's literally a nickel. It's like the old saying, "That and a nickel will get you a gumball, or a ride across Bangkok." Damn, was I born at the age of sixty-five? No wonder I get the "Dad" tag.

I get my Buddhist temple fill for the day at Wat Rakangkositaram Woramahavihan (I definitely didn't have to look up how to spell this), then pay the price gouger to shuttle me back to mainland Bangkok. I return to strolling around the market streets looking lost, when a man approaches asking if I am, in fact, lost. I have such a tendency, call it northeasterner, call it American, call it westerner, call it asshole, to immediately judge and dismiss approaching strangers as a danger or annoyance. But this older Thai gentleman genuinely wants to take a minute out of his day to help me get somewhere with no ulterior motive.

I'm confused. And a bit ashamed at my initially dismissive reaction, but he's not phased as he happily handles my inquiry for a good place with a beer and directs me to a spot in the Maharaj Market. I subsequently set up shop at the upper deck of this riverside location, order a chicken dish and a Chang beer and say a karmic "Cheers" to my helpful host as the sun sets across the river.

As night saunters in, I make my way back and end up next to a ladyboy on the train, an Adam's apple as big as my fist being the major giveaway, but still a bucket list check-off for my first Thailand experience. After initially being thrown off by my false start here, I like this place.

My taxi to the airport in lieu of the claustrophobia machine is worth every baht, even if I'm still trying to figure out how much that actually is right now. As I check my bags, it's crazy to think I was just picking these up from the claim area about twenty-four hours ago.

It gives me an idea for a show: hey, new program development people at the Travel Channel (or HGTV, since I really love *House Hunters*), if you're reading this, send me around the world Anthony Bourdain-style for something called "24 Hours In...". Well, one day is pretty short. Let's make it a weekend, forty-eight hours. We can even loop in Jonathan Taylor Thomas as a co-host. He can't be doing anything these days and I was always a big fan of his, mainly because our names are so close. (My middle name is Thomas) "A Weekend in... with the Jonathans". Or "Spending the Benjamins with the Jonathans". Have your people call my people.

After what seems like a never-ending travel week from Florence to this point (I think it's Friday now?), the last leg down to Bali is only a few more hours. I open up my reading for the new month, the meditation-themed book Zeus suggested in London, *Search Inside Yourself*. At this point, I've been meditating occasionally, but not with any consistency, even though I kind of like it when I do. I figure Bali might be a good place to focus on this aspect, in divinely cliché fashion.

As I'm about to start reading, I realize I'm perched on the aisle next to what appears to be an American couple, so

I break character to say hello. It turns out they live in Hermosa Beach, about thirty minutes, without that dreaded traffic, from my old spot in California. Because of course.

We talk for a bit about the randomness of it all, along with how long they've lived there. The running joke in L.A. is that the first question you ask someone when meeting them is probably "what's your name?" The second question is always, "where are you from originally?"

I'm normally not a plane talker, obviously finding the forced conversation tiresome, but the small world nature of this connection, especially after the lonely month I just had, is as refreshing as the beer we share on the ride down. In the process, I set aside my reading objective and engage.

Eventually the couple both nod off, and since I'm the worst plane sleeper to ever grace the friendly skies, I fire up *The Great Gatsby* on the mini-screen. Leo nails it, of course, but it gets me thinking about the book and author, and the possibility of second chances in life. The plane touches down as gently as an outcast lamb, a new location and new month ready to turn things over. A second act to get this right before it all comes crashing down.

THE OUT OF OFFICE CHAPTER

chapter twelve

"Sorry I'm late, the dial-in code wasn't working for me."

Translation: obviously the dial-in is fine, since I just joined the call. I'm late because I'm in Bali doing other things and my timing is all messed up. What did I miss so far? Nothing? That figures.

"We'll just wait a minute for everyone to join," she says. But I know what that really means: whoever's trying to join a few minutes late so the conference call's already started and they don't have to talk isn't getting off that easy.

While I wait for the conversation to get going, I grab a quick scroll through Facebook. Yet another ex is on her way down the aisle soon.

It's never the guy right after me. It's always the one two after. The guy that gets all the press is "the one before the one". I've got another theory though, based on my history.

The One Before the One isn't really the person that came close. They're just the person, through a failed relationship of stark and apparent contrasts, that made someone finalize their ultimate wants, needs, and readiness for the real thing. That's the purpose they serve without realizing it. But the one before that is the person that actually came close, just not quite all the way there, in agonizingly frustrating fashion. The Two Before the One (the TBO, or "the Tebow"). And much like Tim Tebow, it's the nice, good but not great one, the one we like but don't love, the one where there's something just not right about him. The Tebow sets the tone and prepares the right emotional state and 50 years ago, probably would have been the person to marry at the age of 25, but today would just be a settling move for everyone. The Tebow shows the potential, the One Before clarifies what's missing, and the One happens to be in the right place at the right time.

My mind really wanders a lot. Sometimes in the shower, usually on conference calls.

"Can someone put their phone on mute?"

Oops, that's me. I forgot to switch over, and it is pretty loud at my coffee shop setup on this outdoor patio setting. The roads here in Bali are bonkers, scooters zipping in and out of traffic around slower moving cars, cars driving down the middle of two-lane roads around slower moving scooters, all self-policing, all anxiety-inducing. There are few stop signs or lights so basically, all the cross-traffic of scooters goes for a while, and then the two sides going in the perpendicular direction decide they've had enough of the waiting and they all get their turn to go for a bit. Somehow, it works. But there's no way in hell I'm renting one of these for the month.

I pack up my laptop, with my phone now on mute, and walk the five minutes back to my villa for a quieter setting, past a seemingly endless display of ornate structures of a Hindu persuasion with a tropical twist. The constant stream of temples and religious structures perched timelessly along the road, prevalent enough to make one desensitized to the whole concept and purpose of the features, is surpassed in frequency only by the abundance of scooters that buzz by. Bali is generally busier, more congested, and more developed than I guess I expected, including the disappointing presence of a Dunkin Donuts location. Yes, I'm from New England. No, Dunkin is not good, it sucks. Don't @ me.

The service on my phone cuts out and I drop off the call, then scramble to find the dial-in info to jump back on.

"Did someone just join?"

"Sorry, I don't know what happened, my phone cut out for some reason," I respond with a smirk, as if it's not abundantly clear that I'm doing *anything* more important at the moment.

My home for this month, arranged through my new digital nomad group, "The Remote Trip" ("TRT"), is located in the central "city" of Ubud, which is less of an actual metropolis and more of a collection of mainly north-to-south running throughways that all flow from the range of mountains and volcanoes at the top of the island as if someone tipped the whole thing on its edge one time and the streaming rivers and parallel streets all fell into place and stayed there. There is no central downtown area, but instead a mild sprawl that never seems to start or end.

Up the hill about half a mile is a monkey sanctuary that has an aggressively lax policy of containing its guests, as monkeys overflow onto fence posts, walking paths, cars, and streets in a scene that some find frightening, but I find adorable. My walk home is canopied with decorations, fifteen-foot-tall yellow and white ceremonial flags and penjor, bamboo poles with offerings that hang over the street creating a runway-like atmosphere as if welcoming someone in. Since this is Bali, of course it has some kind of religious meaning, and my host explained to me that it's the Galungan festival for the next ten days. It's the period where, two times a year, all the dead relatives come back and chill at their former homes, so the current occupants wild out in celebration. It has something to do with Dharma defeating Adharma, but as soon as I hear that reference, I make a *Lost* connection and start wondering again about what really happened on that island.

"Which project are you talking about? Sorry, I didn't catch the number... Oh yeah, that one's on hold." (I go back on mute).

The unit I have is located at the back of a development off one of the few east-west streets at the southern edge of Ubud. I'm not even going to try to explain in too much detail how these compounds are structured, because they're pretty goofy to the western mind's sense of housing. I remember reading Gilbert's attempt at a compound description in *Eat, Pray, Love*, and having a completely different picture in my head than what I'm seeing here.

My host is named Wayan, of course, because most first-born children in Bali are named Wayan, the second child is named Ketut, and it doesn't matter whether the child is male or female. My Wayan is married to a woman named Wayan, and their compound initiates from an outer wall at the street with a three-foot-wide cement path down a small hill into a jungle-like setting. To my right is a 200 square foot temple pavilion, with open walls and a pitched ornate terracotta roof. To my left, an interior wall with more modern housing behind it, presumably for Wayan's family. All of this is more densely constructed than I envisioned, everything from walls, to trees, to buildings on top of one another. A modern cottage sits just off the path to the right behind the temple, then the walkway cuts to the left. Interior concrete walls of the compound compartmentalize more family housing, with a cottage through an open gate to my right and a two-story house to the left, all close enough that if someone takes a dump in the house to the right, they still need to light a candle at the house on the left side of the wall. At the very end of the path through doors too narrow for a regular-sized American, maybe a three-minute walk all within the same compound, is my mini-sanctuary.

For the record, the current temperature today is "Sweat".

Our four-unit facility is centered around a gorgeous stone infinity pool, an open-wall outdoor kitchen, a separate guest house, and three units in the main building, all of which Wayan built himself and is very proud of. My domain is the master bed and bath upstairs, with a huge wooden balcony overseeing this jungle palace. I share the space with a handful of folks from the TRT group, made up of fellow remote workers from Italy, Canada, Romania, the Netherlands, and back in the States.

In the morning, we are greeted by an old Balinese man in traditional sarong and head cloth lighting something on the doorstep to our house. He is Wayan's father, the patriarch of the large compound here, performing the morning offering to the gods. A four-by-four-inch banana leaf base is folded into a small dish that contains flowers and incense and is lit by match as part of a daily ritual to appease someone up above. He does the same at each of our doorsteps and at the religious statue next to the pool that I'm just now noticing. At no point does he stop smiling from ear to ear with unmistakably surpassing joy, so whatever homeboy is doing, it's working.

"Sorry, I was on mute."

Narrator: He wasn't on mute. He just wasn't paying attention again.

"Yeah he still hasn't gotten back to me. I think he mentioned he was gonna be out of pocket for a few days." But really, I just forgot to call him after last week's meeting, so I'll call him right after this, probably. I'll just be over here kicking back on the pool lounger first.

This high heat, no-sock, bathing suit-heavy life reminds me so much of being a kid in summer, wearing out a path from our backyard wiffleball field to the pool for reprieve and back again. As with New England summers, the mosquitos here are unbearable, the requirement for bug spray application on a regular basis being crucial to surviving the day. But it's not just mosquitos, it really is a bug's life in every way. There's a certain adjustment period to the presence of little critters everywhere to accommodate for in this jungle atmosphere. The comfort and safety of the indoors, within the saving graces of air conditioning and bug netting, is only a temporary haven mainly for this reason- Netflix is banned in Indonesia. There's basically no choice but to be outside all the time, which is so much better than being an inside bum anyway.

"I've got another call to jump on, I'll talk to everyone later." Actual meaning: LOL suckers, no I don't. I'm jumping in the pool.

After enjoying my first day in this new #poollife, I head down the road for dinner with no lights along the way, making the narrow egress a bit more precarious. I meet a few people from the TRT group in front of this Vegan restaurant, we customarily leave our sandals at the door and walk in barefoot, observe a few dozen geckos scattered on the dimly lit walls of the restaurant, immediately begin sweating from the humidity, order something with avocado from an interesting menu while the power cuts out intermittently, and alternate between slapping mosquitoes on our ankles and obsessively spraying restaurant-issued and clearly ineffective bug spray to our legs. If I thought I was a fish out of water in my first days in Puerto Rico, my initial entry here has been a shock to the system on par with finding a flounder somewhere on Pluto (which is still a planet, I don't care what anyone says).

I'm really trying to get out of the habit of typecasting, but the crowd at this Vegan restaurant in Bali is exactly what I expected. Exactly.

I find my place in this setting quite humorous, if only because I've never been one that conforms to the dress, mannerisms, and mindset that might befit my historically reserved, unassuming personality. I'm a bit of an enigma in that regard, a social chameleon that likes a little bit of everything in eclectic appreciation, getting along with a variety of people and trying to avoid being boxed into any one stereotype. In high school, you might have called me a poser as I transitioned from the Green Day skater character early on to Eminem and American Eagle (with my hat tilted to the side). Yes, that was a combination for us in preppy-but-wannabe-edgy CT. It might be a social identity issue or just a deep desire to fit in, but I prefer to call it non-conformance to expectation.

My friends and I went to a taping of *The Colbert Show* during high school, and the guy warming up the crowd asked if anyone in the audience was a Republican. I raised my hand because I was at the time, though now I operate more in the realm of a yet-to-be-created political party in the fiscally conscious-socially liberal persuasion best described as a "hands off my money and my genitals" mindset. The emcee took a look at my long shaggy hair (from hockey) and thick hemp necklace (no, I can't explain that one), and said "You?? You look like the biggest hippie in this place!" Something about not being able to be figured out right away, keeping things mysterious, a "fuck you" for trying to pin me down, is an odd point of pride.

For that reason, I try not to judge anyone here. Who knows their back story or what they're going through in life? If someone saw me in a Vegan restaurant in Bali, what inferences might they draw on spec that would probably fall flat? But still, I'm enjoying throwing myself right smack in the middle of my own downward-dog-posing, barefoot-walking, peace-and-love-talking, where-do-I-get-my-Sanskrit-tattoo cliché.

Our group at TRT is similar in design to other remote programs with the one-month-at-a-time travel structure and coworking focus, while adding more elements of community building. Our first activity is an authentic Indonesian dinner across the street from the monkey forest. The multiple course meal consists of Balinese staples like chicken satay and Nasi goreng, a delicious fried rice dish. As dinner winds down, the emcee gets us ready for the upcoming show.

In the history of people warming up a crowd, has anyone ever *not* done the routine of "how we doing out there?.... aw come on, you guys can do better than that... I said how we doing out there?!"

We are treated to that enduring introduction, obviously, followed by the main event of some kind of frog-themed presentation that's more confusing than a Japanese game show. I think the woman character fell in love with a frog who becomes a man... who knows really. It calls back memories of that hula show in Maui, a story-telling medium generally outside my comfort zone. I wonder if the people in the show are proud to be showing off their culture, or if they too are thinking to themselves "WTF are we doing here?"

The group heads back for some night swimming, but we're cut short by a flash rainstorm that descends on us not quite as quickly as these things are shown in the movies, with all calm followed by a flash of lightning followed by immediate downpour, in stupidly unrealistic form. In the real-life version, I have time to gather my things and head to my room, listening to the last gasps of the stormy season in Indonesia on my pitched sirap roof, the monotony of the rain helping me pass out quickly within the confines of my mosquito-netted quarters.

In keeping with recent habit, I quickly establish a work-out routine for the new location, typically running and exercising on the poorly-maintained soccer field a few minutes up the hill, under the blazing sun, heavy humidity, and curiously watchful eye of the locals.

I swear on this, I'm not sure any of the people driving by on their scooters and staring in confusion and amazement have ever seen a jumping jack before. The scrutiny involved in working out on display is motivating though, and now that results are starting to peak through after a few months of dedicated effort, I want to keep the good times rolling. Running suicides in the park while sweating and drenched as if I already fell in the pool that day is a great way to do that, even if I have to put on a show for the neighbors to do so.

The question I keep having around here, as everyone seems to be on the move at all points of the day, is where are you going? Scooters never stop passing, at home, at the restaurants, at the field here, and yet I see very little industry, very little by way of regular working hours, so I'm curious where everyone is off to. And in such a hurry. Everything else in life is happily done slowly and peacefully, but get the Balinese a scooter or van and watch them risk it all as they road rage aggressively around a single car in a line of traffic. I'm especially curious, and more concerned, by the family of five who has opted away from the classic minivan in favor of a clown car scenario, piled on top of each other on a single scooter: child in front of the dad driver, another child in between the parents as mom casually holds a baby in one hand and the back of the scooter with the other. I suppose that's one way to do it.

Another of our group activities is an authentic Indonesian cooking class in the rice fields a few miles out of town. Green stacked on green stacked on green, which I believe are not the lyrics of a Lil Wayne song but very well could be, the paddies set an appropriate backdrop for our foray into the native cuisine under this thatched roof, open-air pavilion that seems to be Bali's venue style of choice. It feels so good to be social again, even if it's much more Little House on the Prairie than Animal House. Hitting up the WhatsApp group chat at the end of the workday and having someone to meet up with for a quiet dinner helps to put much of the Florence social anxiety behind me.

My favorite new place to work is in the tranquil setting and consistent smiles of the folks at my regular coffee spot, Barong Bridge Café, which you might have guessed, is located next to the Barong Bridge. Open air seating on a front porch setup, with decent WiFi, delicious, healthy, and cheap food balancing authentic Indonesian and western fare, a rice cookie coming with each espresso order, potable water, and the sweetest waitresses who quickly recognize my increasingly frequent visits. Some people consider the prices relatively costly for the area, but since I could eat every meal here for about ten bucks a day, I'll call it an upgrade from my usual cost of living. The décor feels rustic and homey, a colorful display of repurposed wooden and metal window shutters making up the walls of the restaurant, providing an outpost oasis in the middle of the jungle.

I finish my iced green tea and acai bowl and head across the street to meet the TRT group at the actual Outpost, the aptly named coworking facility that serves as our work-home for the month. The facility is packed with entrepreneurial types best described in the hardcore raps of Will Smith: all ages and races, real sweet faces, every different nation; all of whom are required to ditch their sandals at the door before starting the workday on one of the large open space tables. Lunch can be ordered-in directly to your seat, or if you're that type of person (and I am), you could just go down to the Outpost pool and drink a coconut while waiting for your Mie Goreng dish to be delivered to you in the water. Yes, the coworking space has a pool. Our TRT group schedules a pool-side lunch date every Wednesday, a much-needed timeout from all the stress and hard work we clearly encounter daily.

After a few days at the Outpost facility, I'm not really feeling the vibe, even though the community pool was a big selling point for my presence here. There's a little bit too much of a head down, in-the-zone mentality amongst the remote workers that I both appreciate and avoid. It feels like any typical office, just with completely atypical surroundings, like a pool that no one really uses. Who comes to Bali just to slave away in another office?

Working in hushed conversation with intent and focus in a confining environment for the majority of the day is the exact reason I went out on my own and started working re-motely in the first place, to avoid that very setup. I like to be outside if I can, and barring that option, at least out amongst the people in random public places, with action and distraction occasionally buzzing around me. Mostly, the sight of other people working just makes me uncomfortable, so I do my own thing and take my business, in more ways than one, back over to my café across the street.

In the few hours I spend at Outpost, though, I immediately notice an attitude that really challenges the idea of the legendary and unmatched American work ethic. As I look around at the crowd, some American, but mostly a combination of European and Australian, the faces and effort are all the same and raises the question: why is everyone here so happy and motivated in their work? What have these folks all figured out that many, myself included, haven't yet?

The modern workplace is certainly changing. In location, in expectation, in structure, in the entire understanding of what a "job" and "career" actually mean. The End of Jobs argues that the current educational model, the collection of credentials through fancy degrees and buttloads of debt (raises hand), has long fueled a knowledge economy well-suited for the growth of corporations during the twentieth century, but is now outdated. The replacement model is one of creative thinking and reasoned risk-taking, resulting in an entrepreneurial economy that has no place in the workplace of our fathers and forefathers (well, maybe your father; mine's been working from home for twenty years).

Our natural wiring is not compatible with the jobs of yesterday. I, like most everyone, enjoy working, but don't like it framed as a job or obligation. It's what Daniel Pink calls the "Tom Sawyer effect", which is a term I love and can smirk at. So, the less workplace constraints and definitions we have, the more likely we are to work hard and enjoy what we do every day.

The nature of jobs is evolving, but also the way that we approach how we function within them. Modern tech founders, while challenging the man and the industry and conventional wisdom and anything else they could make better, also began to challenge workspace concepts. Now we have a trend towards open-floor concepts, more comfortable and casual environments with obvious conveniences like a coffee bar, nap pods, and of course a foosball table. The idea behind this arrangement is to remove daily stress in the office and foster more relaxed and focused workers who don't have to worry about where they go for lunch or at what point in the day their cubicle walls are eventually going to cave in on top of them.

Coworking facilities like WeWork have many of these same open designs incorporated into their model, allowing small startups or one-person operations a place to find consistent work space without a classic office vibe. Innovative remote service companies in New York City are maximizing square footage efficiency by renting space in restaurants that usually only open for dinner, and setting up WiFi, power cords, coffee and refreshments while workers utilize previously unused tables during the day as another alternative office form. In these environments, work can get done without a focus on office politics, or of "being on" and obliging surface level relationships with people you wouldn't give two shits about in any other setting but are forced to under the guise of idiotic buzzwords like synergy, impact solutions, and cross-functionality.

Even in more traditional office settings, the rising workforce is challenging many of the hierarchal structures and rigid conformity handed down from on high many decades ago, probably by one of the Rockefellers. There's a general disrespect for the status quo of "well, that's the way things have always been done". The forty-hour work week has become seventy or eighty, perpetrated by successive generations trying to one up each other to avoid the stigma of being thought of as lazy and entitled, until we stand up and call out the stupidity of the whole premise. Working longer does not mean working harder, or better.

An honest question remains, though, that with all these seemingly progressive changes, does that get me to the point of a happy professional life?

It would be difficult to imagine a better daily schedule than the one I've set up for myself in Bali. I generally survive a night mildly tossing and turning, fretting over the time difference or a mosquito/killer spider inside my bed netting or a gecko on the wall (although I'm slowly acclimating and improving on all of this), wake up around five and check emails and voicemails from people living in the past on the other side of the world. I do that for about an hour in my bed, returning any calls and getting caught up on six hours of the standard workday in about a quarter of that time. As the sun rises, I make tea and complete consulting work for another hour or two, grab my shoes from the front step, shake out any potential ants or other invading creatures, and run up to the soccer field. After working out, it's time for a mid-morning swim to cool off for twenty minutes, dry off in the sun, then apply a healthy amount of bug spray and walk down the street to the café. I grab myself an espresso to manage the next few hours and a superfood bowl that rocks my world and looks so basic when I post on Instagram, but shoulder shrug emoji. I take in the contrasting sights of thick green jungle scenery and heavy scooter traffic, while squeezing in some work or note-taking. I return to the house after to meditate, read, write, and tan by the pool, the Pacific coast workday ceasing to bother me at this point. When I get hungry again, I head back to the café for some protein if I can find it, and focus on writing without distraction. I may pop into Outpost for an hour, or work from the pool there or at home. An afternoon nap in the A/C, and a little more writing and a shower follow, before meeting up with some of the guys from TRT for dinner, outside our tiny three restaurant bubble if we can. Bali Rob and I may venture out to a spa for a cheap massage and possibly a night swim. As the day wraps to a close, there might be a couple emails to address as the western world wakes up and starts pestering me with their day, followed by a completely reasonable bed time and a very similar day tomorrow.

Yeah, I woke up like this.

As much as I love my day, there's still a piece missing. And wouldn't you know it, but my current reading is up to the task again.

When people generally ask me if I like my job, my response is some variation of, "It's alright. I love the freedom and flexibility I have, and being able to work from wherever. I mean, look around. But I just don't really give a shit about building cell towers." Well, now I can put a little bit of research and understanding behind that.

I want to be rich. I think we all do, though it's always downplayed by the classic "money isn't everything". Obviously that's true, but it's still nice to have. Most studies show, however, that money as a motivator can actually be a disincentive. The only time it seems to have a positive effect is when it's in conjunction with equity, with having a direct financial stake in the work being done, like the entrepreneurial economy of tomorrow shows.

So, if money isn't everything, what is? Just about anyone who has ever researched or wrote about motivation and happiness in the workplace has basically come to the same conclusions on the necessary factors, or elements, if you will. And I will, because I love breaking things down into elements.

Broadly speaking, there are two general and connected elements: 1.) some combination of related factors of autonomy, freedom, mastery, and responsibility, and 2.) overall meaning, passion, and purpose.

There are some twists on the features within each, but roughly, the first element involves a strong level of ownership and control over the work, and the second is a factor of feeling like you're taking on challenges, overcoming them, and contributing in some way to the advancement of yourself and society as a whole. Most nerds when discussing the second element cite Mihaly Csikszentmihalyi's work *Flow*, which argues that we are naturally advancing, goal-setting and goal-achieving beings, and that by striving for what we seek and overcoming challenges to get there, we cultivate happiness by finding value in our work and in our selves.

These are the motivating factors that lead to peak performance and resultingly, happiness in the professional life. The lessons, and elements, stay very much the same when applied to our overall happiness in life as well. Taking on challenges through acceptance of personal responsibility leads us to the most satisfying sense of fulfillment that we can find. That's what they tell me, anyway.

This is why the people around me at Outpost seem happy, even when buried in their laptops in a tropical paradise. They have control, autonomy, mastery of their craft, whether they're starting a marketing business or managing an engineering project, but they also have a passion for what they're doing. Maybe it's something ground-breaking and unique to the market, or a twist on a classic business plan, there must be a level of passion and purpose that fills the second portion of the professional love bucket toward fulfillment.

And that's what I'm missing. There is absolutely no higher purpose in advising my client on the feasibility of relocation for their cell tower assets. I just fell asleep typing that sentence. Freedom and autonomy I have up the wazoo, hence my pin position currently. And though I shy away from calling myself a master, I'm good enough to be given the flexibility to continue consulting from afar even if no one in the telecom industry has ever heard of a digital nomad. What I haven't had in the many years I've been at this is a feeling of a real challenge, a real contribution to something bigger.

It's in the supplemental work of late, the "second job" as a writer and pondering millennial of the adult condition that I've found a deeper passion, a challenging and worthy cause that fills that missing piece for me and that you now get the benefits of. You're welcome.

The entire combination of setting, timing, professional responsibilities and objectives allows me to set a schedule here that I thoroughly enjoy waking up to every day, even if limited or slightly monotonous. Choices that I make without a hint of "what if" weighing in. One of my new friends at TRT puts it best, when I tell her during a group pool session at the house about the happiness in my day: "I love that you can set work around your schedule, instead of the other way around."

Fuck the nine-to-five, and whoever came up with it.

Now, you might be saying, "Hey dummy, that's all well and good, but I'm a teacher or a whatchamacallit, and yeah I love what I do and am passionate about it, but forget about flexibility and autonomy." Or, "Hey dummy, I'm a freelance whatever so I've got all the authority in the world, but man is it boring." Well, we've got step one covered, which is just recognizing the issue and the source. That surprisingly simple yet giant step of awareness has allowed me to now know what I need to target in terms of improving daily happiness going forward, especially as it relates to work, an underappreciated authoritarian influence on life.

Which of the elements is missing? Passion, okay, well, fix it. Be creative. Do what works. It could be volunteerism on the side, engaging in a hobby I enjoy and can be good at, focusing on my own personal development as a "job". One way or another, taking time for myself or for others. If I can't hit both aspects in my daily job, I need to find an alternative source and commit to it, or approach a difficult work situation with an accessible solution within this framework. And maybe then I can stop complaining about Mondays like I'm Garfield with a tray of lasagna.

People often talk about striking a work-life balance that works for us. That notion is fundamentally flawed, though, because it essentially pits the parties against each other in a tug-of-war for the precious and finite time and energy each of us has. It becomes a zero-sum game of emotion and mental output, far too often resulting in a victory for the office, especially in America, leading to feelings of resentment toward our jobs. "If only I didn't have to work so late, I could finally take that Spanish class/read that book/start yoga/eat healthier/have time for dating/not be a miserable crank." Even for the people that have a good relationship with their work, have you ever heard them not add the disclaimer for some reason at the end, "Oh I love my job, but..."? There's always a but.

Maybe what we ought to do, as a generation wresting power away from the olds, is design and allow for a better *blending* of personal and professional life and schedules based on some of these ideas, a seemingly adverse notion that in reality is better suited for our wiring as non-robotic non-industrial-era humans.

The world doesn't all need to move to Bali to figure this out or to implement some of these choices, but I'm certainly glad I did. In the first week or so here, I found a rhythm better than any I could create before, firing on all cylinders professionally, socially, and personally, soaking up sunshine, pool water, superfoods, and self-awareness.

With that kind of setup, how could anyone not be happy? (He said, ominously.)

THE CHAPTER BEFORE HOMETOWNS

lucky 13

There comes a point in every *Bachelor* or *Bachelorette* season, usually five or six episodes in, when the pressure and exhaustion of dating so many people at once seemingly becomes overwhelming. It's typically accompanied by some drama involving a person not there for the right reasons or who has a penchant for overemploying the "can I steal you away for a minute?" strategy, when the audience is made to think our swinging hero is ready to give up on the whole concept of ever finding love and move somewhere dark and depressing like Antarctica, or Cleveland.

This is reality television's best climax point, as shamelessly predictable as it is. The trope works because every love story, every journey has that period of ultimate doubt in the mission. Everything seems to be coming up roses, right up until the moment you're left empty-handed wondering when things went wrong, facing disaster seemingly out of nowhere and despite reassurances of development along the way.

But really though, I just watch the show for the articles.

Over a week into Ubud now, the group joins me in a bucket list activity right up there with all my other adventure sport challenges: whitewater rafting. Hiking a few miles through the freshly drenched and precariously steep jungle paths we eventually find our raft at the base and venture down the moderate rapids of the Ayung River, perpetually surrounded by towering forests upon lush green cliffs. Our stops along the way are either to grab a chilled and oversized Bintang beer on the riverbanks, or because TRT-mate Marco the Italian Conqueror has again ignored the guide's directions and paddled us straight into a partly-submerged rock from which we must awkwardly wiggle ourselves away. The densely vegetated river atmosphere looks like a scene from Disney's Jungle Cruise ride, just without the well-appreciated nonstop puns and questionably-appropriate Native sets on the shore.

At the risk of extending the *Bachelor* metaphor too far, this is the type of group date activity exotic enough to get someone feeling all kinds of randy toward the position they find themselves in. So much of the premise of dating on the show is predicated on placing people in extreme scenarios designed to elicit elevated emotions, particularly toward an otherwise dud of a person or connection. The tales of many a showmance failure are serving their cautionary purpose now, as I try to manage my emotional attachment to this experience as a whole, seeking to avoid being blinded by the false light of the novel and exotic in this current situation.

Don't get me wrong, the Bali experience so far has been quite enjoyable, but as good as I feel, I can't shake the notion that a threatening cloud looms over it all with a darkness and rapid imminence matching the afternoon storm that greets our arrival into base camp at the end of the river run. We escape to the van to take us back home just before the skies open up in classic jungle storm and poetic form.

I can't place where this gloomy sense of pending doom is coming from. Perhaps it's innate in me from the surroundings of my upbringing, hammered by two decades of training in the New England curmudgeon attitude, a product of people that are happier when they have something to complain about. Perhaps it's my grandmother's prudent and frugal mindset, passed on to my dad and partly to us kids, growing up the daughter of a banker in a Jewish neighborhood of Brooklyn during the tail end of the Great Depression, that the highs must always be cautiously counterbalanced by a preparation for the impending fall from grace. Whatever the case, I have still not learned how to just be happy.

So as cool as I find all of this right now, and as theoretically happy as I am in many ways, I'm tempering any notions of feeling myself falling in love, with Bali, with the entire experience, with myself.

That does not stop me from feeling good enough about everything to break my one-month hiatus from dating apps and pop back on Bumble for a few swipes. Though as I do so, again I'm biting straight through my tongue as I try to avoid making any typecasting judgments, because everyone here (seriously, like everyone) is thirty-two, has at least one picture of themselves in a yoga pose that looks like a pretzel, and includes a blurb in their profile about being vegetarian or vegan. I get the "finding yourself" cliché (raises hand sheepishly), but I can't help but appreciate the irony of seeking clarity and personal originality in a place where you can walk outside, throw a stone through the thick jungle air, and hit at least ten people who fit the exact same mold and purpose. I quickly give up on the notion of finding my "one" via swipe in Ubud and go dark on the apps again.

Getting somewhere for any kind of meetup would be a challenge anyway. I made the decision early on that I prefer not to leave this world in a fiery scooter death explosion in Indonesia, but without full knowledge of the complete lack of transportation infrastructure in Ubud. The reason I see a million scooters a day here, some even loaded up with the entire Brady Bunch family, is because there's no other way to get around anywhere. Taxis and Uber are banned from the city by short-sighted protectionist edict, and the only "ride service" is finding a private, unlicensed but designated "taxi van" to bring you somewhere for a predetermined price. It's so 1950's that FoxNews contributors would blow their load over the simple life throwback.

Limited by isolation to old-fashioned foot traffic, options for food and any sort of nightlife are subsequently minimal. A couple of the guys and I have a running joke about the need for additional in-between meals, our American bodies starved for protein and craving some variation from the repetition of our usual haunts. But it's getting late and the time difference factor is catching up to me, pushing me into bed to start the falling asleep process around nine most nights.

I have a big day ahead of doing laundry anyway, which is less sarcastic and more of a challenge than my tone might imply. When almost the entirety of my earthly possessions is my roaming wardrobe, and the only other person to have ever handled my laundry before is Mom, dropping all my clothing off at a rinky-dink facility in a foreign country is a scary proposition. I submit to the leap of faith though, and hand over my prized, mostly sweaty possessions and head over to the soccer field across the street for my regular workout.

I'm still not convinced anyone here has seen another human exercise before. In almost two weeks, I've yet to see someone else running, barely anyone on a bike, and certainly no one else being "that guy" doing burpees and step-ladder plyometrics out in the open. I continue to provide the town with entertainment, people staring at me like I'm doing this all naked or something. A couple on a scooter literally pulls over to watch. If 100 people drive by in the hour I'm out here, 500 will have their heads turned in bewilderment. Don't check my math on that, it works out.

Our TRT family continues with the frequent activities together, and we head to the other group house a few minutes away for a birthday pool party. I've pretty consistently been avoiding alcohol the last few weeks, so one beer for me is all I partake in, although I feel like an old married couple in my lameness, minus the married couple and only partially old. My body can't handle midweek partying anymore, and my mind can't handle another interruption in my pre-arranged schedule. There's certainly the possibility, as is my habit, that I'm turning too structured, the drawback to being type-A and having complete control over my timing being that I become rigidly set in my chosen ways despite the flexibility I have in my power and sought after in the first place.

As I prepare for sleep, the disruption now is in dragon form, as a processional of local kids, fifteen or twenty at a time, all banging drums and ringing bells while wearing a dragon costume on their heads, make their way down the street outside the compound in apparent celebration of something having to do with the Galungan holiday. I see the same thing the next day, but it's noon on a weekday, shouldn't these kids be in school? I ponder this, old and cranky.

The storm clouds continue to circle, as my dad calls to let me know that my grandmother's health is fading fast, and the doctor says it's only a matter of time now. My grandmother has never been the healthiest of sorts, and many of my poor eating habits and genetic... let's say... challenges, come from that pool. But her sweet tooth is far, far outweighed by her sweet heart, and her struggles over the last year and a half, since the Christmas before when we thought we lost her the first time, have been heartbreaking. I've never felt more distant in my travels than I do now, helpless to provide comfort or a tension-breaking laugh. The realization also sets in that I may never see her again. I pray to something up above that she makes it until I'm back, but more importantly, that she makes it to the two remarkable events upcoming in her life: her and my grandfather's seventieth wedding anniversary in a couple of weeks (yes, seventy), and her ninetieth birthday in July. I would be there for that, but mostly I want her to hang on to be with my grandfather, the two of them barely knowing a life apart from each other.

I grab lunch with Bali Rob at Barong Bridge, per usual, and our typically light conversation turns a little heavier as we discuss the weight and burdens of traveling as long as we have. He's coming up on three months, my tally at just about five. A fatigue element inevitably works itself in, even with an experienced level of traveling. The glory and glamour of this life looks nice in cropped and filtered pictures displayed to the masses, or my 500 or so followers, but the personal and emotional toll is not one that I anticipated to this degree. Leaving Los Angeles seems so long ago, and all the negativity from last year that I put behind me has been mostly out of sight, out of mind.

Now, though, I am forced to go back there and relive it all in the form of bank statements and faded receipts, as I waited until the last minute, as my avoidant self always does, to submit my taxes and now the bell is tolling for me. Looking back over bank statements is one of my greatest fears. To riff off of a Seinfeld bit, it always results in a moment of shame and undeserved shock, much like the level of surprise when the bill comes at the end of a meal at a restaurant, despite the fact that the prices are obviously listed and I passed second grade math with my trusty Ticonderoga #2 pencil so I know how to add. Yet, somehow I'm still dumbfounded. And dumb.

My first day of reviewing and sorting business and personal expenses results in two main takeaways: damn I spend a lot of money on booze (you're welcome for all those rounds of drinks, friends), and damn I have a lot of fun. The calculation of fun is primarily represented by my frequent travel excursions, and my initial reaction is one of delight at the walk down memory lane, reliving trips that I barely remembered before the reminder. There was one period in May to July of last year where a string of consecutive weekends consisted of an MDW wedding in Ojai Valley, my birthday in San Diego, Palm Springs for an EDM-lite pool party, Orange County to visit friends, New Orleans for a wedding, Orange County for the Fourth of July, and a birthday party at Malibu Wines. No wonder my savings account balance resembles the temperature of a winter day in Iceland.

The forced self-reflection in that underlying mindset, though, makes for a pretty easy evaluation that does not feel very good or reassuring. This is the escapism of wanderlust conversation all over again, taking place in historical form before I was keen to the habit. Look at all this time and money spent on travel last year, and what did I have to show for it in the form of happiness? Fleeting fun, some of which I even forgot about until I noticed in my statements the bar tab at Mutt Lynch's in Newport Beach or the hotel bill from Palm Springs. Certainly not anything meaningful or soul-quenching.

The second day is even worse, as I dig into the finances that accompanied a pretty depressing and downward spiraling Fall. My main takeaway for today's sorting is total disgust in my attitude and actions only six months prior. One of my accounts is linked to my automatic food payments (DoorDash, UberEats, etc.), and as I run through those charges, I can't stop yelling posthumously at the statements on my computer, "Stop ordering mother fucking pizza, you fatass!" And oh yeah, there are those bar tabs again. How many times in a single night can a person rack up a $100+ bar bill? Seriously.

This quickly turned into an exercise in self-pity and shame, reliving all these clearly surface level attempts at self-medicated whatever during a period that was rougher on my emotions than I could admit, or even realize. It's led me right into a classic uptown funk you up situation, the culminating point of a terrible, horrible, no good, very bad week. Now I am triggered, as the kids say these days.

The return to a personal life I had escaped, but never confronted, is unequal parts reminiscent, reflective, remorseful, and a reminder of the real world that is rapidly approaching on the other end of this business. As I traveled, I have physically and at least somewhat mentally removed myself from that world in an exercise of detachment, only to have it shoved back in my face by Uncle Sam saying, "Deal with this, dude."

This deep dive into the past is causing two parallel paths of reflection, ending now at the same destination. One is the comparison of looking back, where I'm at versus where I was in November, mentally and emotionally. The other, triggered by an infiltration by the real world outside of this nomadic bubble, is on returning to some sort of more sustainable long-term existence resembling the prior life and to what effect, knowing with each day I'm running out of time to accomplish a meaningful change from the obviously broken person I was before I left. There is a faint and looming light at the end of the tunnel I can now make out in the distance, but it looks less like daylight and more like a freight train about to hit.

For the first time, while answering work emails after completing my taxes, I have an actual answer to the question, "When will you be back?", and I absolutely do not think that timing is a coincidence. "A couple of months," I respond honestly. With that admission, though, comes a crunching of the numbers and, also for the first time on this voyage, it hits me that what's in front of me is less than what is behind me.

Now that the end of the road is near and slightly paved, a perfect storm of intense self-reflection has formed in anticipation over our compound in Ubud. The gist of the analysis is this: okay buddy, you've had your fun trotting around the world the last five months, been shown in painstaking detail the many sins of the prior life, realized you tried to press the reset button back then and chased this whole time after an undefined objective away from that setting, learned a few things about yourself and life along the way, so... where are you now?

Part of me has a feeling of regret. There's a little man inside me, or a devil on my shoulder, telling me to continue on in this way for longer with so much more of the world to see and development to be had. While the question I get most from home is about my return, the question I get the most out on the road is "Where are you going next?" Pretty soon, I won't have a stirring response to that.

Part of me has a feeling of excitement. There's still a lot I do have left, including more Bali time to sort things out, my primary destination in Thailand, my return to Tokyo for an extended stay after a brief trip last year, and everything I have in mind for my re-entry. Trips and locations for the rest of the year, dating again, putting some of this theoretical growth from the experience into practice. Going back home to see family and friends again. There are benefits to wrapping this process up.

Part of me has a feeling of lacking resolution. Like what do I have to show for all this? Do I have a prize to return home with, like the conquering and heroic Odysseus? Or will I be viewed as more of a Bertram from *The Sandlot*, who got really into the Sixties and was never heard from again? This writing is supposed to be my battlefield treasure, but I'm in the middle of a massive case of both writer's block and Senioritis, motivation quelled by the finish line in site and the overwhelming burden of writing, unfinished and unaccomplished on the whole, without a clear ending on any front.

Part of me has a feeling of uncertainty. A few months ago, coming out of London, I was riding high about the progress I was making personally and professionally, wide open to a range of prospects and potential. As time dwindles down, some of the windows of opportunity are closing without any real, concrete resolutions for me and my future. I've got some ideas of how to handle my professional life, but I'm not confident in my ability to put it all together. And get paid.

Part of me has a feeling of fear, again. I always expected the end of this process to have some question marks, but I thought I might find more clarity than anxiety when I think about logistics like where I'll live, what I'll do with all my stuff, what I'll do about the job I want out of, and how I'm going to adult for real.

As these pieces swirl around in my consciousness, the very sad realization hits that the things I seem to be questioning and feeling queasy about now are the same worries that I set out in need of answers on at the beginning, the external pieces that I hoped would fall into place in this mixed up puzzle of life.

Well, shit.

Now I wonder what this piece of my life will ultimately mean when all is said and done. Did I completely botch this storyline? Is this now a plot blip that everyone universally looks back on and says, "What were the writers thinking?" Like the Joey-Rachel relationship near the end of *Friends*, or the Landry murder plot in *Friday Night Lights*, or basically anything having to do with Dorne in *Game of Thrones*. That's how misguided this all feels right now.

In characteristic form, I turn to my old pal "travel" as escape from this emotional cyclone ripping a path of disaster and doubt through Bali. To be fair, this is a scheduled group excursion to the Gili Islands, but I couldn't have designed the timing better myself. We start things off right on the top deck of our mini-ferry, a large Bintang in one hand and my phone in the other connected to the boat's auxiliary, somehow tasked with controlling the music for the whole ride. I'm excited for the challenge of keeping this party of a couple hundred people from all over the world amped up for the weekend, and by the time we float into harbor, it's safe to say, it's lit. Maybe I missed my true professional calling as a DJ. But I've seen that

Zac Efron movie, for some inexplicable reason, and I don't look nearly as good with headphones set around my neck.

The TRT group meets up on the western shore at the optimistically named Sunset Kiss Beach Club, where the orange and pink palette of the evening sky rising over the impeccably still waters of the Bali Sea and this pristine white sand provides an extended edition of truly priceless entertainment, save for the costs of these beers at our lounge chairs. Set against this expansive, unfiltered, unfettered vista, the sunset scene never seems to quit, and supplies the perfect backdrop for the hammock in the water picture you've always dreamed of posting. So #basic.

High off life, and not the mushroom shakes that are being pushed incessantly by shady looking characters along the walking path around the island, we make our way to the main commercial area on the eastern shore, partaking in some legitimate night life for my first time since what feels like the Reagan administration. One of the things you read about before coming to a place like this is about not drinking the water, even as ice or while brushing teeth. I've been able to avoid the infamous Bali Belly so far, though, and since I haven't had a vodka soda in forever, I decide to roll the dice with my usual for the night.

We bar hop around to a few spots, all open-air along the beach and heavy on blond girls, so I'm not complaining. Though I do get the impression that this is a playground for the eighteen to twenty-year-old crowd from northern Europe and Australia. We make friends with some other wandering folks roughly our age from South Africa, and after a few games of beer pong, call it a night in relatively tame fashion.

Gili Trawangan is an interesting dynamic of highs and lows. Here is this beautiful ocean scene and beach setup with lounge chairs and cocktails, next to trash thrown everywhere, sometimes floating up next to you in the water. Here are all these bars that look fun and with great scenes, with horror stories online of people being drugged or getting sick. Here are all these cool restaurants with tables in the sand and light waves rolling in steps away, with stray dogs and cats hanging all around. Here are so many friendly people with huge smiles for days, standing next to schemers relentlessly pushing mushroom shakes or ferry rides somewhere.

Along with the no shoes, no shirt, no problem motto, this place also very much practices an "island time" mentality that Buffet would be proud of. Jimmy, not Warren, although I'm sure Warren is a closet Parrothead, too. Our ferry home is nowhere to be found at its scheduled time, and the employees all have a shoulder shrug response to the delay. A casual two hours late, the ferry finally arrives to bring us back to Bali with a more subdued and hungover ride this time.

Back at the house, I feel pretty drained from the weekend, but it was a good mini-reprieve from all the internal drama of the last week. I meet Bali Rob and we walk down to Barong for dinner, which turns into one of our most thorough conversations yet. We've only known each other for a couple of weeks, and he is seven years younger than me, but we've gotten close in this abbreviated time. We're like totally BFF's now you guys.

We dig into past relationship histories, and I take the blame for the failures of my few real ones, while we share tales of heartbreak and the lingering feelings of losses that on paper shouldn't feel so crushing. We talk about our aversion to picking girls up at the bar, and of missing our good friends, and in a different world how our Gili T experience might have played out with our regular crews. And we dive again into the toll of being on the road for so long, with his stint coming to an end in a couple of weeks.

The sharing and open vulnerability with this kind of ease and with this short of a friendship is a new development for me over the last few months, and it feels good to be breaking down my own walls like this. At the same time, a lot of my revelations to him (and to myself) are in an area of self-reflection I haven't touched on much with others or admitted before, especially on relationships. The seeming self-sabotage and immaturity in conviction that doomed what could have been. The sharing of that detail is liberating, humbling, and a bit nauseating, puking my guts out in long overdue and symbolic release.

I immediately need to go home and crash, as the combination of everything has me breaking down. I fall asleep around seven in the evening, feeling some kind of heat stroke, exhaustion, or legit sickness kicking in. My temperature is through the sirap roof of this house, as I spend the night simultaneously sweating and shivering, my muscles aching and barely able to move. Another challenge in an Act full of confrontations.

The fever breaks overnight, but my stomach decides it wants in on the destructive action, sharp pains shooting through my body all night and morning. I spend the day alternating between bed-time and toilet-time, never throwing up but, well, doing the other thing. I feel like absolute ass, the effects and concern only amplified by my position so, so far from home.

Well folks, I think we've reached that critical point in the show. It may be time for me to say my goodbyes, start shilling for flat tummy tea, and wait for my invite to *Bachelor in Paradise*.

PART THREE

"The trails I made led outward into the hills and swamps, but they led inward also. And from the study of things underfoot, and from reading and thinking, came a kind of exploration, myself and the land. In time the two became one in my mind." –ADVENTURE EXPLORER JOHN HAINES

"Happiness [is] only real when shared." – JON KRAKAUER, *INTO THE WILD*

"Be better than the Gap. Be better, than the Gap." – RYAN GOSLING, *CRAZY, STUPID, LOVE*

THE CHAPTER ON PURPOSE

chapter fourteen

Lessons in life are learned in bits and pieces, through false starts and missed moments, points of clarity followed by poorly placed speed bumps, and there's no better time to finally put it all together than while deliriously ill in Southeast Asia after hours of destroying a Balinese toilet.

Mark Twain said that, I think.[1]

Throughout this process, I've had my fair share of stunted successes and bad timing. Periods of productive self-reflection, personal evaluation, and growth, accompanied by annoying setbacks and scattered attention. Ups and downs like the rolling of the tide, ushering a wayward vessel to its ultimate destination. I began working meditation into my life two months ago, but without the consistency and emphasis it deserved. I started learning about the intricacies of the practice,

---

[1] He didn't

only to drop my introductory book out of necessity to handle my tax filing and have a bit of a mental and bodily breakdown. Early on, I had an appreciation for the importance of finding happiness in balance and confidence in my decisions without fear or regret, but have been unable to identify my optimal points or work those concepts into practical application.

From Maui to Bali, the settings have changed for me but the inquiry and ultimate source of adulting anxiety remains the same, and I've flirted with and danced around the necessary recognition and resolutions with the same insecure energy and flailing intention of a high school wallflower at prom, leaving little effect to the queen's fancy, or anyone's for that matter.

As in dating, and everything else in life, timing is everything. Just as one must be in the right place at the right time to meet their partner, the same holds true for any months-long personal journey of self-discovery to meet thyself. Mark Twain actually might have said that too. [2]

In this context, false starts or deviations are not mistakes, but preparation for that moment when you can finally say, I am ready now.

After taking a sick/mental health/unable to leave the bathroom/near-death day, purging myself of whatever was in my stomach and my mind, I wake up with a sense of purpose and intention again that was desperately missing. I'm eager to put the recent events behind me and get back on track. I force myself into an ambitious agenda this week of reading, writing, meditating, thinking, and focusing on the big picture tasks at

---

[2] He didn't

hand, and in doing so, confront head on all the challenges that beat me down the last week plus and in months prior.

As I reinforce dedicated meditation time and dig further into the *Search Inside Yourself* reading, that loud, powerful clicking sound you hear is my consciousness making all the connections that have been impatiently waiting for me to piece together. Things might actually start to make sense now finally. Mostly.

Until now, my relationship with meditation has been surface level and friendly, without any true level of commitment on my part. You might even say we've been stuck in the casual friend zone. I've mostly sought out the practice right before writing, finding at least some moderate effect to my focus and relaxation. There's never been any material objective behind my meditation, as no one ever really explained the full impact or importance of it before, aside from some references in *Eat, Pray, Love* that were too early in the process for me to appreciate.

Well, *Search Inside Yourself* just became the Mr. Miyagi to my Karate Kid, the Mick to my Rocky, the Donkey to my Shrek, the Yoda to my Luke Skywalker. And because I don't want to keep typing the book's full name each time, from here on out it will be referred to as Yoda.

Right off the bat, Yoda drops a Ralph Waldo Emerson line on me: what lies behind us and what lies ahead of us are tiny matters to what lies within us.

Hold up. Was I not just talking about my focus being on what's in front of and behind me like five minutes ago? Now I'm reading those very words, but this time with the punchline attached at the end that I was missing all along. And damnit if that's not some great advice just a few pages into this book. Alright, you have my attention, Yoda. What else you got?

Well, Yoda is a program developed at Google and designed to enhance the mental well-being of its employees, because those stock options, free meals, and matching contribution programs just weren't enough. After experiencing great success internally, Yoda was taken to the public to espouse the benefits of the program globally. It all starts with the premise that at its most basic level, meditation is just mental training, and that literally anyone, through practice, can develop a peaceful, happy, compassionate mind.

The part that stands out to me right away is the word "training". I've always had a pejorative view of meditation, wrongly dismissing it as some new age feel-goodery, but framed in this way as a kind of mental exercise, it seems absurdly simple and intuitive in retrospect. I can think of meditation as equivalent to simply going to the gym to work out, building stamina and muscle. I take half an hour on the elliptical working toward the beach bod. Thirty minutes of meditation "training" is the same concept, a six-pack for the brain.

Yoda runs through a handful of studies for me (always the geeky skeptic) that show that a cognitive exercise like meditation leads to improved brain function in a variety of aspects: anxiety reduction, immunity defense, rational thinking, emotion management, stimuli processing time and efficiency, and possibly the most important, measurable prefrontal cortex activity involved in levels of happiness. In essence, meditation can make you naturally happier. Full stop.

Well, not yet, there's much more to explore.

The comparison to running or lifting weights is even more appropriate when we consider that the brain, though not a "muscle," has the ability to be strengthened just the same through what the nerds call neuroplasticity. Through training, different sections and functions of the brain can develop and advance beyond those brains that are lazy couch potatoes. Yoda was created to tap into and foster this development, and although the program was specifically designed, the principles apply across the meditation practice and life in general.

It's time to introduce a word I would normally hate for its nonsensical and pretentious ambiguity, but which is now all I can think about (literally): Mindfulness.

Yoda and his friends define this term as "paying attention in a particular way: on purpose, in the present moment, and non-judgmentally". So, when we talk about "mindfulness meditation", we're looking at a specific meditation training program, like a plyometric workout or marathon preparation, designed primarily to improve attention ability. Mindfulness meditation at its core is focused on following your breath so that when you're meditating, devoting your entire energy toward the up and down rhythm of the body and against all other distractions and surroundings, the biceps in the mind associated with attention become stronger.

In the age of diverted and short-term attention spans in a world of distractions, what could be better than training the mind to be more attentive in daily life? As great as that benefit is, there's much more to it than that too.

Mindfulness is the foundation for another one of those calculator-holding, glasses-and-suspend-ers-and-pocket-protector-wearing, nerdy-sounding buzz-words or phrases that in reality, is incredibly awesome and important: Emotional Intelligence.

Emotional intelligence is the target of Yoda's mindful-ness lessons, the face to the name of so much that dogged me before this trip. It's also the broader lesson I've been dancing around this entire time, sometimes gracefully, sometimes not, like I do with the beer bottle in the middle of the dance floor in my circle of friends on a random night out. Emotional intelligence deals in both the intrapersonal (self) and the interpersonal (others). Since I need to figure my own shit out first, I'll start there.

Yoda lays out the ports on the passage to Intrapersonal Emotional Intelligence very simply: training in mindfulness through meditation leads to an improved quality of atten-tion; an improved quality of attention leads to a mind that is calm and clear; a mind that is calm and clear leads to a higher perception of our own cognitive and emotive pro-cesses; a higher perception of our cognitive and emotive pro-cesses leads to deeper self-discovery and better insight into ourselves and how we function; better insight into ourselves and how we function leads to better performance and con-tentment in work life, better relationships and social life, and (drumroll please) the ability to create overall happiness in life and the conditions for its long-term sustainability.

Sounds pretty nice, huh? Also sounds a tiny little bit like what I've been searching for from the beginning, exactly what I needed to live that confident, happy, FOMO-free life.

So okay, I get what the potential implications of all this are, and the stakes are sufficiently high enough that Yoda has me locked in. But now that the mind is becoming calmer and clearer, theoretically, how do I translate that into higher emotional perception, analysis, and implementation in the world? Yoda, you're up again.

The first part of the Emotional Intelligence skillset is regular old Self-Awareness, which seems to be a simple and straight-forward enough concept.

The best part about this Yoda is speak in confusing sentence structures, he does not. This Yoda (and his friends) break it down into elements, in formulas that help my linear mind and are surely responsible for my ability to connect all the dots finally. The three pieces that make up this overall Self-Awareness equation are 1.) Emotional Awareness, 2.) Accurate Self-Assessment, and 3.) Self-Confidence.

That looks so pretty to me. It's like being back in Torts class in law school: here are the elements that make up the tort, find their relevancy in the facts, apply them and make your case.

As with mindfulness, Self-Awareness can be trained with the same methods of meditation because we're approaching from the same angle: developing a calm and clear mind that can better perceive emotions. The first component, Emotional Awareness, is a matter of correctly perceiving our internal emotions, knowing why, when, and from where they come, and understanding how it affects our behavior. That understanding leads to Accurate Self-Assessment, where we can apply meaning to that knowledge by diagnosing our strengths and weaknesses, determining our limitations and the importance we assign to certain things, and finding clarity on our goals and priorities. That understanding leads to Self-Confidence, an application of knowing what makes us tick, what we do well and where we need help, and an honest and humble acknowledgment of it all. Developing Self-Awareness is the key to all other emotional development, because doing so activates the neocortex, the rational, thinking part of the brain, in the processing of emotions. With that type of core work, the mind's fitness and balance is ready for an emotional Tough Mudder.

If Self-Awareness is the *knowledge* of one's internal states, preferences, resources, and intuitions (and it is), then Self-Regulation is the *management* of those, and is the second component of this intrapersonal intelligence. So, first there is understanding and processing, and then there is dealing with it. But before we shuffle up and deal, the sun is shining brightly back in Bali.

I can feel the Italian in my skin getting darker by the minute as I provide my daily entertainment on the soccer field to the townspeople. In the middle of my workout routine, a guy actually stops on his scooter and approaches me, introducing himself as the local soccer coach for the kids. He's curious about my exercises and the agility step ladder I'm using. We talk for a few minutes about soccer, the U.S., where he might buy a similar ladder, and some exercises the team can do, before he motors away. It doesn't hit me until after he leaves that I should have just given him mine. There's no way in hell he's going to get one of these anywhere in Bali, and Amazon doesn't make it out this far. Big mind fail on my part.

Bali Rob and I decide to brave the oppressive heat and humidity for the hour-long trek up to the Campuhan Ridge Walk, a cool jungle hike with rivers flowing below on both sides. We stop at the Karsa Kafe for a lunch involving avocado and drinking out of a coconut, because we are just a couple of basic bros apparently. The spa nearby looks even more appetizing, and with the humidity about to break into an afternoon rain shower, we pop into the classy establishment at Lokha Ubud, a Four Seasons-like hotel for non-sketchy Balinese massages. The open-wall cabanas fill with an overwhelmingly natural ambiance, as the rain begins plopping peacefully onto the large palm fronds just outside while the masseuse goes to work releasing a mountain of stress piled into my tightly-wound shoulders.

Still in robes and slippers after, with some kind of fruity refreshment in hand, I fill Bali Rob in on the self-awareness acknowledgment and progress I recently discovered. The experience of sharing my vulnerability is becoming more natural lately. I'm also encouraged by our ability here in the spa to talk about the heart of what this all relates to: mental health. We organically throw personal stories and evaluations out to each other about our own self-assessments with an audacity that would make a shrink blush and an old man grumble about snowflakes. Our generation seems to have a much healthier relationship with this mental fitness topic, operating somewhere between tacit acknowledgment and open conversation that is a giant leap forward in the modern social discourse.

Amongst men especially, this seems incredibly important for a gender that so often has to define our worth by dogged strength and emotional suppression. But legitimate, earned, true self-confidence seems to be a far more valuable commodity than an ability to mask real feelings in the name of manhood. A sincerely self-aware person seems better-suited to handle social circles and career, love, and life.

Knowing my emotions and the actions tied to them, along with my strengths and weaknesses that result from them, is a great start, but the management of them is critical, and that's where Self-Regulation comes in. Yoda confirms that a healthy relationship with our emotions is not about avoiding or suppressing feelings, but properly utilizing the valuable information about ourselves that they carry. This is regulated in five general and related areas of self-control, trustworthiness (maintaining standards), conscientiousness (taking personal responsibility), adaptability, and innovation (being comfortable with novelty). As Yoda says, operating within this sphere of self-aware emotional management ultimately comes down to a matter of making accurate personal choices, the latter a trigger word that catches my attention from earlier conversation.

This is that long-lost rebuttal to FOMO.

Self-Regulation is pretty self-explanatory, but there are two relevant aspects worth calling out specifically now. The first is dealing with triggers. We all have them and they all manifest different reactions within us, whether in bodily effects like elevated heart rate or clenched fists, experiencing a fight or flight response, or through negative thoughts. Obviously, it's beneficial to know how to better react to this sort of stimuli (self-regulation), but the more important place to start is with knowing the root of the trigger itself (self-awareness).

Most commonly, we are triggered by something we feel self-conscious about, like my inability to avoid crying at the end of *Miracle*, or from something from my past. Hey, look at that, another callback topic: dealing with the past. And Yoda and Elsa both advise to let it go.

One trigger I've allowed to exist for far too long, literally, is the old hair situation. It's time to ditch any lingering delusions that I can still pull off a sort of messy mop like early-*Office* John Krasinski, especially with the jungle air doing the opposite of wonders for the look. In the interest of embracing the unavoidable, I tell my hairdresser at the salon to kill the curls in favor of the tight shaved look. And to wax some straggling hair off the back while she's at it, because what the heck, I'm feeling adventurous.

I enjoy the wind in what remains of my hair as Bali Rob and I walk back up the Campuhan Trail to the Karsa Spa for another day of bromantic luxury and massages. Continuing with the exploratory theme, I give ear candling a try, and wow the wax. I can actually hear the birds chirping and bees buzzing again. Lying on my side in this oddly vulnerable and submissive position while a small lighted paper burns a few inches from my head, being pet by the tiny hands of the technician like a furry family friend, this release makes slaving away all day in the office worth it.

The general practice of all this letting go involves freeing myself of two sinister sisters: grasping, where we desperately hold on to something and can't let it go, and aversion, where we push something away and don't let it come. Together, these assholes account for almost all suffering that we experience.

Yoda makes the important point, though, that these pains, although oftentimes seemingly coinciding with suffering, are actually separate sensations, and that we can train ourselves to perceive displeasure without the resulting negative, hurtful, emotionally upsetting effect. Losing aversion allows for pain without the suffering. Ditching grasping allows for pleasure without the aftertaste of loss when the good feeling inevitably ends.

So, the moral of the story, I think, is just unfollow your exes on social media.

The other important note of Self-Regulation is that, again with training, we can and should recognize the moments when we are not in pain. Having an appreciation for normalcy and stasis goes a long way toward being able to manage the variations from that set point, as well as developing the ability to accept and embrace the idea of "just being happy" that's often a struggle for me on the daily level. You can basically become your own constant, like in a science experiment, as a point of reference for when you're trying to bring life into balance.

There it is again. Balance, a word I've used frequently to the point of annoyance without a true command of the concept, now makes more sense as an application of these principles. A few months ago, I was reading in *Eat, Pray, Love* about what the author calls "the monkey mind", swinging from thought to thought in an active brain like the ones going limb to limb in the park down the street. The problem with this natural function is in the emotional attachment that piggybacks the swinging thoughts, because as the mind wanders into highs and lows, chasing certain feelings, so do the emotions and the moods, actions, reactions, and decision-making that go with it.

This trip has certainly been indicative of this in practice, as just Bali alone has been a wild emotional roller coaster. The promise and excitement of the opening scenes, followed by the recent overwhelmingly negative reflective period, with the hope that this current episode of enlightenment can bring it all into healthy balance. But that's the nature of Bali, which has proven to be an exercise in the extremes, and a perfect battleground in the struggle between finding happy and mismanaging adulting into a midlife crisis.

The limitation of options here has taken some getting used to, as the over-abundance of choice did in New York on the other end of the spectrum. A paradox exists in this realm of decision-making where having too many options or too few creates an adversarial arena for resultant happiness. Better emotional intelligence can shift the mindset out of a loss avoidance or fear scenario into one where no matter the options, I can be at peace with each choice and without regrets, for getting me to my present place and a feeling of happy with the moment.

And maybe it's a self-fulfilling prophecy, seeing what I want to see since I've heard so many references to it, but Wayan's family and all of the Balinese people I've met really do have this aura of happiness surrounding them at all times. When the taxi drivers at the airport pestered me about needing a ride when I landed, a part of me believes they weren't just peddling for cash but were actually looking out for me, generally concerned that I was being taken care of and getting where I needed to go. I can see why it's so easy to find and keep happy here.

This place just wants me to be a happier, healthier, better version of myself, helping to guide the choices that are best for me and nudging me toward peace of mind.

Putting it all together, I now have a fun-sized roadmap to take with me wherever I go, a strategy for calming down and just living life, on purpose. It's included now with the cost of your admission.

The Emotionally Intelligent Guide to Adulting without FOMO, Sponsored by Mindfulness

1.) The default state is happy. When the mind is calm and clear, through meditation or otherwise, I'm more likely to be naturally, scientifically joyful, as Yoda points out. So, if I can find ways to actively reset to the happiness default, and to appreciate the normal, non-chaotic parts of life when I'm not in pain or distracted by a Twitter thread, that regular state of elevated bliss will help adjust my starting point. Since that state of Zen is not really feasible all day, every day as things happen, decisions need to be made, life unfolds, I can use the training of a clear, attentive mind to cultivate a better approach through the competencies of Self-Awareness and Self-Regulation.

2.) Know Myself: Get to know and understand the self, and be confident in it.

3.) Manage Myself: Know how to manage my emotions, strengths, weaknesses, and act with control.

4.) Choose Happy: Know my core values, what is important and what makes me happy, then make choices to align those personal qualities with the world around me, in job, love life, social life, life. From there, everything should fall into place. Or not. But that's okay too, because I'll be better prepared to deal with it all.

Meditation is just one way of developing self-awareness and understanding. But the end game is always the same, and it all starts within, with honesty, openness, and vulnerability. With that comes self-confidence. From self-confidence comes the ability to keep my emotions light, and life fun. To incorporate humor and self-deprecation, and a belief that as long as I've got the right foundation and approach in place, I can realize being happy is not that difficult.

The last piece to tie it all together: 5.) Find Balance. If I know myself well, where I am and where I'm going (ironically), then I can find equilibrium, and a constant for dealing with the changes all around me at any point in time. I don't want to be entirely set in stone, and should always be growing and evolving appropriately, but at least with a base point from which I can let life present itself.

I lean back in my chair at this new restaurant I'm trying down Monkey Forest Road and smirk in unfinished accomplishment. I push my coconut aside and take a note in my pad about NYC. Sinatra's "New York, New York" is playing over

the speakers of the restaurant and I make a point to reference the lyrics of the song into one of the section titles, considering the relevance of the words to me and this trip. Not
two minutes later, after picking Yoda up for a read, I come
across a line where the book references the same lyrics, "If I
can make it there". I pause, look around for a Russian/Face-
book spy, shake my head and laugh at the oh, I don't know,
thousandth timely "coincidence" sent my way the last few
months. Paying attention pays off, it seems.

Our group hits the beaten road for our last major activity together, surfing in Canguu on the southwestern shore of
Bali, where the crowd is densely populated with even more
Australians somehow. Since I now consider myself a surfing
expert from my experience in Maui, and have no desire to
enter the ocean ever again, I use my time to drink a Bintang
on the beach. I think I like this area and its pace better than
Ubud, where the only thing that moves fast is on the road
causing me heartburn. My ideal location is an active, medium-sized city near the water. That's my sweet spot, preferably also with mixed use developments of a beachy but brick
aesthetic, many golf courses nearby, is ATV-friendly, and gets
300+ days of sunshine a year with no humidity. If you find this
paradise, my contact info is at the end.

I snap some GoPro shots of the group surfing before
grabbing sunset beers on the beach as reggae music that
no one actually likes plays in the background. Randomly, we
run into our South African beer pong friends from Gili T and
laugh about the silliness of that night, and of coincidences.

It's time to start saying some goodbyes as our month in Bali dwindles down to its final days. A few TRT people take off in the morning, so we throw a goodbye party at the villa. In true high school pool party fashion, amongst the fifteen or so of us, there's an appropriate dose of adolescent-level flirting, splashing around, chicken fighting, and keeping the neighbors up. We're joined by new friends from Outpost, some digital nomad girls from Serbia we recently met, including the tall and gorgeous Bali Mia, with whom I form a solid connection.

Next, I say goodbye to Snapchat. I know, shocking given my rave reviews for it here. How will I ever survive not receiving snaps with dog filters or missing a stupid story of a friend at a concert where everything is dark and I can't hear lyrics but I can hear my speakers being blown out of my phone? I'm going to guess, I'll survive just fine. With my new push for managing stimuli, options, distractions, this is an easy one to cut, escaping the mindset of "well I might miss something" that overtakes so much of life.

The goodbyes continue on our penultimate day, and I feel a bit weird and desensitized to this process at the moment. I've been so focused on myself that dealing with others has really taken a back seat for now.

I still go through the platitudes that keep everyone happy, the "keep in touch, let me know about X, we're a family now" lines, but in reality for most people I'm leaving here, there's unfortunately a 95% chance this is the last time I'll ever see them.

I pack my bags again on my last day, ditching my unnecessary hairdryer, the agility ladder I plan to leave with Wayan to give to the soccer coach, and an extra backpack I can do without since I'm carrying so much less with me now.

I grab my workout gear for one last show in the park before I leave. In the middle of my workout, I spot the soccer coach driving by on his scooter with his son and wave them down. I have to repeat myself about four times when I tell him he can keep the ladder for his team. Eventually the shock wears off that I would just give him this, and his smile is heart-filling. He calls over his son to learn a few different exercises, invites me to lunch and dinner (which I politely have to decline), and asks for photos of all of us, his thumbs-up sign and smile never wavering. It's such a small thing to me, something I really didn't think would have an impact to the point where I barely made the gesture. But now if we see Indonesia in the World Cup in ten years, carried on the backs and swift feet of some really agile Balinese players, we'll know the background story.

Still surprised by that rush of paying it forward to good karma, I grab a late morning acai bowl at my café, where three of my favorite waitresses are all working. I say my good-byes to them also and leave extra as a tip, just doubling the price of my meal. It seems like a lot at the time, especially since tips aren't customarily given, but really only amounts to about $8. They are so taken aback and thrilled though, they too come in for multiple hugs and photos, with a promise that I will definitely be back some day.

With that, Marco the Italian Conqueror, Bali Rob, and I are off to Seminyak to party for our last night in Bali with the three Serbian girls. We rent a huge Airbnb house with a pool in the center, and pregame with many Bintangs, every bag of chips available in the country, and a dance lesson for the others on how to do the Wobble. We spend the rest of the night dancing at a Caribbean-themed bar called Mexicola and Brazilian-themed club called Favela, all very-well ordained in their respective settings and open until four in the morning. At that hour, we spill into the street as the party somehow continues on behind us. Avoiding the questionable prostitutes and even more questionable hot dog stands across the road, we end the night with a few of us all in the master bed spooning until we fall asleep. I met these people less than a month ago, and the girls about a week ago, but something about it all feels different. Sharing this Airbnb, and now a bed, with people I barely know feels weird that it doesn't feel weird, the similar mindsets of a more relaxed, open personality shining through.

In the morning, we do what millennials do best and brunch over mimosas and eggs in an outdoor setting. Slowly, people start to make moves to their next destinations, dropping off one by one like it's the end of summer camp and parents are arriving for pickup.

I drop Bali Rob off at his hotel for the night and continue my taxi to the airport, first giving a good bro hug to one of the five-percenters I hope to keep in touch with. As my taxi makes its way through the fading sun, the magnitude of the moment, leaving this formerly foreign country for another new one, alludes me. Maybe it's the ridiculous way I'm dressed as I arrive at the airport: bright yellow LSU t-shirt, red flower print board shorts, neon blue running sneakers. Most likely, though, it's a feeling of inevitability, a positive mindset, let's do it, the band marches on, on to the next one, carrying the momentum forward, onward and upward... alright sorry, I ran out of cliché expressions.

The spirit of the moment holds true though. As I board my flight to Singapore on my way to Thailand, somehow passing through Indonesian customs dressed like a clown, the feeling inside is unusual to me, but dare I say it, possibly self-confidence? I think it would almost have to be, given my attire.

I like this feeling. I want to chase this feeling. And maybe even share this feeling.

THE CHAPTER WITH ALL THE CLOSURE

chapter fifteen

My favorite kind of exit is of the Irish variety, the one that involves never actually having to say goodbye. I use this maneuver most often at the tail end of a long night out where my energy level and interest in anything going on around me has reached its breaking point, and rather than put up with pleas to stay or friendly taunts, I just bounce instead. That makes all the goodbyes recently, which are noticeably more frequent of late, all the more curious. Closure is surely nice to have in many instances (hello past relationships), but I generally prefer the positive open-endedness of a "see you next time" vibe to the "this is the end of this encounter" exchange.

I FaceTime my grandmother in the States on what I believe is now their actual anniversary date, though I'm still figuring out all the days and time changes. I congratulate my grandparents on their seventieth, but it takes about all of the emotional muscle I have not to break down on the phone when I see her laid up in a hospital bed with her children from Maine, Connecticut, Idaho, and New Mexico all gathered at her bedside. She's surprisingly upbeat despite knowing her remaining time is measured in days now, not months or years. I've always provided her comic relief and regaled my grandparents with my stories from all over, so they get a kick out of my tales from Thailand now. It takes me a lot to say goodbye and hang up, knowing that very well may be the last time I talk to her.

I head out for a walk on the beach to clear my head and process, before I turn back toward my villa at this small resort complex on the western shore of Railay Beach in the Krabi province. The Railay peninsula is cut off by impassable mountains to the north, so the only accessibility is by longtail boat, a quintessential, welcome-to-Thailand experience. It takes all of about ten minutes to walk around the entire village. The small shops and restaurants are all rustic beach huts and as authentic as it gets, aside from the music, which is oddly just awkward covers of popular American love songs. The isolation is strong in this one, and as I pass dive after dive, I wonder if it's possible to be a hole-in-the-wall spot if the whole island is. The views, though, are everything I imagined when I put Thailand at the top of my travel wish list. The clear, peaceful waves rolling in between huge out-of-place rock formations in the water, gently caressing the cushy, clean sand on their way back out to sea. This setting is just as good in person as the stock photos show, and way better than my terrible iPhone camera can capture or any of those word things I string together can describe.

My bungalow villa, steps from the beach one way and pools the other way, is a little taste of first class living in another world setting, the luxury of my small cottage balanced out by the bathroom warning sign about flushing paper material due to the poor plumbing of the area. The resort staff is always smiling and friendly, so much so that on arrival, my bag valet made sure I was all set on my weed needs for my stay. It turns out I don't need a weed source anyway, as "skunk" delicacies are aplenty on the northern walking path connecting the commercial areas.

While unpacking, I get a text from back in Connecticut that a good friend from high school has died of an apparent overdose related to opioids. I had fallen out of touch with her over the years, but this hits the closest to home in a desperately destructive trend that's obliterating good people across our area and a generation at the hands of predatory pharmaceutical companies.

I don't handle death very well, and I've never been great at understanding other people on the whole either, never knowing how to really pay attention to that stuff. I'm a good listener, but I think it's pretty obvious by now I'm not great with the nonverbal signals, which luckily for me only make up, oh, about 90% of all communication.

But that, my friends, is part of what we call Empathy, the first of the Interpersonal Emotional Intelligence skills used when competently dealing with others. Being able to understand and share in the feelings of those around us is a critical social skill, and directly correlated to one's own self-awareness. If I have strong self-awareness, I'm likely to have strong ability for empathy, because both use the same equipment in the brain, called the insula. As Yoda advises, when we strengthen our insula through a practice like mindfulness meditation, we improve both aspects of emotional awareness. If we're able to make connections and find similarities in another, we're likely to then be more empathetic and treat another person with kindness. And by transmitting kindness, we physiologically improve the ability to achieve sustainable happiness. It's science.

I close the Yoda book and set it aside for now, as I'm tired from holding it straight up above my head to block the sun from my face on this poolside lounge chair. It's time for a quick dip in the pool and some more tanning.

I decide to commit myself to the social experiment with a night out at the bars on the eastern side of Railay, passing new neighbors of kittens, monkeys, and skunk shops aplenty. I post up at Last Bar, which is literally the last bar on the northern end of the commercial area, complete with dance floor and Muay Thai boxing rink. A couple attractive girls from Texas order drinks next to me, and all it takes is a move by me for a "Cheers" clinking of Chang beer bottles to open a lively conversation. Imagine that.

After making the "Americans in Thailand" connection and explaining my solo status as part of a larger travel experience, they ask what I do for living. I'm feeling bold at this point, and for the first time, drop the "I'm a writer" line on them, detailing the idea behind this book in your hands. It

may not have been the best time to try that route, as one of
the girls is drunk and asks about twenty times for me to put
her in the book. Well, here you go, Nikol.

We share enough laughs and stories and contact information to meet up the next day to explore our surroundings
together in Railay. For a long, familiar second, I contemplate
passing and doing my own thing, but I want the social connection, even if with new people. We start in the Diamond
Cave, because women and their diamonds, am I right? In exploration, we then discover hidden beaches, one of which we
have to wade through water to another island to reach, get
lost without the necessary machete in the jungle paths trying to find a pirate-themed bar near Ao Nang Beach, give up
and drink in a mountaintop infinity pool instead, and enjoy
smoothie cocktails and a joint at Bang Bang Bar, appropriately named after the proprietor, a dude who literally goes by
Bang Bang and is very generous in both liquor quantity in his
drinks and in lighting up with his guests. The girls don't survive past Bang Bang's place and retire to their room for the
night. I continue on for another go at Last Bar, but get frustrated by a group of Canadian girls who timidly dance around
me without making a clear move, and a beautiful Brazilian
who I keep up with for a bit but is way out of my league and
enjoying the attention of every guy in the bar standing around
trying to swoop. I call it a night, happy with both the solo social
baby steps and the dance floor moves laid down.

Back at the villa, I FaceTime the family in Connecticut,
where everyone is gathered for the anniversary party for my
grandparents. I get passed around the room to all my sib-

lings, all my mom's siblings, my grandfather, and eventually my grandmother, who I can immediately tell is not going to make it much longer. Even from a few days before, she looks much worse, much more bloated, and I know for certain these are my last words with her.

She seems at peace though, and that makes me at peace. She made it to her seventieth anniversary, and now to the party with her family around her, and I can tell she's content to go now. I try to keep things light as always, telling her about my day in Thailand and the Canadians I just met. They aren't from her native Quebec, but she loves the story and the connection. Our goodbye is longer than usual. I'm uncertain how to do this, unsure what to say or how to let go. We say "I love you" enough to the point that I lose count, before I feel selfish that I'm hanging on to her and tell her to go cut up the dance floor at her party. I hang up, slowly. The smile I fronted for her in my last goodbye quickly turns to tears of release in my resultant solitude and crushing silence of the otherwise empty room.

Shaken up the next day, I lay low with a little reading, not straying far from my cottage.

Yoda hits on an interesting topic that presents a chance for a little more self-evaluation. The topic is specifically about person praise versus process praise. Studies show being praised for being smart (person) is considerably less effective than praise for working hard (process). This seems like something that probably hampered me over the years, as most of my appreciation was for the former. I was always one of the smartest kids in the class and things have generally come

easy to me. That means I've rarely had to work hard at anything or am ever challenged. In the past when I've been test-
ed, though, I've been known to shy away in avoidance, and
take the path of lesser resistance. This experience as a whole
has taught me to steer into the adversity now and embrace
it, putting an end to the flight mindset.

The tests of my emotional fortitude continue overnight,
as the Pad Thai I ordered for dinner makes a violent come-
back. The food here is annoying me, and the cautionary tales
littered throughout the online restaurant reviews already se-
verely limit the options. Unfortunately, I can now add another place to the do-not-touch list. As I spend the day in the
villa again, alternating between bed and toilet, the increas-
ing homesickness and travel exhaustion are triggered again.
Having just gone through this process, though, and come
out stronger on the other side, I use it again as an opportunity to cleanse and refocus, rather than feel sorry for myself.
Yes, I feel isolated here and exhausted like in Florence and
parts of Bali, but that's not going to bring me down anymore.

Even walking around the island, recovered from whatever bug Thailand injected into me, seeing couples all over
the place, hand-in-hand and wine-glass-clinking-wine-glass,
a sight that would normally trigger a sad longing within me
is instead a chance for me to continue to find closure. My
mind turns to the failed relationships that have haunted my
past and finds another moment of clarity to exorcise prior
demons. In what feels like a final round of post-mortem analysis, it hits me that the sense of balance I've learned and implemented of late was clearly missing from both of my major

relationships. I think I became almost addicted in my daily consciousness, caring so much about a person without the understanding of how to have a healthy relationship that includes the appropriate amount of balance between me, her, and us. And that all comes from a place of self-awareness, especially self-confidence, that I never found before but am building toward now.

As I read again by the pool, Yoda's last note on empathy is on how critical it is for a leader to possess that level of emotional intelligence. In high school, my senior year politics teacher was my own Robin Williams in *Dead Poet's Society*. She stuck me with the lesson that the best way to succeed in politics, in business, in law, in life, was to understand where the other side was coming from and know their position as well as my own. In a way, that's empathy, and something I need to apply more if I want to get along better with others and be someone people turn to with trust. Just imagine if a leader was so emotionally and mentally stunted that he suffered from extreme narcissism, only caring about himself and not the well-being of others he's supposed to lead. That person would probably be a fat racist disaster of a conman with a hair piece trying to over-compensate for competency and physical deficiencies and go down as the worst president in history.

That was a well-deserved point, but not kind, so I take notes on a number of practices suggested for being more empathetic, open, and sincere, in listening, and in building trust. I head back to the villa for my afternoon meditation and a possible nap when the phone rings.

It's my dad, at four in the morning in Connecticut, and a knot immediately builds in my throat. I know what this call is.

I stay strong and matter of fact with my dad, mirroring the steely demeanor he always carries in these situations. My mom is not ready to talk at first but eventually gets on the phone and describes her mother's last moments, and the waterworks start to pile up in my face, ready to empty out. She tells me about the other night when I called and was saying goodbye to my grandmother, how she was holding on tightly to the phone and then petting the back of it in an eager attempt to hang on and make a final connection with me, almost close enough to touch but so far away.

How I interact with my parents is very much a direct reflection of each of their personalities and influence on my own. My mom brings out the emotional side in me, and when we say we love each other very much and goodbye for now, I hang up the phone and start bawling in a way I don't think I ever have before.

The release of emotions goes in all sorts of directions. Even though we all knew it was coming, her actual passing is obviously very sad. I'm also broken up about being so far away right now, about my mother's grief, and of my own personal self-doubts about how I'm handling it all.

I honestly get worried sometimes about being selfish and uninvested emotionally, especially in this sort of moment of trial. The caring and loving feelings pouring out of me right now are somewhat reassuring as an expression of an empathy I'm not familiar with. I work out the emotions and sit in meditative silence, not timing myself like normal and just allowing the thoughts to wander for a long, long time, before saying one more goodbye and letting her go.

It's still a while longer before I'm able to pull myself off the floor. Since Yoda has been so timely on point, I turn to reading again for understanding, and today's final installment on emotional intelligence, particularly in the interpersonal space. On my relationships with others.

"Social skills" is a broad domain that encompasses a range of abilities in relating and dealing with others, the most important being compassion. Compassion is very closely related to our good friend empathy, but adds an additional element of desire for action. Yoda and friends break down compassion into cognitive, affective, and motivational components (respectively): I understand you, I feel for you, I want to help you. As Yoda identifies studies that show the neurological impact of compassion on the section of the brain that's connected to happiness, one line sticks with me: the happiest state can only be achieved with compassion, which requires engagement in real life with real people.

All the self-analysis and understanding will only take me so far. It's in the interaction with others, the relatability, humility, common purpose, shared human condition, and the resultant physiological reward, that peak happiness is achieved on the interpersonal level.

Combined with maxing out our own personal competence and contentment, we reach that emotional intelligence thing that sounds very evolved and high class. I may even add it to the Special Skills section of my resume on LinkedIn. Yeah right, LinkedIn.

In so many ways, these lessons combined are further evidence for letting the past go, and saying goodbye appropriately. It also means allowing the self room to learn and grow and act along the way non-judgmentally and without anxiety, and in dealing with others with watchful understanding. It's abundantly clear to me now that no one (including myself, for which I'm frequently guilty) should be judging the life choices of others. Everyone has their story.

It's time to move on, and I load my awkward but lighter gear into the longtail for the quick ride to the ferry sitting offshore, ready to break me out of here to the islands of Koh Phi Phi. All of my packing and storage practice to this point has led to this moment of ultimate confrontation as I hop my way now through the Thai islands. My worldly possessions get bunkered down on the top deck of the ferry, covered with a tarp in preparation for the nasty storm we're headed directly into, while I duck below deck with my laptop as *Jonah Hex* plays with Thai subtitles on the monitors. Needless to say, I pass on that gem of a film-watching experience for some writing instead during this hour-long ride. The rain starts to pour, crashing with violence into the windows of the side of the ship. Despite all of my preparation, I didn't check to see that I'd be visiting the area during the May rainy season. Whoops.

As I write on the ride over, I catch myself naturally sitting weirdly with my legs crossed in an open and unusual way, thrown carelessly across the row. I'm pretty sure I've never sat this way before, certainly not in public like this. But I immediately recognize the noticeable physical change, the haphazardness of my legs strewn about, a small, subtle, and silly scene.

On a friend's recommendation, I exit the ferry in Phi Phi and sign up for Bob's Booze Cruise, despite the light drizzle that still permeates the air. The captain (Bob?) assures me this weather is normal and we'll have a beautiful afternoon. Bob's speedboat has about fifteen other partygoing travelers and the beers start flowing almost immediately as the sun reigns down true. In our aquatic travels, we stop at Monkey Beach and feed peanuts to the ones hanging on the side of the cliff, snorkel around a reef, and park in a lagoon at Phi Phi Leh, the smaller of the two islands. We hop into the water with life vests strapped around our legs like diapers so we can float around the lagoon with beers and mixed drinks in hand. When we're empty, we toss the cans back in exchange for a fresh cold one someone flings at us from the boat. But in a very classy way.

I spend most of my time with an attractive couple from Hermosa Beach. Unable to escape L.A. per usual, playing third wheel per usual. The guy's an actor, recently in *Workaholics*, and I won't use his name here but it makes me think of the song from *Euro Trip*. His girlfriend is a bosslady, originally from Brazil, doing big things in L.A. too.

We form a little three-person clique as our boat continues to another nook in the island, unloads us onto a rock formation to climb over and through to a short path in the jungle, and then out of seemingly nowhere, we hit The Beach. Like literally, from the Leo movie. The first steps onto Maya Beach are stop-in-your-tracks beautiful, a panoramic paradise of natural wonder with climbing, jagged, forested cliffs softly surrounding a pool of hidden tranquility. And tourists. Ever the wordsmith, all that can escape my lips is "Wow". We spend the golden hour here taking pictures together and admiring the magnificence of the backdrop, sobering up a little before the ride back to the main island, where the drinks start flowing again. Bob didn't lie about the booze on his cruise.

Back on land, we meet up after dinner at a Muay Thai bar where if you sign up to fight, you get a free booze bucket, the ones famous around here for being infamous. In the annals of weekend stories that contain the words, "What a mistake that was…", the act in question is almost always a round of tequila shots, or here in Southeast Asia, the ordering of a bucket. With that in play, we sit firmly and unmovably planted in the crowd with our simple beers before heading out to the beach bars and their evening fire shows.

Along the way, I'm more tempted than ever to finally get that obligatory tattoo, passing shop after shop open to the walkway, people pulling over into the parlor chair with the nonchalance of grabbing a slice of pizza. I make it through needle-free and slightly regretful, but the three of us find our way to a dance floor and partake in a bit of awkward swaying. This is the type of situation where an odd number only works when the group size is over six. Anything less, and it's not possible to dance in a group and describe the scene as anything besides awkward. We make it work, though, as I break out my patented Dad dance, a stiff re-creation of the moves you'd see if your dad was at a wedding and "Footloose" came on.

On a related note, it's a sad day in any man's life when he comes to the realization that he's just too old for the random drunken dance floor makeout. For me, that moment is distinctly now. It was such a huge part of my life for so many years through college and law school and beyond, but it's time to put that behind me now. Goodbye old friend, whatever your name was.

We make our way over to the bar and kick back with a few rounds of beer, chatting casually about life in L.A., my travels, and this writing project for long enough that our green bottles form a river of sweat bubbles on their sides in tropical splendor.

Deep into the conversation, as I'm relaying some learned lessons about professional happiness, my new buddy smiles back at me shaking his head and says, "Man, you just have this air of relaxed confidence coming through you. It's awesome to see and be around, I love it."

I almost break down right on that bar stool. That is exactly what I'm going for and exactly where I want to be. It's been a long six months and a mountain of effort, to get to that point where a new friend can read it like that in my voice and in my vibe. I tell him how much that means to me to hear, a manifestation of self-confidence that I know has sorely been lacking for... forever, possibly. We make a point to keep in touch and meet up in L.A. sometime, and say our goodbyes.

After a pretty poor round of golf in Phuket that doesn't annoy me at all, my next Thai destination is the island of Koh Samui, most famous for its role in the climactic turning point of *Meet the Parents*. The airport in Phuket is so basic, and not in the usually lovable and charming way. You can tell it, along with many other tourist-exploding destinations in Thailand, is going through a modern facelift to better accommodate the increased traffic, like a kid in high school who makes the varsity football team and has to figure out what to do with his newfound popularity.

Thinking to myself "okay cool, so this is how I die," I board the fun-sized propeller plane on the airport tarmac, bound for either Koh Samui or that island in *Lost* finally. My oddly dark fantasy of meeting up with Jack, Kate, and Sawyer falls flat though, as we make our approach onto the Thai island clear across the mainland. My eyes are locked out the plane's window as we descend over small islands, vibrant waters, smooth sand, and gently-rising green mountaintops. Something indescribable hits me deep down, the sensation of serenity immediate. This place already feels right, and we've yet to hit the runway.

Since I'm puddle jumping around Thailand a few days at a time, far too bougie for questionable accommodations and far too old for a hostel anyway, I opt for a luxury beachfront hotel in my neighborhood of choice, Chaweng Beach. My biggest obstacle to reaching the sand is crossing the resort's massive pool and bar area, but once there, the impeccably cushy white sand sits surprisingly undisturbed by the soft-breaking aquamarine waters of the Gulf of Thailand. Oh, I think I might be able to find some use for these lounge chairs looking over the bay this week. I grab a drink and kick back on one, toasting myself to the sixth month anniversary of starting this crazy, choppy, completely necessary voyage.

It's Mother's Day, so I call home to Mom, who I'm viewing through a new lens for her overwhelming compassion toward others. She's doing well and seems at peace, getting to say goodbye to her mother and seeing her off into the stars above. I'll look out for her up there now too.

I then call over to my grandmother on my dad's side. I tell her about my recent adventures and tentative upcoming plans for the next few weeks. My grandmother's funny because she's always trying to get off the phone before the conversation starts. She's the only person I know that when you call her, she starts the conversation with, "Well I know you're busy, I don't want to keep you." A New Yorker on the move, through and through. As I update her on everything going on, she stops me to tell me that I sound great, and very assured and confident.

It's an observation she wouldn't normally make to me, coming from someone that knows me so well and just a day after my new friend says the same, so I have no choice but to get up and do a little Snoopy happy dance. I jump into the infinity pool overlooking the beach, lean over the edge, and smile.

You guys, we made it.

THE PRESENT CHAPTER
chapter sixteen

The taste wasn't overly strong or distinguishable. My initial impression on contact was that it must have been at least a few days since she'd last brushed her teeth. Certainly not the minty freshness you'd expect from someone who did this for a living. As I wash my face in the bathroom, I smirk at the irony of the off-brand gum and mints that the peddler at the door has laid out for display and sale on the sink. Or maybe they're the top of the line gum and mints. It's hard to tell with everything written in the goofy Thai letters with products I don't recognize.

I've recently made a life decision. A decision I think I'll look back on many years from now with relief. I have chosen to call an audible and run away from the Thai woman who just assaulted my mouth with her tongue, rather than go home with her. I do feel bad though. She had bested about four other "waitresses" for my money, attention, and eventual affection, followed by more of my money. But a quick TripAdvisor search from my table at Henry Africa's in Koh Samui makes no secret that the girls going around dressed in cowboy outfits and barely-there shorts, who are all really good at Connect Four for some reason, are on the job "working the crowd". Single American male drinking alone at the bar, they were swarming and fighting over me while feigning legitimate interest harder than the girls in the Bachelor mansion.

After a few high-pitched verbal altercations I don't understand and some light shoving, the alpha of the bunch won out and comes in to close the deal. But I'm definitely not ready for Fifty Shades of What the Hell is Happening Right Now?, so instead, my mouth retreats from the attack and I pull the "I just need to go to the bathroom for a second" play and sneak away. Now it's a matter of ducking out of the bar, unnoticed and untarnished, for the most part. I peek out from the men's room door. She's turned the other way, so I run out onto the main strip, bound for home and smirking that this is the second time in my life I've had to run away from a "lady of the night". Maybe my days of random public makeouts aren't completely over with after all.

I still need something to get this taste out of my mouth though, and the Burger King open at three in the morning up ahead is calling my name. I grab some chicken nuggets and a double cheeseburger, scarfing down my first fast food order since I started running around the world six months ago.

Strolling back to the resort down the slim sidewalks of Chaweng Beach Road after escaping some very poor decisions, I pause along the way to dip a nugget into the BBQ sauce cup in my bag. This area is much more commercial than my last few stops, large enough to not require warnings about flushing toilet paper, but still mostly limited to one active main road that hugs the beach to the east, with trucks running up and down the street constantly advertising Muay Thai fights "to-night! TOOOOOOONIGHT!!" In the short breaks between the trucks blasting their megaphone messages, vendors on the street, mostly taxi drivers, holler sweet nothings to every passerby. To a very small extent, I can better understand the annoyance women go through with catcalling, minus the overt sexual aggression. My street walking experience is limited to an inquiry every twenty feet, as if I said no to the guy just before but now that I'm actually closer to my destination I would say, "Sure pal, I wasn't feeling it eleven seconds ago, but *now* I'm ready for that taxi."

In the morning, I'm supplied with no shortage of happy places to work from, no limit to the incredible views to take in during downtime, no pause in my desire to rescue all of the random dogs, sleeping in weird places around the island, back to the States with me. The nearby coffee shops already recognize when I come in and know my usual order, wondering where along the way to the beach I got lost in my board shorts and laptop bag. At this point, I have my passport number memorized, its use being constantly necessary to unlock the gate to all the WiFi treasures on the other side.

My favorite spot is sitting outside on the plaza at The Coffee Club, chatting up the barista staff on occasion. I've noticed my interactions with locals has changed, an adaptation to be better understood by limiting my vocabulary. American colloquialisms, minor as they may seemingly be, like "sure", "it's all good", and "I'm all set" fall on deaf and confused ears around here, so it's necessary to tighten up the conversation and speak directly, a tact that helps me communicate more efficiently in general (as you shake your head and ask "where was that 200 pages ago?"). Either way, almost any conversation I have parts ways with prayer hands, an understated act of grace and gratitude that elicits a calming feeling in the closure that I very much appreciate now.

My solo travel skills have gotten better in venturing out for social activities, and I take a day to explore more of Koh Samui outside of my Chaweng bubble. My guided tour starts with petting elephants, and then trekking around on one (I'm sorry! I didn't realize it was bad for them until after). That's followed by a show where one of the elephants scores a soccer goal, and then a crazy man puts his head inside a crocodile's mouth. Because entertainment, I guess. After some ornate Chinese temples, we hop in a 4x4 truck, where I'm volunteered by the guide to ride on top in a makeshift two-seater above the cab, speeding through the jungle on washed out dirt roads to the top of a mountain viewpoint that is worth all the gray hairs added during the trek. From the vista, I look down lovingly on the beaches and northern part of the island, out to the archipelago in the waters off mainland Thailand. The route down the hill is really just massive rock clusters that the truck somehow traverses without splitting into pieces, on our way to check out the island's natural beauties: waterfalls, tigers, and a mummified monk. Our last stop as the sun sets is at the infamous Grandfather and Grandmother rock formations, which are aptly named because the former looks like an old man's you know what, and the latter like a woman's you know what. I learned so much.

As I stroll down the beach for what is my new nightly activity, the sand wispy-soft under my feet while I walk off the day and unwind before bed, singers croon at two-top tables on the beach, romance present in abundance as couples take in the scene overlooking the sea. Soothing lights run up the southern hillside of the bay surrounding Chaweng Beach while off in the distance, flashes of lightning from heat or faraway storms provide a natural show to the crowds of two at a time. A hint of bass-bumping house music somewhere down the beach entertains the reveler crowd, much smaller this season but with venues that tease a livelier nightlife in another time. From both aspects of social interaction, just a short month or two ago I might have felt longingly for one or the other, or both. But right now, I'm unapologetically content on my own.

For a solo traveler with an extroverted tendency, embracing being alone has been one of the hardest parts of all this (what's up, Florence?). I think I may have just figured out how to be happy in that place and really appreciate that time, while simultaneously coming to the conclusion that I'd prefer to do this all with someone by my side, if I can find her. I've learned there's a difference between being alone and being lonely, and how to be okay by myself but accepting that I'm finally ready for something more now. As much as I love this place and doing my thing, when I come back here next time, I'm bringing someone with me.

The resort staff would appreciate that as well. Almost every time I interact with them, they're confused by my lack of companionship, a single unicorn on a beach known for its tendency for pack life. The two champagne glasses in my room when they present my complimentary bottle, the references to the plural in the hotel material, the welcome to "Mr. Restivo and party". It feels like the scene in *Forgetting Sarah Marshall*, when Jason Segal's character shows up at the resort's restaurant in Hawaii and Jonah Hill isn't sure how to handle seating and serving a single guest, asking if he wants a magazine to handle the boredom and depression of not having anyone to join him.

The art of dining alone is a skill I've had to develop for most of the last half year, and well beyond that given my remote work life. In some ways, modern communication lines help, where I can carry on a conversation with someone via text while not spitting all over them when talking while eating. My mom always told me people don't like that very much.

More importantly for me, being one who struggles heavily with my relationship with food, it allows for an opportunity of mindful eating. Far, far too often I choose meals thinking too much in the short term and impulsively based on what looks good on paper, and then when it comes, I eat distracted by any manner of outside stimuli and appreciate the food with minimal effect. So the calories are never really worth it.

But dining alone so much, it forces me to be more conscious both in meal selection and when actually eating, and by physically enjoying a meal it adds to the old happiness tank. Like this appropriately sized pasta dish I'm loving at this decent Italian joint on the main road, sipping slowly on chilled white wine like it's an endless summer, which it sort of is.

Koh Samui is the perfect blend for me right now, with just about everything I envisioned when I first developed an idea for my remote work life in the Pacific islands. I walk out from my beachfront pool onto a serene but active setting and stroll through the sand, passing bars, restaurants, resorts, and massage huts along the way. The activity is manageable, at least during the slow season. The resorts are clean and well-kept without breaking the bank, and mine has a nice gym for a morning workout. I cool off after at the beach or the pool, sometimes both, grab healthy and good eats at one of the many open-air spots nearby, and frequent one of my regular coffee shops with WiFi, necessary afternoon air conditioning, and menu items with avocado. All the essentials in life.

Almost all of the bars, beachfront or not, have a fun island theme, and a laidback vibe permeates the area. There are modern conveniences and a little taste of the west with places like the always reliable 7/11 and the omnipresent Hard Rock Café, ignorable for the most part but enough to make a basic American bro feel a pinch of comfort. And of course, those trucks screaming about Muay Thai fights with a regularity that almost seems welcoming to the natural aesthetic. Even though I'm probably part of a very small group, possibly a group of one, that's actually doing the digital nomad act here, this porridge may be what our Goldilocks needs: not too quiet and food poison-y, not too wild and druggy, but most of all, just feels right.

Given how much I catch myself saying the word "vibe" lately, my perceptors must be operating at full capacity. What I've learned from meditation and recent emotional intelligence training is to pick up on the moments when I'm not in pain, and be happy because of that, through an appreciation for the normalcy. It's a matter of tapping into that natural state, creating this sense of subconscious contentment. From that starting point, I can more fully notice and value the feelings of pleasure when they arise, raising emotional perception across the board and an opportunity to create those moments more frequently.

As the emotional intelligence increases and gets put into practice, I notice I'm journeying inside less with existential pondering, being much more self-aware and confident in my mental state. My notes lately are trending toward a focus on the external happenings around me, further evidence that the heavy lifting internally has been completed for now. The recognition and applications are coming easier, the missing pieces all along now falling into place as I understand myself better.

Instead of heading up to Chiang Mai as originally planned in continuation of the chase, I embrace what's working for me and extend my stay in Koh Samui for another six nights, moving to a new hotel down the road closer to my action: the coffee shops during the day, social activity at night, and superfood bowl spot at all times.

I still hate the word settling, especially when used in the context of life choices. It just has such a negative connotation to me, an insinuation of giving up and defaulting into what's in front of me at a particularly random point in time. I've talked a lot about chasing happy, with my lingering concern there being the ability to stop chasing and start embracing when it gets to that "know it when you see it" place. But I'll consider that moment my version of choosing to settle, when the feeling is right and only then, and only for as long as it's right.

Even though I'm generally anti-"day at the beach", I step out from my treetop villa at Buri Rasa Resort and set up for the afternoon in the loungers in the sand in front of the hotel. While taking a quick dip in the water to cool off, the moment rushes over me as I walk back to my chair to lay out in the sun. This is now my favorite part of the experience. Sorry London, and to a lesser extent, Bali. I'll always appreciate those spots for what they are, and how they set the course for my development. But being here now, near the nadir of this trip, so much further along in my personal progression and with such a different perspective, in this near-perfect surrounding that I might've drawn up in an act of fiction, I know we've reached this journey's peak and come to the other side. This is my reward for a life well-challenged and well-lived these past six months. When I originally contemplated the concept of Love Languages and theorized whether the idea of a Happiness Tank could similarly be implemented, from conscious choices I make to achieve what is right for me, my own tank filling to the brim at this moment was what I manifested in my mind.

It makes me wonder for a minute what this feeling is that's so unfamiliar to me. Is it that ever-elusive present? That forgotten friend in the middle that constantly cedes attention in my mind to the wonders of the past and future. I think I found it. It's right here. Now.

All this time I've been chasing happiness, trying to find a way to be okay with where I was in my adulting life, anxious and unable to let go of both the good and bad of my past, anxious and unable to decide what to do with my future. But the only way to really experience that sought-after contentment is by paying attention in the now. It just makes sense, too. Right now, in this very moment, whenever that is, is the only time it's ever actually possible to experience that feeling.

Walking the beach at night now, I physically feel an overwhelming flow of positive emotions, and know I still need some practice to get used to this new sense of internal balance and understanding.

As I glide across the pillow-light sand, the darkness of the night sky cut by the neon lights of Chaweng's commercial vendors, lazy rolling waves off to the side sending a faint smell of the sea wafting into the senses, I get sent into a reflective and contemplative mood, but with much less pressure or stress guiding the inquiry, almost from a place of completion. From living my best life.

This is all a lot of words to basically say, I feel really happy right now.

One of the absurd things in my mind is thinking back to L.A. and how I lived there for so long, in one of the healthiest and most laidback but active outdoor places in the world where it's always beach season, a setup that obviously can make me happy with the right outlook, and yet I never carried this mindset I have now. Here I am, getting out, exercising properly, meditating, eating acai bowls and making healthy choices, sleeping and living well on the road, but in L.A. I never used to think this way. Of course it was all available to me, but the bad habits I had established were so hard to break. It's the same approach that was missing in the emotional intelligence department as well, never taking the appropriate time to pause, think, and act wisely. The regular lifestyle has a way of quicksanding into monotony, losing track of bigger picture considerations. I look back on that period partly with regret, but more so with relief that I made the decision to break the chain in decisive fashion, and hopefully bring a new attitude back with me, wherever that may be.

This is adulting with mindfulness. Paying attention, on purpose, non-judgmentally, in the present moment. Happiness may not be luck, but it doesn't have to be a struggle either. It's a matter of making the right choices, putting myself in the right settings, and allowing it to just be.

On my last day, after a little work hustle (yes, I'm still working at this point, kind of), I kick back on the loungers in between the pool and the beach and pick up my copy of *Into the Wild*. I've read this before and seen the movie a few times, but have been saving reading it again until the near-end of my trip. The message of the book is one that I use to check myself and my often-wandering, often-independent mind, my cautionary tale and reminder not to stray too far and stay grounded in my roots and my base.

I close up shop as the sun goes down and spend my last night in Chaweng with a relaxing dinner at the resort and a long walk on the beach again. The celestial majesty of the midnight sky calmly shines its guiding lights, beacons, calling the wanderer home.

Now that I've seen all of Koh Samui and affirmed my love, it's always good to check out the neighbors and make sure I can get along with them too. For my last few days in Thailand, and ringing in my last weeks on the international road, I add a couple of quick nearby trips to the itinerary and head to sea, bound for Koh Tao.

There are times when this experience has left me utterly speechless and in awe of my surroundings, and the top deck of the ferry from Samui to Tao is one of those instances. I sit in admiration of the expansiveness of everything around me in 360-degree form, the water stretching as far as the eye can see, only disrupted by random rock formations curiously emerging to punctuate the horizon line. I have a weird craving to explore all of these islands, especially the uninhabited treasures. It reminds me of the summers as a kid, taking the canoe out with my grandfather and invading the shores of any tiny islands in Long Island Sound that we could reach without capsizing. Who had been there before, what could we find? The thrill of the newness and exploration into the unknown and untouched. Alright yeah, I most definitely was a pirate in a prior life.

We pull up into Koh Tao, a playground for divers and Europeans, sometimes at the same time. As I sign the ferry's required manifest, no other American is listed and I'm almost emboldened by my discovery of this still relatively hidden gem. Although, it's also possible they didn't sign out of defiance or naivete, both very on brand.

The island is much smaller than Samui and far less commercial. The beach isn't as nice as others I've been to recently, but it has character, and I hate myself for saying that, but it's the first word that popped into my head. Longtails are parked off-shore and banyan trees reach casually out into the airspace over the sand, stretching their arms just far enough for an old wooden swing to hang as if directed by an Instagram influencer.

My number one bucket list travel experience is staying in a hut over the water in Bora Bora or Tahiti, but I'm saving that for a trip with a special lady, probably honeymoon related. Somewhat similar, but available to me in my single state, is a cottage on the beach in Thailand, in the sand with waves crashing thirty feet away through the palm trees and beach pines. These are my digs for my night in Koh Tao, a hammock on the front porch of the cottage available for me to properly absorb this storybook scene. I'm thrilled to have this moment, but a part of me continues with that growing feeling that I wish I had someone here with me, less from a place of loneliness and more from a desire to be able to share this experience in real-time with someone.

I'm able to catch a few hours of the fresh ocean air from my hammock in the morning, looking up obsessively from my reading and writing to soak in the scene. Keeping with the spirit of my island adventuring of late, I grab a taxi boat longtail to Koh Nang Yuan, a small island formation just a touch off the northwest coast of Koh Tao.

The island setting is a not-so-hidden gem marrying beaches and cliffs in an impressive display of God's creative hand. Nang Yuan is just as stunning and colorful as it is congested by Chinese tourists in neon-orange life vests attempting to snorkel the crystal waters on all sides. The prevalence of all the tourists doesn't deter my beach day, which is a perfect amount of time before I normally get bored anyway, in one of the best locations I may ever visit. Even the way in and out is mesmerizing, along a picturesque wooden maze of boardwalks over cool steel-gray rock formations, white sand, and ridiculously clear teal water. I meet my Uber boat driver there to take me back to the mainland and the ferry for the next island.

Koh Phangan is home to the world-famous Full Moon Party, a regular rave taken to another level like it's on steroids, or more accurately, ecstasy. I doubt I can handle that level of rager anymore, but my timing doesn't match up with the lunar calendar as it is, so I'll avoid that potential pitfall. In any event, I figure the Haad Rin area around the beach party scene would still be active and cool to check out during off-dates, though.

Nope.

Block after block is a deserted ghost town that boggles the mind for a Friday night. Hostels are dark without even bothering to open their doors for business. Restaurants and bars are closed, with the few that are open showcasing staff just sitting around playing Solitaire or something. Big fail on my part. But at least I don't have any FOMO by staying in while something epic goes on nearby. I grab a light poolside dinner back at the hotel and am in my room early to relax and watch a movie, choosing *Crazy, Stupid, Love* on Netflix, a flick I normally save for airplane rides since it's always available and always satisfying.

Back in Bangkok for a couple of nights on my way out of Thailand, I'm open to a little adventure this round. I check the swipe apps quickly, but the unexpectedly high presence of ladyboys is a game-changer, causing me to pause for a second too many times out of uncertainty, before I just give up on the idea entirely. I'm still in the mood for a "one night in Bangkok" experience, though, so despite some rain and a thirty-minute Uber ride (that somehow only costs four bucks), I bounce around to some bars on Khao San Road of *Hangover II* fame. After a few beers, Thailand's equivalent to New Orleans' Bourbon Street starts to get predictably rowdy, but I'm riding solo in an area of mostly large groups, both Thai locals and western tourists. I'm not getting much traction meeting anyone, but I'm also not trying too hard, content to hang back and take in the absurdity of the scene.

Planning on calling it a night after one more beer, I head into my last bar and find an old Thai man, pushing eighty years old, out on the dance floor and living it up on his own. A preview of my future flashes hilariously before my eyes.

My man is a big hit, and as I'm sitting back watching him work, another group of Americans is doing the same nearby. A gorgeous girl breaks free of that group to come over to talk, and we hit it off for a good twenty minutes or so, laughing and having good conversation back and forth. She's young though (22), fresh out of Georgia Tech, and frankly way out of my league but for some reason, it's all working. We teach the old man the moves to the YMCA song, but after the song she fairly abruptly ends our rendezvous with a, "Well, it was nice talking to you."

I'm a bit bummed and confused, and alone again, so to stall and figure out my next move, most likely to the exit, I take a bathroom break. While I wash my hands at the mirror, I realize that I'm drenched in sweat from the summer humidity, bar heat, and dancing, and this light purple dress shirt I'm wearing is now a dark purple. I look ridiculous, and we very quickly have solved the mystery of the disappearing hot coed. At this point, what can I do but laugh, shrug my sweaty shoulders, head back to the hotel, and leave the country entirely?

It's on to the next and theoretical final stop in this expedition, Tokyo, the land of sake, great public transportation, karaoke rooms, fast food curry, being efficient at stuff, Mario Kart, Wipeout-style TV game shows, ramen, and puppy cafes. And sushi, I guess.

The Roam location for my stay is perfectly centered on a hilltop on the border of the Akasaka and Roppongi neighborhoods. A left turn out of the house and down the hill brings me into Akasaka, a clean, shockingly quiet, business-friendly area with a ton of small restaurants, shops, and cafes. The taxis catch my eye, with a classic style as if they're suspended in time from 1974, but with doors that the driver can pop open and close with the push of a button from 2074. Japan things. My favorite Japanese fast food curry place Coco Ichibanya is nearby, past a gym along the way that I quickly sign up for to combat any curry trips I'll be making this month. A right turn out of the house and down the hill brings me into Roppongi, a livelier, more touristy area with oodles of bars, nightlife, and places for noodles.

The Roam facility is a bit of a shock to the expectations, compared to the London experience. The building is more "apartment complex-y" than "Real World house-y," a little less homey and welcoming, but with great Japanese flair through-out that gives it some character. The operation and the people here, in true Japanese fashion, seem to be a bit more com-partmentalized than the London crew and setup. It still has the modern-thinking features of a Roam property that I ap-preciate: my own private space in a Japanese-style bedroom, common work areas, and a huge, open space kitchen.

As I get myself settled, I head through my Hinokicho Park backyard to the grocery store in the Tokyo Midtown shopping area and play a somewhat successful game of "what the hell is this?" through the aisles, stocking my fridge and counter space at Roam. In another example of Japan doing things bet-ter than the rest of the world, the grocery checkout process is efficiently designed so that the slower part of bagging goods is handled at a separate stand after checkout, so that people can move more quickly through payment without holding ev-eryone else up behind them. People hate grocery lines, make them quicker. People want more puppies in public, give them puppies to play with. Japan just gets it.

The land of the rising sun is a fitting tagline, as my all-white, eastern-facing room with huge windows and curtains that barely contain the sun let all of the light in bright and early each morning. As a result, my day starts before five in my authentically-styled bedroom, mattress on the floor, shoes at the door, with minimal furniture or knickknacks for decoration. I'm gladly in bed by ten like a good soon-to-be thirty-one-year-old on a weeknight.

One of my favorite parts of the Roam experience is the weekly community dinners; one of my favorite meals of all time is breakfast for dinner. When those two are combined into one setting, it makes for a happy American boy in Tokyo. So, if you're keeping score at home, go ahead and add "breakfast for dinner" to day-drinking and being on the beach at night to things that are better when done out of order, in true rule-breaking form.

My task tonight is pancake duty, and for a house of twenty plus with awkward cooking supplies, it gets a little heated in the kitchen, but I can stand it. Over eggs and sausage and some damn good pancakes, our housemates exchange recent travel stories and future plans, and it hits me that I'm the seasoned vet at this point, on the other side of the discussion from where I was early on in London.

The new Roam crew organizes a night out on a Thursday, finding a small open-air food truck plaza in Omotesandō with a healthy mix of locals and ex-pats. Our squad is a UN-style collection: our Japanese community manager, forty-five-year-old Homer from Ohio who's gay, at least six foot eight, and my closest friend in Tokyo now, a Polish woman, a couple from Canada, a Singaporean woman visiting for the week, and a handful of young Germans who have taken to me rather quickly. The more adventurous of the bunch stay out as we continue on to bars in Shinjuku, joining Homer as he meets up with someone in Tokyo's LGBT-friendly neighborhood. I bail after performing my proper wingman duties, swinging first through the historic Golden Gai area on my way home as a reminiscent stroll down narrow memory lanes. I find my favorite dive karaoke bar and pop in for a laugh and an Instagram story before heading back to the house.

Going out on Thursday allows me to set up my preferred weekend activity schedule: staying in for a quiet Friday night, having a productive Saturday morning, and either day-drinking the afternoon or doing something else fun before a night out.

This particular Saturday is the day before my thirty-first birthday, and my new German friends have decided to head up the celebration. Normally, since I'm the planner in my friend groups, I take the lead in these situations and organize the birthday as an excuse to get people together. But the Germans are happy to coordinate, so I lean back and enjoy the ease of instinctually making new friends like this and becoming close enough right away to take trips together without hesitation.

Early Saturday morning, the three Germans (all of whom are about twenty-two from Munich), and I board a train to the southeast coast of Japan to the small beach town of Kamakura, an hour outside of Tokyo. We grab coffee at a local hole-in-the-wall before strolling around the neighborhood through unique and quaint shops and residences, shrines offering quickie wedding services and the granting of wishes with a donation and proper prayer protocol, touristy areas with more Japanese structures, a hidden lunch spot behind a house, and eventually to the beach overlooking Sagami Bay. It's tough for me to get excited about a relatively plain beach like this, considering the ones I'm just coming from (not humble bragging,

I swear), but the experience is still really cool as we take in the sunset with drinks on the water while Mt. Fuji smolders in faint perspective off in the background.

We catch the train back to Tokyo, regroup, and grab dinner at my new favorite ramen restaurant Ippudo, around the corner from Roam. I implore these guys not to sing the birthday song to me, because it sucks and I'm starting a movement against it. I'm also starting a movement to bring "LOL" back after it fell out of favor the last few years, so get on that. Sitting around while people chant and sing terribly in unison at you for far too long is a dreadfully awkward and unnecessary tradition that needs to go. Can we agree from now on to just do a shot together, and call that sufficient birthday acknowledgment? Especially for birthdays after twenty-five (when you can finally rent a car) or thirty (when you're officially old).

The celebration continues from there, birthday song-free, to a small market area in the Ebisu neighborhood called Yokocho, a compact indoor shopping street with a low ceiling and tiny restaurants on both sides of the walkway. People sit at squished picnic tables or bistro settings, drinking on the "street" and carrying out very un-hushed conversations. We order beers and sake while taking note of the heavy presence of drunken Japanese businessmen in the crowd, a surprising amount of whom carry handbags or clutches. The latter is so pronounced that we order a bottle of wine and play a game of "drink when a man walks by with a purse", and the bottle goes down very quickly.

While we play our game, three businessmen join our table, only one of whom speaks English. They play their casted roles well with the senior statesman, the junior next-in-line, and the young up-and-comer, deferring to the elder manager to call the shots, even if he's hammered and leading the group sloppily around the streets. After the boss orders drinks for the gentlemen, we engage in some quickly escalating personal detail, learning about his divorce and his inappropriate opinion on American airline stewardesses. He's very complimentary of the girls in our foursome, using his broken English to repetitively call them models, but is mostly harmless and we share some laughs. He wins my heart when he calls me "sexy Bruce Willis", which I don't entirely get, but I'll take it. We do a shot with our new friends as midnight brings in my thirty-first year, then make our move out of that scene to a classic sake bar before finding a karaoke dive with all sorts of available costumes. We don Mario hats, wigs, blow-up guitars, and other props, crush some Backstreet Boys on the mic, and call it a night around four in the morning, as even sexy Bruce Willis has his limits.

My stay here is passing quickly, as I go about my business with mostly uneventful tranquility. It's not quite gym, tan, laundry, but it's pretty close, with less hair gel and more ramen and curry. The Akasaka neighborhood is incredibly clean and so quiet that I just realized after all this time that I've yet to see a homeless person on the streets or hear a car horn. The peacefulness is readily apparent.

My workspace venue of choice during the week is the outdoor patio that fronts the park in the Tokyo Midtown commercial complex. There's a casual contentment I find in the non-confinement of working outside in a city landscape, business carrying on all around me, while taking in unobstructed sunshine. Plus, there's the benefit of seeing in a single work session a group of go-carts speeding by and dressed as the characters from Mario Kart, followed by cameras chasing a couple on a reality TV "date" which appears to be the Japanese version of *The Bachelor*. Even in Tokyo, I can't get away from the show spoilers.

In more *Jersey Shore* fashion, my new family here adopts a Sunday group dinner policy, this episode at Da Michele Pizzeria, a spinoff of the famous original joint in Naples and just as good. Our squad walks the pizza off exploring the Ebisu and Daikanyama neighborhoods together, past so many cool-looking coffee shops and outdoor areas to try. Every time I walk around a city like this, I reconfirm my feelings that I need this type of development in the place I live. Maybe it's my appreciation for good real estate design, or seeing people be productive or social in a community, but something about that surrounding makes me happy in that moment. And I don't even really like coffee.

One of the guys leads us around and I hang back a bit chatting with one of the German girls, Arete. My relationship with her is entirely platonic, and I feel really good about that. Despite the ease in which we get along and her beauty, dark features, thin, and tall with kindness bursting from her face, at no point is there any kind of tension there. It's an unusual place for me, still recovering from decades of anxiety, acne, bad hair, and weight yo-yo's. But through regular conversation with her now, there's a shift in my mind that I don't have to feel like every moment, thought, or statement I make in a situation with a female or prospective beau is critical and needs to be perfect. From a place of newfound confidence, I can be myself without games or hiding my personality, and if it's not right, I'll know it and that's okay.

The feeling of connectedness through all the birthday shout-outs back in the States last week, combined with the care of new friends and housemates, some even going out of their way to put on a celebration for me here, really helps to change my definition of "home". That terribly lame cliché that home is inside you, is kind of, sort of true. A state of mind more than a state of place. At times, I've been able to form levels of connectedness that feel like home, even without a residence. It's why my heart breaks a little harder right now when I see video of a terror attack on the London Bridge, a place I walked over in my home city just a few months ago.

On a much lighter note, it's also why I feel happy helping Arete cook an important dinner in the kitchen for her boss and coworkers, chopping veggies and prepping her German dishes. I generally like to cook, but it's tough to be motivated to do so with complexity or in bulk like this when I'm only sharing it with the Tupperware in my fridge.

Being on the road alone has forced me to get better about being less territorial and more welcoming to letting new friends in more quickly, as I have here and recently. A new position of openness and vulnerability. And maybe, just maybe, I hate everyone a little bit less now.

And his heart grew three sizes that day.

I continue to poke around a bit on the swipe apps, though the only one which seems to be active in Tokyo is Tinder. I also sign up for Hinge again in New York, planning on heading back for real this Fall, and make a few promising connections.

I can't even with the girls on Tinder in Tokyo, though.

The app is pretty humorously useless, as I end up swiping left on about a hundred profiles in a row before giving up and deleting it. In my not-that-small sample size, the trending themes of the profiles are faces hidden intentionally by some object, back of head photos, distance shots only, cat pictures, weird cat filters from Snapchat or something, and a written message making it clear she REALLY doesn't want to just hook up, be a tour guide, or give language lessons. I get a match with a normal profile and attractive girl named Saori, but I never send a message. Is it too late now to say Saori (for this joke)?

Crickets chirp wildly in the background.

Moving on.

There's been a bit of a thought process shift of late as I ready for what's next. I find myself taking considerably less notes and pictures, sharing less on social media in search of validation, and just living. McConaughey-style.

That aspect of being in the present is where my motto of "what's next?" wasn't getting it quite right. While I love the idea of putting the past behind and looking forward, I didn't give enough appreciation to the now part of it. In reality, even though it implies a future focus, what's next is just another way of saying, "What can I do *now*, let's go, bring it on."

By being in the moment, with a level of understanding and mindfulness, that should allow me to confidently deal with everything that life throws my way going forward. No matter the end result or choice, that may be the only silver bullet I have in this life for dealing with things appropriately, and finding happy. And hopefully along the way, I can handle it all without taking life too seriously, making fun of myself a bit, but with love, as I continue to learn and grow.

When I originally sketched out what my big picture theme in Tokyo would be, I thought I might discuss in painfully thorough detail my feelings on having kids as part of a larger conversation on the modern family. Japan is a good backdrop for that topic because of their critically dwindling marriage and birth rates. I would then relate it back to the U.S. and our modern trends, like dating longer and marrying later, or potentially viewing the institution as a whole as an outdated construct, while choosing to have less kids than previous generations if at all. But while it's an interesting subject, it's not really relevant to my travels as I anticipated it might be, so I'm passing on that deeper dive.

Many moons ago, a part of me thought I might get some clarity on my feelings toward that future question, and while to a minor extent I confirmed my general inclinations against the prospect right now, it hasn't played a major role in this journey. That's because I'm not ready to answer that question, and I don't think I could or should without a partner. Just like all the important choices I make as I adult, it's a decision that should come from a place of strong emotional intelligence, from solid self-awareness, and with this one in particular, made in conjunction with another I understand as well. So, there's no need to make grand proclamations just yet. I'm confident I can deal with that as the topic arises, without forcing the issue here. I will say, though, these Japanese kids running around the park right now are really damn cute, and darn it if they aren't really well-behaved too. Kind of makes me warm to the idea a bit.

What I do have going forward, though, is a game plan, my trusty *The Emotionally Intelligent Guide to Adulting without FOMO, Sponsored by Mindfulness* pamphlet, and the start of learning and knowing how to approach it all properly.

One of the most important things is a happy work life, finding that right situation that combines my desired flexibility and lack of oversight with a more purposeful challenge to find flow. Resolving that situation is going to instruct so much of the direction and next steps for me, from where to be located and for how long, to taking dating seriously again and developing future objectives personally and socially. I might be able to develop a rough sketch to satisfy my planner personality, but it can't be with too much rigidity, a weakness in some respects that I'm realizing through the challenges of this voyage. I need to be better at managing my anxiousness and frustration when I'm off schedule. I consider myself a Yes Man, but really those moments mainly come when I'm not mentally committed to another idea already.

Along similar lines, finding a healthy balance of social and personal time is something I need to be mindful of, choosing appropriate spots for enjoying each that match my extroverted attitude. That goes for managing all options and potential distractions too, whether in the overabundant city atmosphere or the isolation of a more limited setting. And nice weather doesn't hurt.

Across the board, though, the most important application for me has been and will be self-confidence, a term I never truly appreciated until now. In so many aspects of my previous life, whether in dating, social anxiety issues, or professional and financial status, this basic quality has been lacking. I can feel mine starting to grow, even just from the knowledge of the problem in and of itself. But with a target now on the root of so many issues, and a better understanding of what to do, I may not feel so lost anymore.

I learned in law school and on the bar exam, the standard way of structuring a test answer is through the IRAC formula: identifying the *Issue*, supplying the relevant *Rule*, *Applying* the presented facts to the elements that make up the rule, making a *Conclusion* based on the application of facts. Recognizing the issue in the first place, knowing the breakdown and roots of that issue, and applying the principles to the case at hand are where all the points were scored, a lesson I wasn't so quick to learn in my forever impatient mind.

In so many ways, the ending I come up with now, the conclusions I draw are not nearly as important as the process to get there.

As I prepare to return to the U.S. and test out all these grand theories I've developed with my new set of tools, the only thing I'm worried about now is preparing my speech for the thousand inevitable questions of, "How was the trip?" As un-penetrating a question as, "How was your day?" and "Do you like pizza?"

But it's time to set sail on my overnight flight to LAX. It's going to be tough for me to sleep, being terrible at it anyway, but with the added excitement of seeing all my friends again after months of clamor from home of my return. I try my best with a sleeping pill, a round of sake, and two glasses of wine on the plane, and still only get about four hours of sleep, time-traveling so that I land before I left. I Uber up to the Valley to pull my car from storage, check into the Viceroy in Santa Monica, and while everyone is still working and whatnot on a Friday afternoon, I nap and wait. I shop for new clothes for the first time in months on the Third Street Promenade and meet up with a few friends for dinner, but we all lay low with a big party planned at Malibu Wines the next day for a birthday and my welcome back. We share a few laughs, a few beers, and after some initial stories from the road, it all sort of returns to normal. I'm back at the hotel ready to crash around eleven.

This is the way the trip ends. Not with a boom of undisputed and triumphant conquering, but with a whisper of quiet resolution. The world around me remains intact and largely unmoved, doing their thing while oblivious to the personally monumental lessons learned and demons slayed on my now-concluding epoch.

I realize now that everyone is likely dancing their own tango with adulthood in an unspoken grind. But guys, we're going to be more open about it now and get through this adulting thing together. And we may even open our own retirement portfolios someday. Not this week, though, because we have that boozy brunch on Sunday first.

I unpack the remaining items from my much more manageable baggage, now a guest in a place I called home for so long. As I reach the bottom of an empty suitcase, I say it again, that familiar question I ask myself often as I look to the future, this time with the apprehension dissipated, leaving only appreciation and resolve, along with my trademark smirk: what's next?

TLDR

Clear eyes, full hearts, can't lose.

THE NEXT CHAPTER

epilogue

Pop-pop-pop-pop-pop ...

"Well, it looks like North Korea's here to attack us."

The short burst of popping sounds land a few dozen feet behind us near the concession stands, sounding like firecrackers from some asshole kids and prompting my sarcastic initial comment.

Up on stage, Jason Aldean continues with his set, pumping country music out into the open desert air on a perfect Fall Sunday on the Las Vegas Strip. It's been an incredible reunion with my California friends, our first time at the Route 91 Harvest Festival. The lineup was amazing for a country music fan, much better than the competing Stagecoach Festival in Palm Springs that we usually attend every April. With my being in Asia at the time and with Nestor's sister Helen about to give birth in May, our group opted to try this concert in Vegas instead. Three days of music and drinks, sun and fun, culminating in the final act of the festival with the always enjoyable Jason Aldean wrapping up a legendary weekend.

The pops behind us accelerate in pace, intensity, and proximity. We pause our conversation and turn in growing confusion. Right away, Helen picks up on something really wrong, maybe tapping into the new mother intuition, and yells at our group of twelve that we need to get out of there. The next few seconds go by instantly and eternally, a lump builds in my throat, and my instincts finally catch up to me. The music stops and the band scatters off stage. People around us drop to the cement of this converted parking lot venue. We turn and run for our lives.

I always anticipated that this post-script section would be a collection of tests to the new psyche, a series of speed humps, hiccups, turbulence, or any other appropriate synonym that might cause a bumpy landing on my reentry into the world of old. I felt it from the first night as I jumped right back into my friend circles in L.A. and Orange County in my initial weeks back in the U.S. The idea that nothing had really changed was both hugely comforting and disappointedly terrifying at the same time.

Granted, in the grand scheme of things, being away for a little over seven months isn't a crazy long time or anything, especially considering the availability of contact through social media and some old-school texting. The problem I face, that no one else knew or could understand, was that the time meant so much more to me. To me, the experience was such an impactful, life-changing and defining opportunity, taking place for many months while everyone I know went about their usual business, admiring the romanticism and adventure of the journey from afar via Instagram and the like. But coming back into that world, their world now, with all of the emotionally-driven personal development, the freshly-inspired self, and wild tales from places previously unknown, suddenly the normalcy and familiarity of being back amongst the usual takes a big whack at that supposedly new and improved person, knocking me back into an unwanted reality.

I approach my return with caution, a fearful and watchful eye to preventing a failing letdown after all the hard work, doing my best to carry the lessons with me in my cargo. But I'm quickly anxious to get out of L.A. again, and even just this mini-return is enough confirmation for me.

Out with some friends at my favorite Santa Monica beachside bar Big Dean's, I run into an old law school classmate. He's a new father now and tells me how jealous he's been living vicariously through me in following my travels. We talk a bit about Thailand and about my writing, which is odd because other than my family, a few close friends, and random people on the road, I haven't really been releasing that latter detail to other friends. Before he says goodbye, he tells me not to stop, to keep doing what I'm doing because it's inspirational.

For some reason, that little exchange with a friend I haven't spoken to in years is a kick in the ass to get me going again. I'm not sure why I've been holding back with the rest of the world about what I'm doing and the reality of my emotional experience, but sharing that little bit opens me up again. From there, I start to have more conversations with friends on a deeper level about our collective struggles in adulting, realizing that most everyone is in that same boat, and offering my amateur, dime store psychology advice when I can.

In a conversation with my friend Bali Mia about this re-entry process, I pose the question to her about falling back to our natural self after traveling, and her response floors me. She thinks her truest self is the one away from her past, away from the place where so much history, and pre-determined obligations, and the trappings of entrenched habits, and fear of judgments, and expectations of her, are formed. It's outside of that "comfort zone" where she's able to act naturally, free of those burdens.

I think she's right. And that's the challenge to sort out from here.

I happily leave L.A. behind for good after roughly nine tumultuous years. Staying that long is the weird exception to the rule. Most people come, have their fun in the endless summer, and move back to something more "real". Nine years is too long, and too much time to develop bad habits that I fall back into in my short return, involving the standard booze overload, bad food, and unproductivity. I pack it all up again, selling and emptying out my storage unit, and loading up the car before it finally hits me in anticlimactic fashion in my last few hours that this is really goodbye. And a bit of good riddance (not to you, friends, just the city).

My intro into the New York City apartment scene is rough and eye-opening, and my original idea of spending three months in a furnished sublet in West Village for a decent price quickly falls apart piece by piece. I end up paying a buttload to take over a lease in the Village for eight months and having to furnish it myself. But as soon as I sign the lease, I feel good about establishing a bit of a base to work from, and date a bit, and have a social life again. My best female friend is just a PATH ride away in Hoboken, and I easily fit in with her group for weeknight kickball games, along with many non-kickball nights out and about. At the end of September, I head to Las Vegas to reunite with old friends.

Pop-pop-pop-pop-pop-pop-pop-pop-pop-pop...

I don't have much experience with guns. I shot a couple one time at an indoor range in L.A. My mother always ruled against them in our house after dealing with my grandfather getting mistaken for a bear and shot while hunting when she was three. Violent video games weren't really allowed, and water guns were okay, but I could tell she wasn't happy about it. So it takes me a few seconds to realize that the rapid fire "pop" sounds are bullets flying at me.

At this point, our entire group is running toward the exit opposite of Mandalay Bay, a few hundred feet from the centerstage area where we stood most of the weekend. We scatter frantically. I see Nestor drop about ten feet in front of me, in between and on top of two of our friends, but in the haze of my mind I can't tell if they were dropping for cover or if someone tripped. I think it's the latter and continue on, calling out in search of Helen as my main priority while bullets buzz all around us, ricocheting off the ground and coming from seemingly all directions. She's about fifty feet ahead and near the exit already though, and yells back at me to grab our friend Kay. I run back and grab Kay's hand, looking past her toward the ground where Nestor and the girls are still down, wondering why they've yet to get moving. [3]

My first instinct is to find a place for cover, so we run another hundred feet and crouch behind the front right wheel of a police SUV parked at the concert exit as the pops continue from somewhere and everywhere across the venue. The rest of our crew seems to be booking it down the street or over the fence and onto the airfield across the road, but I'm unsure if everyone is safe in the chaos of thousands. In the moment of pause, my mind begins to run wild. Given the volume of the attack, we have no clue how many shooters there are and suspect there's at least someone on the ground, but that the police would get him soon, and we'd be safe and could check on all our friends. I'm not sure where the feeling came from, but I just knew the fire was coming from above. Unused to the sound of an automatic rifle, in my mind I think there's a helicopter above us because of the cadence of the bullets. Although it made absolutely no logical sense, the thought I have is, "Are we seriously getting shot at by a fucking helicopter right now? What the fuck is happening?"

This is the moment of my greatest feeling of fright and helplessness, that we were now pinned down behind this car as bullets zoomed by, and something was going to get us

---

[3] Some of this story had to be pieced together after the fact from various people's recollections. This middle section was particularly spotty for me originally.

from above. The initial helicopter feeling was wrong (though there may have been one there, I still don't know), but the notion that this was coming from an elevated position that could reach us was unfortunately right, and we needed to move.

We weren't going to be able to go back for anyone at this point, so I grab Kay's hand again to make a run for it. We pause until there's a break in the shooting and sprint out of the exit and up the street a few dozen feet before the peppering from above continues and we dive behind a fence just outside the gate for cover.[4] The attack is relentless, and we need to get farther away still, so we get up and start sprinting again to the north along the back street, instinctively toward our hotel at MGM. Kay is struggling to keep up, so I pause with her and the words fall out, "If you don't run your hardest right now, we're dead. This is the time to give everything you've got."

Whatever recognition of the situation I had before, it pales in comparison to the moment those words unconsciously come out of my mouth. But once that realization hits, we absolutely fly as best we can in cowboy boots, and we'll never run harder in our lives. The adrenaline starts to take over as we sprint together down the street, so many others doing the same. The cotton mouth I feel is unlike anything I've experienced before or hopefully ever will again. I go to say something to her as we get farther away from the scene and seemingly into safety, and no words come out. I physically cannot talk.

We finally hit the backside of Tropicana and see a

---

[4] Again, this part I blacked out and did not realize until a few hours later when I noticed my shirt was dirty and knees were bruised from diving on the cement.

stream of people flowing into a service entrance. Knowing there's something coming from above and we need to get cover immediately, we follow them inside. On the way in, blood lines the door and is pooled on the floor. As we turn the hallway to the right, a man is on the ground with a bullet wound and a group of people tending to his midsection.

My initial thought is "Shit, there's a shooter in the casino too," and we run across the hall to an employee locker room and find a place to hide in the back.

For the first time, I feel like we're going to make it.

Not knowing what will happen with the cell coverage, I immediately call home (at 1:21 EST, about thirteen minutes after the shooting started) and tell my parents I love them and am okay and to turn on the news. Kay does the same. We begin exchanging texts within our group, keeping everyone informed of our status. After a few minutes, a message from Nestor lets us know that our friend Jay was hit and they're trying to get her into an ambulance.

I do my best to put on a brave face with Kay, acting like it wasn't tearing me up inside as we waited for more updates. Everyone else in our group checks in safely from random places they had scattered. Over the next few minutes, a couple dozen more survivors come into the room, and as we hear more conflicting stories about active shooters in Luxor, Bellagio, and even Tropicana, we knock over a handful of the eight-foot-tall locker stalls and barricade the door. The guys in the room pile on way more defense than is necessary, feeling like we need to do something, anything, to contribute to the moment. The survivor's guilt and feelings of helplessness are so strong in a situation like this, it's impossible to explain. Some even go through lockers and pull knives from the kitchen staff to lay out by the door. If whoever was out there was going to bust through the barricade, we were going to war with butcher knives.

Finally, the text we had been waiting for from Nestor comes that Jay was at the hospital, they had stabilized her, and she was going to be okay.

I lose it. I mean I absolutely lose it.

This was my fault. We were here because of me. This group came together because of me, the center of the social circle I cling to so tightly. My best friend from Connecticut, his sister and brother-in-law with an infant at home, a friend from work, and a bunch of law school mates for which I was the hub connecting all the spokes of the wheel. I was the one that brought these people together, and into a life-crushing hellscape.

All the penned-up emotion of that scene, that night, the status of my friends and myself and all those poor people out there, comes crashing out of me after bottling it up for the last couple of hours.

As things settle on our end, and news flows in that the single shooter is dead and it's just a matter of making sure the area is safe, Nestor fills us in on their story from what can only be described as a war zone. When the three of them had gone down for cover, a few seconds later, Jay was hit with a stray bullet through the left side of her back while Nestor tried to shelter both sisters. They applied pressure to the wound, removing her from the active shooting scene as best as possible until they got to the street and tried to flag down an ambulance. The EMT drained the blood from the punctured lung on scene and the ambulance was off. They wait with Jay at the hospital after successful surgery, and a collective relief is felt by all.

It's another hour or more before we're finally released from the locker room by Tropicana security. In a moment of dark humor, I have to smirk at the look of sheer confusion on the security guard's face once we finally break down the locker barricade and open the door. As he surveys all the locker stalls tipped over, uniforms thrown in the corner, and knives everywhere, I will always remember his facial expression of, "What the hell did you guys do in here?"

Just surviving, bro.

We get back to the hotel around 5:30 Monday morning, entirely unable to sleep. I spend an hour on the phone with American changing my flight that's scheduled to take off soon, as I can't even imagine getting on a plane at the moment. I really want to see Jay, and to decompress with the rest of the group. The whole night and through most of Monday, I am crushed by emotion. I feel guilty that Jay was shot, that I didn't do more, that I wasn't with the rest of our group, that I was stuck surviving in a bunker and not out helping others, and most strongly, that I was so emotional and that I was selfish for being so, wishing I could devote my energy toward praying for and helping the victims like Jay.

Later Monday, we're able to visit the hospital and see her in recovery. I'm overcome with relief as I see how well she's handling everything and powering through, talking and even joking as we always do. I can start to let myself off the hook a little bit and begin to turn the corner, finally falling asleep a few hours later. But there was still more struggle ahead.

In the aftermath that followed that horror, I leaned heavily on the lessons learned over the past year that prepared me to handle an emotional challenge that's about the worst anyone can face. If the Vegas shooting had happened a year ago, before I went on this journey, there's absolutely no way I handle what comes next as well as I did, or with the same approach. The advanced emotional intelligence, better self-awareness and understanding of my triggers, especially new ones related to a PTSD I've never known, and the reactions and feelings moment-to-moment, was absolutely critical for being able to process all of the turmoil and anguish that was going through my head, and to try to help others in my group do the same. People around me were dying all over that night, my friends and I barely escaped, Jay inches away. That's a survivor's guilt that doesn't dissipate easily, if ever, and takes a lot to manage.

The other related piece is the lesson I learned about the importance and benefit of sharing feelings and being open, honest, and vulnerable, to myself and to others. In the hours that followed the shooting, holed up in the Tropicana, through the weeks and months later, I must have received a thousand messages through text, call, or otherwise. Without realizing what I was doing at first, but knowing it was helping me process, I decided to take the time to answer each one that came through. So many messages arrived from all over, from good friends checking in regularly to people I hadn't spoken to in years. From long, emotional messages, to quick "thinking of you" notes. No matter the person or the sentiment, I started to pause, reflect, and respond thoughtfully to each one. If someone asked how I was feeling, even if it was a cursory inquiry, I actually self-assessed where I was at in the moment and wrote back with exactly how I felt. Again, sometimes getting into deep conversations with people who were out of my phone or life at the time, whether they had expected to or not.

That combined process was hugely cathartic. Being able to, first of all, actually know and recognize the emotions I was feeling, and two, convey them to another in conversation, I thoroughly believe got me through the mental aftermath. Within a few days, I continued with the sharing concept and wrote a small summary of the night, some of which appears here in parts, and posted it publicly. The reaction of support from my community was incredibly strong and heartening, and the whole process so cathartic again. I encouraged the others in my group to do the same, whether they wanted to share or not, even just writing down facts or their recollection of the night. The entire exercise is a step toward emotional understanding and recovery.

And eventually, we get better.

That's a line from *The West Wing* that followed a character's shooting, and a thought I carried with me in the months after Vegas. It's a simple, strong reminder of our ability to overcome.

As I got back into a normal life, dealing with this new kind of emotional upheaval, I wanted to take the positives that I could from that whole experience forward with me, further committed to the idea that a strong emotional intelligence willing to be open and vulnerable is so crucial for what life throws at us at any time. It helped me to finish a book that was stalling out, and to try to send that message of the importance of our own understanding.

A few months later, a friend shared my story with one of the organizers of the March for Our Lives rally in New York City. After reading my account, she asked me to share my experience in Vegas and a message moving forward. I was proud to march after having to run for my own life not so long ago, wanting no one to ever have to face what we all have gone through.

Despite my passion on this subject, my heart constantly breaking for a country whose flag is perpetually at half-staff, I know a toxic and sometimes violent debate is not going to get us there. The appeal I want to make is one of compassion. That only through a collective and concerted effort from a place of understanding can we achieve meaningful positive changes to make the world safer.

In front of the microphone, looking out over an endless sea of people, the crowd doesn't get to me but the emotion of revisiting that moment chokes me up a bit. I tell our story of that night, and make an appeal to address the roots of this issue on the human level, being open about mental health and a culture of violence that has caused us to lose respect for each other and life. There are many things we can and should be doing in our laws to prevent tragedies like that, but for me, it starts inside. The message I leave is something

I know I need to improve on in myself, but it's in that striving every day, in that struggle and in overcoming, that's where all the meaning waits.

I exit stage right to a massive hug from the organizer, one of the most compassionate people I've ever met, tears cascading down both of our faces in prevailing release.

That initial hesitation in getting some dumb tattoo while out on my voyage was in being apologetically cliché. But as I ditched that sensitivity, I still couldn't come up with anything that actually meant something to me, until recently. Now, I carry with me constant reminders of the benevolent struggle and beauty that each day brings.

On my left arm in Sanskrit writing is the word Sukha, meaning bliss. A symbolic trophy earned during my odyssey of the heart and mind, a mantra of long-term happiness, and reminder to always be aware and growing and grounded within myself.

On my right wrist are two connected marks. First is a dash, inspired by a poem from Linda Ellis. On our tombstone are two dates, the day we're born and the day we die. In between the numbers, in small and forgotten form, is a dash, and in that dash is our entire life. Everything we did and saw and experienced. Everyone we met and loved and lost. To fill that space is to live.

Below that and related, is a "91" and my nod to the Vegas experience. Not of that night and that terror, but of the lessons gleaned and reinforced in the aftermath. That everything we have, everything we've done and hope to someday achieve, can all be ended in one unexpected instant. So experience each moment we have to its fullest, and, whenever possible, don't leave for tomorrow what can be done, or said, or lived today.

I'm not sure how everything would have gone had I not taken the opportunity to meet myself last year, but I do know there is no time for regrets in this life.

ACKNOWLEDGEMENTS

Holy hell, putting a book together is really fucking hard. The whole time I was traveling and writing, discussing my rambling and poignant thoughts of the day with the people around me, everyone would say, "Oh wow, you're writing a book, that's phenomenal." And when I got back and finished writing, and editing, and writing some more, and editing some more, people would say, "Oh wow, you wrote a book, that's incredible." And the whole time I was thinking, "Yeah, what's the big deal? It's just 130,000 words and 3 years of my life", until the magnitude eventually hit me when I finally said, "Oh wow, that was 130,000 words and 3 fucking years of my life."

Easily the hardest part for me was not knowing what the hell I was doing when I started. I tried to convey some of that inexperience, uncertainty, and writing frustration into the story without it being an overwhelming factor. I had an editor early on who told me to remove all of it; writing about the writing wasn't important. And to a large extent, or at least to the extent I had included that aspect into the original story, she was right. But for me, the writing experience itself, an ambitiously inquisitive dive into a personally novel world, was critical to any development I was going to make and became an actual character in the story. Without the writing as a driving force, there's no story to tell here.

Early on, I wasn't sure what that story would actually look like or where it would take me. I just kind of wrote, a lot. Writing without knowing an ending created a structural mess that took years of surgical reworking to fix. It also resulted in a way too long behemoth requiring trimming of about 1/3 of what I had written, and much more surgery. And then, when I finally got it to a place that I thought was ready for broader consumption, I ran smack into the brick wall that is the traditional publishing industry. At various times throughout the whole process, through writing blocks and a constant stream of rejections, I teetered on the edge of abandonment as if I was any Trump kid trying to get their father's approval.

Along the way, though, I found my voice and everything improved. Both in this book and in life, even through the most difficult of struggles. And if I've said it once, I certainly have said it one million times now: yes this is my story, but in so many ways I think it's our story. More generational than it may seem on its face, and not about the "Myself" but about the "How". Maybe I'm wrong in that, but I've had too many conversations in these three years with friends and lovers and strangers alike who seemed to share that unspoken sentiment of an anxious and potentially unhappy world, and a hope for something great. And that helped me carry on to this point, to finish this product for real. If I can change just one person's life for the better, make one person laugh along the way, have just one person read this story and find commonality and understanding, it will all be worth it. It was for me.

I need to thank my parents, first and foremost and always, for being gigantic boulders of strength, steadiness, and support, my entire life and especially these last few years of self-inflicted mayhem. They read this story and provided guidance, but also helped to live it and get me to where I am today. My brother Anthony and best friend Phil have read every one of these many words multiple times, as well as all the ones left on the cutting room floor, and for their input in the process I am incredibly grateful. Eric, Ryan, Spencer, Nicole, Jay, Dane, Avidahn, Amy, Rob, Mia, Scotty, Kristen, Bri and all my friends and family who gave encouragement or feedback on certain pieces or helped add to the story, I thank you for contributing and helping me in life and in this endeavor. For any friends, exes, passers-by who were converted to Greek characters and made it into this odyssey, I hope my recollection of events is true to form and that I was much harder on myself than you. To Mark and Trisha, and your lovely hospitality at Uncle Jon's Cabin, thank you for providing me a peaceful and productive place to perform oh so many edits to this book. I need to thank my editor, Philippa, who had the unfortunate pleasure of breaking down my first draft and setting in motion the restructuring process, and my publisher Jeannie, for bringing this all together and seeing my vision through to the end.

Lastly, to my lovely reader who has somehow made it to this point in the book, thank you. Not only is writing a book unbelievably daunting, but also very scary. Especially a memoir of this sort, being open for all the world to see. Thank you for taking the leap with me.

About the Author

Seriously, you want to know more? The 300 whatever pages you just read wasn't enough for you?

*For the continuing story, I can be found living in San Diego, on the world wide web at **jonathanrestivo.com**, or follow me on Instagram at **jrestivo12**. Or don't. I'm over it now anyway.*

CPSIA information can be obtained
at www.ICGtesting.com
Printed in the USA
BVHW071432270820
587359BV00002B/118